COMPUTER SCIENCE, TECHNOLOGY AND APPLICATIONS

T0076021

EMULATING HUMAN SPEECH RECOGNITION

A SCENE ANALYSIS APPROACH TO IMPROVING ROBUSTNESS IN AUTOMATIC SPEECH RECOGNITION

COMPUTER SCIENCE, TECHNOLOGY AND APPLICATIONS

Additional books in this series can be found on Nova's website under the Series tab.

Additional E-books in this series can be found on Nova's website under the E-books tab.

COMPUTER SCIENCE, TECHNOLOGY AND APPLICATIONS

EMULATING HUMAN SPEECH RECOGNITION

A SCENE ANALYSIS APPROACH TO IMPROVING ROBUSTNESS IN AUTOMATIC SPEECH RECOGNITION

ANDRE COY

Nova Science Publishers, Inc.
New York

For permission to use material from this book please contact us:
Telephone 631-231-7269; Fax 631-231-8175
Web Site: http://www.novapublishers.com

NOTICE TO THE READER

The Publisher has taken reasonable care in the preparation of this book, but makes no expressed or implied warranty of any kind and assumes no responsibility for any errors or omissions. No liability is assumed for incidental or consequential damages in connection with or arising out of information contained in this book. The Publisher shall not be liable for any special, consequential, or exemplary damages resulting, in whole or in part, from the readers' use of, or reliance upon, this material. Any parts of this book based on government reports are so indicated and copyright is claimed for those parts to the extent applicable to compilations of such works.

Independent verification should be sought for any data, advice or recommendations contained in this book. In addition, no responsibility is assumed by the publisher for any injury and/or damage to persons or property arising from any methods, products, instructions, ideas or otherwise contained in this publication.

This publication is designed to provide accurate and authoritative information with regard to the subject matter covered herein. It is sold with the clear understanding that the Publisher is not engaged in rendering legal or any other professional services. If legal or any other expert assistance is required, the services of a competent person should be sought. FROM A DECLARATION OF PARTICIPANTS JOINTLY ADOPTED BY A COMMITTEE OF THE AMERICAN BAR ASSOCIATION AND A COMMITTEE OF PUBLISHERS.

Additional color graphics may be available in the e-book version of this book.

LIBRARY OF CONGRESS CATALOGING-IN-PUBLICATION DATA

Emulating human speech recognition : a scene analysis approach to improving robustness in automatic speech recognition / editor, Andre Coy.
p. cm.
Includes bibliographical references and index.
ISBN 978-1-61942-914-7 (soft cover)
1. Automatic speech recognition. I. Coy, Andre.
TK7882.S65E48 2011
006.4'54--dc23
2011053524

Published by Nova Science Publishers, Inc. † *New York*

Contents

To Indianna

I can only hope to be for you what you have been for me.

Acknowledgements

The work presented was carried out at the Speech and Hearing (SpandH) Group in the Computer Science Department of the University of Sheffield. I would like to express my appreciation to the members of the group for all the support, good times and great memories. Special thanks go to my Supervisor Jon Barker, who greatly assisted in my academic development and will continue to be a source of inspiration. His patience and willingness to share his knowledge and insights made this journey less challenging.

Special thanks also to Prof. Phil Green who offered me the opportunity to join SpandH and arranged for my study to be funded. I must say thanks to the past and present members of SpandH for the support, the good times and the great memories. Thanks to James, Yasser, Bala and Ning for your support over the years and for simply making time to chat.

Acknowledgement is made of the EPSRC for funding the Multisource project (GR/R47400/01).

Thanks to Indianna, Sue, James and Rochelle for proof-reading. Your comments and suggestions have served to improve the quality of the book.

Most importantly, I have to thank my parents, whose love and support have given me the confidence I need to do anything.

Foreword

Anyone who has even a modest exposure to the genre of science fiction literature and movies will be readily aware that the future is expected to be populated by speaking and listening machines with whom the human race will engage in conversational interaction in order to achieve their everyday tasks. Whether it is commanding a shipboard robot or ordering pizza, it is assumed that the natural means by which people will communicate with machines will be spoken language. Even today we see some primitive foretastes of such a technology – it is possible to dictate text into your PC or iPhone using software for automatic speech recognition, and you can book cinema tickets using an interactive voice response system over the telephone.

However, as most people who have experienced existing speech technologies will readily testify, it hardly seems natural to engage in spoken interaction for some of these tasks, and the state-of-the-art seems to be a long way from the vision portrayed in science fiction and thus is far removed from what customers actually expect and want. The problem, it turns out, is much more complex than originally thought. Despite over 50 years of dedicated research into recognising human speech in which huge strides have been made in our understanding and ability to process speech, scientists are still scratching the surface when it comes to dealing with the everyday reality.

Spoken communication very rarely takes place in perfect laboratory conditions. Most conversation takes place in a social context in busy locations. The normal acoustic environment is full of extraneous sounds and noises, as well as the buzz of other people's conversations and activity. Human listeners are spectacularly good at recognising and understanding what is said to them in these conditions, yet contemporary automatic speech recognition is very fragile when placed in such circumstances and recognition accuracy deteriorates dramatically.

Research into methods for overcoming these difficulties is thus a priority for making progress in automatic speech recognition, and this has been acknowledged by the many surveys that have been conducted into the key elements of scientific work that need to be addressed. Of course it is not the case that scientists have been ignoring the challenges posed by realistic environments – far from it. Over the years there have been many excellent research projects that have attempted to tackle this area. However, very few have taken on the complexity posed by an acoustic environment containing multiple voices – and this is exactly what is presented here.

In this volume, Dr. Coy presents a systematic approach to the automatic recognition of simultaneous speech signals using computational auditory scene analysis. Inspired by human auditory perception, Dr. Coy investigates a range of algorithms and techniques for decomposing multiple speech signals by integrating a spectro-temporal fragment decoder within a statistical search process. The outcome is a comprehensive insight into the mechanisms required if automatic speech recognition is to approach human levels of performance.

Roger Moore, University of Sheffield

Chapter 1

Introduction

Despite the advances made over the past 30 years, automatic speech recognition (ASR) is still fragile. Human speech recognition (HSR) however, is robust to environmental noise; arguably, because it benefits from the auditory system's ability to decode a signal of interest in the presence of noise. The differences between HSR and ASR stem partly from the fact that ASR systems generally do not consider the task of source segmentation – segmentation here refers to the process of decomposing the signal into parts that are deemed to be either dominated by the source of interest or by the sources of noise. This is evident in early systems, which focused on the recognition of 'clean speech' – speech recorded with a high signal to noise ratio. In contrast, HSR, which is typically performed in acoustic scenes populated with a variety of noise sources, employs processes that segment noisy speech signals in order to facilitate the recognition of the message therein. Thus, it is possible that a noise robust recognition system can be developed by taking inspiration from the approach of HSR.

This book presents one approach to developing such a system, specifically designed for the recognition of monaurally presented mixtures of speech. Taking inspiration from an account of auditory perception known as *auditory scene analysis* (Bregman, 1990), details of which will be presented throughout the book. The work proposes a two-stage system that: i) provides an initial segmentation of the speech mixture via primitive processes and, ii) employs a recognition engine that jointly selects the correct segments of the mixture using schema-driven processes, and performs a decoding of the message represented by those segments. By thus coupling the segmentation and recognition stages, the system aims, not only to achieve noise robust ASR performance, but also to emphasise the utility of incorporating principles of HSR in the development of a robust ASR system.

1.1. Auditory Perception and Automatic Speech Recognition

Bregman's Auditory Scene Analysis (ASA) account of auditory perception presents a theory of how listeners perform the task of recovering separate descriptions of each source in the auditory scene (Bregman, 1990). In the account, Bregman posits that this ability is based on an interaction between *primitive* grouping rules that partially organise the incoming data using Gestalt principles, and *schema-driven* processes, which link partial sound source descriptions to models of complete sources that have been learnt from the environment. The recognition stage completes the partial organisation performed by the primitive processes.

This approach of combining primitive and schema-driven processes to describe the auditory scene confers several advantages on the auditory system. Firstly, it allows flexibility in the primitive segmentations that can be proposed. While the constraints provided by an accurate signal-driven (primitive) segmentation can greatly improve the final schema-driven grouping, incorrect segmentation can equally degrade grouping accuracy. The combination of these complimentary processes enables a more cautious approach to primitive segmentation; if there is no need to identify the individual sources at the primitive stage, then the system can present a segmentation in which fewer elements of the scene are grouped, as this lack of constraint can be overcome by the schema-driven grouping performed later on. Secondly, it allows the system to correct errors made by the primitive processes. If two segments of a signal that belong together were incorrectly separated, they can be regrouped by the schema-driven processes if the evidence exists to support grouping them. Finally, the auditory system does not need to know the composition of the sound scene beforehand, specifically, it does not require prior knowledge of the nature of the sources in the mixture. Schema-driven processing allows for the active selection of segments of interest, so that the system can attend to a particular source in the sound mixture and ignore the others. Thus, if one source is speech and the others noise, then the combination of primitive and schema-driven processes will allow the system to group the regions of speech and ignore the noise.

Bregman's work also highlighted several characteristics of sound (cues) that could be exploited for primitive segmentation. Among these cues are: fundamental frequency differences, common onset/offset time and locational cues. These allow for the acoustic scene to be decomposed based on the elemental properties of its components. This is an attractive prospect that gives some insight into the flexibility of the auditory system in performing source segmentation in unfamiliar environments. These powerful cues can be used singly, or in combination, providing the listener with a wide range of techniques for making sense of the sometimes, severely degraded, message that arrives at the ears.

The schema-driven processes select and group components of the initially segmented acoustic mixture that best match to learnt models of the components of the sound scene. By employing well trained models, the auditory system allows itself the opportunity to make grouping decisions informed by experience and knowledge of each component. Such decisions are likely to be more accurate than those based solely on primitive processes.

An ASR system that was designed to incorporate such processing could benefit from the considerable body of research that has been conducted into primitive source segmentation as well as the power of statistical ASR. The outcome would be an ASR framework in which primitive segmentation cues are employed to perform an initial segmentation which is refined with the use of statistical models of speech. This is completely different to the approach taken in traditional recognition systems.

1.2. The Scene Analysis Account and Automatic Speech Recognition

Bregman's theory that the auditory system combines both primitive and schema-driven processing strategies to decompose an auditory scene, has the potential to inspire a new generation of speech recognition systems that react in a more human-like way to the presence of competing noise sources. However, despite the potential of the fusion of ASA and traditional ASR techniques, little progress has been made in this direction. Previous attempts to combine ASA and ASR have proved largely unsuccessful. The earliest approaches attempted to use primitive grouping rules to separate the sound sources, and then to re-synthesise the target source for input to a conventional speech recogniser. This approach was first taken by Weintraub with disappointing results (Weintraub, 1985). Weintraub identified the fundamental weakness in this technique as being a decoupling of the segmentation and recognition systems. Unlike the ASA account, where primitive and schema-driven processes interact, in Weintraub's system the segmentation and recognition were performed independently.

An advancement of this work has been seen with the *missing data* techniques that have adapted this framework to perform recognition without having to first separate and resynthesise (Cooke et al., 2001b; Raj et al., 2004). This class of techniques first segments a spectro-temporal representation of the mixture into reliable regions (those dominated by the target source) and 'missing' regions (those dominated by the masking source) and then employs adapted statistical ASR models to recognise the target speech based on the incomplete reliable regions. In the missing regions, rather than reconstructing the data with a best guess, recognition proceeds by considering all the possible values the speech may have had in these areas. This 'marginalisation' approach allows a more principled integration of the bottom-up ASA front-end and the ASR back-end. However, this approach does not recouple the segmentation and recognition processes. The front-end produces a single foreground/background segmentation and passes it on to the recogniser which is powerless to change the segmentation decision.

In order to fully access the power of ASA the recognition system must be presented with a number of possible segmentations from which to chose the one that best fits to the statistical models employed for recognition. Such a system, the *speech fragment decoder* (SFD) was proposed by Barker et al. (2005), however, the lack of a systematic approach to source segmentation precluded a demonstration of the full power of the technique.

1.3. Objectives

The main objective of the work presented here is to develop a robust, signal-driven segmentation system – inspired by studies of the human perceptual system – to be employed as the front-end of a framework for noise robust ASR. The work describes a fully functional system: from the development of a primitive segmentation system, which decomposes the sound scene into a set of spectro-temporal fragments, through to the recognition engine that employs schema-driven processes to perform the final segmentation and output the correct word-sequence hypothesis.

Within such a framework there are several stages (see Figure 1.1). Each step is essential to the final outcome of the system. Thus, another objective is to examine the issues arising from each stage of the process, with a view to assessing the utility of each component in the attempt to improve ASR accuracy.

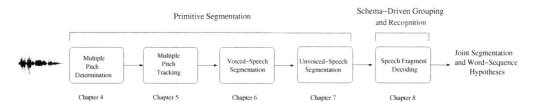

Figure 1.1. An illustration of the coupling of primitive and schema-driven processes proposed.

There have been several calls over the years for the development of ASR systems influenced by HSR (Lippmann (1997); Hermansky (1998); Huckvale (1998) see also Scharenborg (2007) for a review). However, little effort has been made to develop such systems. The final objective is to examine the overall claim that incorporating knowledge of human sound scene processing can enhance the noise robustness of ASR systems.

1.4. Overview of the Book

Chapter 2 discusses techniques of robust automatic speech recognition inspired by the scene analysis account of auditory perception. After introducing the basic concepts of automatic speech recognition, the chapter goes on to discuss the traditional approaches employed to achieve noise robustness; sub-dividing them into feature- and model-based compensation techniques. Perceptual approaches to noise robustness are motivated by surveying the theoretical principles of auditory scene analysis (ASA) and the computational implementation of these principles – computational auditory scene analysis (CASA). The *missing data* approach to noise robust ASR is then discussed. This approach employs low-level processes to remove corrupted regions of noisy speech and uses uncorrupted regions for recognition.

One limitation of the missing data framework is found in the approach employed to detect uncorrupted speech. Typically, these systems attempt to achieve this segmentation by employing solely low-level processes, which often produces incorrect segmentations. Chapter 3 discusses the *speech fragment decoding* framework, which proposes an approach to overcoming this limitation. Inspired by studies of the human auditory system, the framework combines low- and high-level processes in a principled manner to achieve the required segmentation, and ultimately, improved robustness to noise. The chapter surveys ASR techniques informed by low-level processes as well as those informed by high-level processes. It then examines the motivation for coupling these processes in such a way as to harness the power of both. This is followed by a detailed discussion of the theory of the speech fragment decoding technique.

The main contribution of this work is the development of a systematic and general approach to the fragment-generation processing performed by the front-end of the SFD. This processing is broken into sequential stages (illustrated by Figure 1.1) that will be described and evaluated in Chapters 4 through to 7. Chapter 4 focuses on multi-pitch determination. Pitch is one of the characteristics of speech most frequently exploited for the segmentation of voiced speech; it is also employed in this work. The chapter begins with a survey of the techniques proposed for single- and multiple-pitch determination. It continues with the development of a novel algorithm for multiple-pitch determination. The algorithm works in tandem with a multiple-pitch tracking algorithm to recover the pitches of all the sources in a mixture of voiced speech – the current implementation focuses on monaural mixtures of two speech sources. This coupling ensures that the proposed approach – retaining multiple peaks from a summary autocorrelogram – maximises the possibility of detecting the pitches of both sources. In the instances where the pitch of a source is missing and the algorithm detects a harmonic at half or double the fundamental frequency, the algorithm does not correct these 'errors', but rather accepts them as evidence of the source, which can be useful in the final segmentation stage. An evaluation with fully- and partially-voiced speech mixtures is then performed.

The pitch determination algorithm will detect and estimate the pitches of the sources in a mixture of voiced speech, however, it is essential to impose a degree of temporal continuity on these estimates. Chapter 5 proposes a novel multiple-pitch tracker that tracks the pitch estimates across time. Systematic modelling of pitch doubling and halving errors facilitates the formation of smooth pitch tracks, even where the pitch of a source is missing. The tracker assumes the candidates output by the multi-pitch determination algorithm are generated by a number of voiced sources and a separate noise source. A generative model consisting of models for the voiced sources as well as a noise model is developed and the pitch tracking problem is recast as one of inferring the most likely way in which the model might have produced the candidates output from the pitch determination algorithm. When attempting to assign a pitch track to a source, errors are often made when there is a break in voicing, leading to mis-assignment of the track. The proposed algorithm avoids this by not imposing strict temporal continuity where a pitch break occurs. This is permissible, as temporal continuity is imposed in the decoding stage, where segmentation is completed by schema-driven processes. The tracker is evaluated with both fully-voiced utterances and utterances which contain breaks in voicing. A comparison is also made with a state-of-the-art multi-pitch tracking algorithm tested with the same data.

Voiced-speech segmentation is the subject of Chapter 6. The chapter begins with a review of the role of pitch in segmentation. This covers perceptual studies of the segmentation of tones, synthetic speech and real speech, showing how these studies have influenced the development of speech segmentation systems. A unique segmentation algorithm is then presented, which employs the outputs of both Chapters 4 and 5 to decompose the voiced regions of speech into coherent spectro-temporal fragments. The algorithm outputs fragments for all sources as well as a confidence map, which indicates how likely it is that a spectro-temporal point in a fragment belongs to one source or the other. This confidence map will assist the decoder in assigning a fragment to a source, which is essential for correct recognition. A novel evaluation metric, a gauge of the fragment's coherence, is developed to measure the quality of the fragments derived.

The majority of existing CASA-based segmentation algorithms focus on the segmentation of voiced speech only. This is partly because those studies that evaluate the output of their segmentation algorithms on speech recognition tasks typically do so with small-vocabulary tasks, where unvoiced speech is not as important as it is in tasks with larger vocabularies. Chapter 7 proposes a novel algorithm for the segmentation of unvoiced speech. The chapter reviews the cues used for classification and segmentation of unvoiced consonants, with a view to developing a segmentation algorithm that exploits these cues. However, it was found that the majority of these cues are not robust enough to be utilised in a segmentation system. The algorithm developed employs image processing techniques to segment unvoiced speech based on the shape of the spectro-temporal energy profile. An evaluation, using de-voiced speech, is carried out to measure the coherence of the fragments.

Chapter 8 presents an evaluation of the full system in the form of recognition experiments, where the speech fragment decoder (SFD) is used with the fragments derived from the segmentation system. Two sets of experiments are carried out: Firstly, a challenging task of decoding monaurally mixed digit strings is presented. The next experiment involves a more challenging *alpha-digit* recognition task. The performance of the SFD is compared to that of listeners on the same tasks.

The final chapter (Chapter 9) presents the conclusions, where the major contributions of the book are highlighted and an assessment is made of the work leading to a discussion of future research directions.

Chapter 2

Scene Analysis and Robust Automatic Speech Recognition

2.1. Introduction

Given the significant advances that have been made in the field of automatic speech recognition, it is surprising how poorly state-of-the-art systems perform in the presence of modest amounts of noise. Juang (1991) identified the single most debilitating effect on automatic speech recognition (ASR) performance as a mismatch between training and testing conditions.[1] This has led many researchers to develop methods to reduce the mismatch. The two sources of mismatch typically explored by researchers are: noise - additive and convolutional, and speaker adjustment (Holmes and Holmes, 2001).

Many mechanisms exist whereby the speech signal can be corrupted; a noisy background, a poor transmission channel and reverberation, are examples. To deal with these effects one can either adjust the speech so that both the training and test environment match (a feature-based solution), or adjust the speech models or the recognition process to accommodate the noisy conditions (model-based solution). Traditional approaches to noise compensation tended to make strong assumptions about the nature of the noise affecting the speech signal. These approaches work well in cases where the assumptions made are correct. In the scenarios where the assumptions are wrong, the techniques do not work. This suggests that there is need for a general approach to noise compensation; one which is less dependent on detailed knowledge of the nature of the interference.

Noise compensation methods based on the scene analysis account of auditory perception aim to achieve this. These methods treat both the speech and noise as equally valid components of the auditory scene, either of which can be isolated from the other by exploiting the fundamental characteristics of each sound. This approach to noise compensation holds the promise of facilitating the recognition of speech corrupted by noise, about which little is known.

This chapter will review both traditional noise compensation approaches and those ap-

---

[1]It is noteworthy that the word *mismatch* implies that improved global *signal to noise ratio (SNR)* in the testing conditions can produce worse results than for matched conditions - a result that has been established (Juang, 1991; Gong, 1995).

proaches motivated by auditory scene analysis; discussing the benefits and drawbacks of each approach. The chapter will be organised in the following way: Section 2.2. will outline the basic theory of ASR. This will be followed by Section 2.3., which discusses feature- and model-based noise compensation techniques. Section 2.4. then examines noise robust ASR inspired by computational auditory scene analysis (CASA). The chapter concludes with a summary in Section 2.5..

2.2.   The Statistical Basis of ASR

This section serves to present the basic concepts of ASR, as well as introduce mathematical notation that will be used throughout the book; it does not aim to be an exhaustive account of ASR. For a thorough study of ASR the interested reader is referred to one of the many excellent textbooks, such as Rabiner and Juang (1993) or Holmes and Holmes (2001).

Consider a sequence of feature vectors derived from clean speech, $X = x_1, x_2, ..., x_T$, presented to a standard recogniser. The recogniser is tasked with returning the most likely word sequence, given the feature vectors. Formally, the aim is to derive the probability that a word sequence W, was uttered based on the observed feature vector X, i.e., $P(W \mid X)$, and to find the sequence W' that maximises this probability.

$$W' = \underset{W}{\operatorname{argmax}} \ P(W \mid X) \tag{2.1}$$

The *a posteriori* probability, $P(W \mid X)$ cannot be easily estimated, and it is much simpler, and more practical to estimate the *likelihood*, $P(X \mid W)$. The likelihood can be interpreted as the probability that a set of features were generated by a particular word model. The posterior is then computed from the likelihood using Bayes' rule:

$$P(W \mid X) = \frac{P(X \mid W) \cdot P(W)}{P(X)}, \tag{2.2}$$

where $P(X \mid W)$ is the *acoustic model*, as it encodes the variation of the acoustic feature vectors for a given sequence of words in the vocabulary and $P(W)$ is the *language model*, which specifies the probability of particular word sequences. $P(X)$ is the probability of observing a sequence of feature vectors. This is independent of the word sequence and does not impact on the maximisation, thus it is dropped from the calculation. That is:

$$W' = \underset{W}{\operatorname{argmax}} \frac{P(X \mid W) \cdot P(W)}{P(X)} \approx \underset{W}{\operatorname{argmax}} P(X \mid W) \cdot P(W) \tag{2.3}$$

Under the stochastic approach, the acoustic feature vectors can be associated with a sequence of states $Q = q_1, q_2, ..., q_T$, which is traversed in an orderly manner based on the transition probabilities associated with each state. Equation 2.1 then has to be modified to reflect the search over the set of allowable state sequences Q_W for a given word sequence W:

$$W' = \underset{W}{\operatorname{argmax}} \ \underset{Q \in Q_W}{\max} \ P(X \mid Q) \cdot P(Q \mid W) \cdot P(W). \tag{2.4}$$

Each state sequence models some segment of a word, thus it is assumed that a state sequence determines the word sequence. This assumes that there is no context-dependent modelling, or pronunciation variants. Within this framework, the task of the decoder is to find the most probable state sequence; this is equivalent to finding the best word sequence.

$$\hat{Q} = \underset{Q}{\text{argmax}} \ P(X \mid Q) \cdot P(Q)$$

$$= \underset{Q}{\text{argmax}} \ P(x_1, x_2, \ldots, x_T \mid q_1, q_2, \ldots, q_T) \cdot P(q_1, q_2, \ldots, q_T) \quad (2.5)$$

Time variability is handled by allowing a model to remain within a state for more than one frame, or to skip a state if necessary. The sum of all transition probabilities for a given state must be 1 so as to preserve the stochastic integrity of the model. Transitions are governed by the state the model was in at the previous time step, ignoring all other information about prior state occupation. This behaviour describes a *first order Markov process*. Each state has a *probability density function* (pdf) for the feature vectors that is used to determine the probability that a particular feature vector could be emitted by the model when it is in a given state. This probability is referred to as the *emission probability*. In order to simplify the model it is further assumed that the observation x_t is dependent only on the state q_t. Thus:

$$\hat{Q} = \underset{Q}{\text{argmax}} \ P(X \mid Q) \cdot P(Q) = \underset{Q}{\text{argmax}} \ \prod_{i=1}^{N} P(x_i \mid q_i) \prod_{i=2}^{N} P(q_i \mid q_{i-1}) P(q_1). \quad (2.6)$$

The fact that the exact state sequence that determined the output is not known makes the model a *hidden* Markov model (HMM) (see Rabiner and Juang, 1993, for a full treatment of HMMs). The Baum-Welch algorithm (Baum et al., 1970) is used to train the HMMs given a set of labelled speech data. The Viterbi algorithm is used to perform the search over the state space for the most probable state sequence given the observed features and the trained HMMs. An exhaustive search over all state sequences is effectively performed without the need to calculate all possible paths. The search makes use of the fact that the probability of generating the first t observations and being in state q_t, depends only on the state occupied at time $t-1$, i.e. it exploits the first order Markov property on which the models are based. In this way the algorithm effectively finds the best path through the utterance without evaluating all possible paths.

2.3. Feature and Model Compensation Techniques for Noise Robustness

The procedures proposed for improving the noise-robustness of speech recognition systems are many and varied (see Juang, 1991; Gong, 1995; Benzeghiba et al., 2007, for reviews). They can however, be broadly grouped into two categories, namely: feature-based and model-based solutions, which are implemented at the feature extraction and recognition stages, respectively (see Figure 2.1). The following sections will briefly outline some of these proposed techniques.

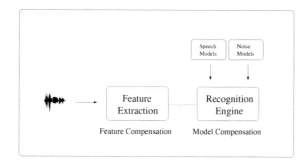

Figure 2.1. Illustration of feature and model compensation, which highlights the domains in which each type of compensation takes place. The feature compensation techniques are applied at the level of the features, either through the development of noise-robust features, or by removing the noise from corrupted features. Model compensation takes place within the recognition engine, where the models are adjusted to deal with the intrusions. See the text for details.

2.3.1.   Feature Compensation

It has already been suggested in passing, that certain feature types are more robust to noise. For example, Mel-frequency cepstral coefficients (MFCC) are known to be more noise robust than coefficients based on *Linear Predictive Coding* (LPC) (Lockwood et al., 1991; Holmes and Holmes, 2001). Gong (1995) also states that auditory-inspired features are in general quite noise resistant. Perceptual Linear Prediction (PLP) derived features have been shown to improve noise robustness (Hermansky, 1990). PLP features are similar to MFCC features with the major difference being that many of the processing steps involved in PLP derivation are motivated by psycho-acoustic studies. *Linear discriminant analysis* (LDA) is also suggested as a means of making features more tolerant of noise (Siohan, 1995). LDA is a supervised feature extraction method, which attempts to de-correlate the features used for ASR by minimising the intra-class variance and maximising the inter-class distance.

The domain in which the features are adjusted depends on the type of noise to be dealt with. Additive noise is handled most easily in the spectral domain because it simply adds to the existing spectra; this is based on the assumption that the signal and noise are statistically independent.[2] Convolutional noises (processes that effectively act as filters applied to the speech signal) are best tackled in the log spectral domain because convolution reduces to addition in that space.

One technique for dealing with additive noise is *spectral subtraction* (Boll, 1979). Spectral subtraction is the removal of the noise signal by way of subtracting an estimate of the noise from the corrupted spectrum. An estimate of the noise is acquired by averaging the energy of the spectral components of the frames in a region where there is no speech.[3] It is possible, however, to overestimate the noise, which causes the energy in some channels to

---

[2]This assumption is often true, or approximately so, though the Lombard effect provides one counter-example.

[3]There are also techniques for estimating the noise spectrum even where there is voice activity. For example Martin (2001) tracks the minima of the spectrum across frequency in order to improve the estimate of the noise.

fall below zero after subtraction. The channels that fall below zero can be replaced by zero or some other threshold value. In the *general spectral subtraction* approach proposed by Berouti et al. (1979), an overestimate of the noise is subtracted from the noisy speech spectrum if the value lies above a set threshold (some fraction of the noise estimate), otherwise the noisy speech is replaced with the threshold value. Removal of a static noise estimate can lead to removal of many areas of speech; therefore, some researchers apply an adaptive noise estimation technique that updates the noise estimate as the utterance progresses (Lockwood and Boudy, 1992). For example, the new estimate can be calculated from time-frequency 'pixels' that are judged to be dominated by noise (Barker et al., 2001a). As the noise involved becomes more non-stationary, then it becomes more difficult to estimate.

Convolutional noise is often dealt with by employing *cepstral mean normalisation* (CMN) (Furui, 1981). This technique is an analogue of spectral subtraction for cepstral features. The noise estimate is taken from speech regions of the spectrum because the noise and information are convolved. The estimate is taken as the long-term mean of the spectrum. The utterance and noise spectra are then transformed to the cepstral domain and the noise is removed. CMN will work well for slowly-varying noise signals; non-stationary noises pose a problem as an estimate of the noise can be difficult to obtain.

Relative Spectra (RASTA) processing is an extension of the above technique where the components of the corrupted speech signal, which are not changing in a way characteristic of speech are removed with the use of a bandpass filter applied to the modulation spectrum (Hermansky and Morgan, 1994). This only deals with convolutional noise. However, a variation of RASTA for cepstra and PLP, called J-RASTA, has been developed to deal with both additive and convolutional noise.

Several other techniques have been proposed - see Gong (1995) for a review. These include Comb filtering, Bayesian estimation, and parametric spectral modelling. A unifying thread running through these techniques is the application of some signal processing method, which makes several assumptions (sometimes incorrect) about the nature of either the noise or the speech signal. These techniques have limitations in the types of noises that can be handled. In particular, the majority of the techniques mentioned above work only if the noise characteristics are sufficiently different from those of speech.

2.3.2. Model Compensation

Rather than attempting to develop speech features with properties that are invariant in the presence of noise, there is an area of research that focuses on attempting to adjust the models at recognition time, in order to compensate for the effects of noise. One particular approach to model compensation employs models of both the clean speech and the environment in an effort to explain the noisy speech signal – see Figure 2.1. *HMM decomposition* (Varga and Moore, 1990) involves creating a noise model that captures all the variability expressed in the noise. This noise model is decoded in parallel with the speech models. In order for it to be feasible mathematically, it requires that the noise and speech be treated as independent (Holmes and Holmes, 2001). Another model compensation technique is *parallel model combination* (PMC) (Gales and Young, 1996). PMC combines the models for speech and noise to derive a 'noisy speech' model using a 'mismatch function' that approximates the effect of the noise on speech. Given that a single 'corrupted HMM' is derived from the noise and speech HMMs, there is no need to modify the decoding framework, whereas some modification is necessary in HMM decomposition. PMC has also been shown to handle both additive and convolutional noises (Gales, 1995). These techniques can produce remarkably good recognition results, however there are some issues that need to be highlighted. Firstly, they require detailed knowledge of the noise source; a prerequisite that can hardly be met in all circumstances. Secondly, the techniques are extremely computationally expensive. The state space explodes for relatively simple recognition tasks, even those with small vocabularies. While hypothesis pruning may alleviate this to some degree, recognition performance is likely to suffer as a result.

Roweis (2000, 2003) proposes a technique that is similar to PMC and HMM decomposition. The algorithm employs log-power spectral vectors and models the speech and noise separately with banks of Gaussian mixture models. The noisy speech is reconstructed by combining the models of noise and speech using a factorial HMM (Ghahramani and Jordan, 1995). In each sub-band the maximum of the contributions of each source is taken and the entire spectrum is thus reconstructed. The *ALGONQUIN* algorithm (Frey et al., 2001; Kristjansson et al., 2004, 2006) implements similar ideas, but makes use of a high frequency resolution for modelling the individual signals in the mixture.

HMM adaptation is a method of making HMMs with more robust noise characteristics. Gong (1995) states that duration characteristics for speech produced in low noise levels, greater than 10 *dB* SNR, tend not to change significantly. What this suggests is that duration characteristics can be exploited to reduce the impact of noise masking on ASR recognition performance. This was confirmed in an experiment which employed explicit duration models which led to a significant reduction in recognition errors (see also Siohan et al., 1993). Speaker adaption techniques use examples of noise corrupted speech to find a mapping that will transform models trained using clean speech into models that are more robust to the particular environment. Two of the most common approaches are maximum a posteriori probability (MAP) (Gauvain and Lee, 1994) and maximum likelihood linear regression (MLLR) adaptation (Leggetter and Woodland, 1995) (and their variants). These techniques adjust the parameters (means and/or variances) of generalised (speaker-independent) HMMs to match those of a specific speaker, creating speaker-specific models that offer improved discrimination and greater noise robustness. MLLR clusters model parameters and estimates the parameters of the transformation function from the adaptation data using maximum likelihood. The model parameters in each cluster are transformed using an affine transform. With MAP adaptation the new parameters are estimated using a combination of prior knowledge (in the form of the parameter of the speaker-independent models) and the adaptation data. The limitations include: i) the difficulty of modelling large variations in the parameters which can arise, for example, in high noise levels; and ii) the relatively poor performance when small amounts of adaptation data are available. Several recent studies have attempted to address these and other limitations (Chesta et al. (1999); Kuhn et al. (2000); Mak et al. (2005); Gibson and Hain (2007), for example).

Multi-condition training is a method which trains HMMs on data that have been corrupted with different kinds of noise (Morii et al., 1990; Dautrich et al., 1983). The aim is to have a model that generalises well, eliminating the mis-match between training and testing conditions, and gives good performance in any noise condition. In practise, the technique works well with data corrupted with noise that matches those used in training (Furui, 1992);

the recogniser will generally do worse when tested with speech contaminated with different noises (Gong, 1995). Another drawback is that performance on clean speech is sacrificed, because the discriminative capacity of the HMMs trained with noise is reduced.

2.4. Perceptually Motivated Approaches to Noise Robustness

The methods outlined above range from the creation of noise robust features to incorporating explicit models of the noise into the recognition process. Each of these techniques is useful in a specific domain – working on some noises, or in certain conditions, and not others. What they all lack is a systematic approach to handling speech that is distorted in unexpected ways; this points back to the template of human audition.

The mechanisms of human speech recognition (HSR) can provide useful input to the continued search for techniques to improve machine recognition of noisy speech (ten Bosch, 2001; Moore and Cutler, 2001); also, (see Scharenborg, 2007, for a review of research on the links between ASR and HSR). The central goal of both areas of research is the decoding of the speech signal to recognise the words therein. Humans, however are more adept at detecting and recognising speech in the presence of interference (both speech and non-speech). Further, the auditory system is flexible enough to adjust to different listening environments, accents and distortions (Moore and Cutler, 2001). Human speech recognition has consistently been found to be significantly better than machine recognition for various vocabulary sizes and environmental conditions, especially in low SNR conditions (van Leeuwen et al., 1995; Lippmann, 1997; Sroka and Braida, 2005; Cooke, 2006; Meyer et al., 2006). Given that there is such considerable evidence of the superiority of the HSR system, coupled with the fact that both systems are trying to solve the same problem, it seems likely that incorporating principles learnt from studies of human speech perception should improve ASR, however this is not always accepted. In an oft-cited study, Hunt (1999) suggested that (at the time of the study) direct modelling of the human auditory system had contributed little to the improvement of ASR systems. He made this observation while making it clear that, "... despite the present evidence, it seems that there must surely be much to learn from what the human auditory system does in representing the speech signal" (Hunt, 1999, pg. 7). Schlüter and Ney (1999) suggest that it may be more beneficial to employ the *principles* of human audition than to directly apply detailed models derived from perceptual studies.

2.4.1. Auditory Scene Analysis

Bregman (1990) coined the phrase *auditory scene analysis* (ASA) to describe the way humans organise the coexistent sound sources around them. It is hypothesised that the human auditory system employs a coupled, two-stage processing mechanism. In the first stage, (primitive grouping) sounds are segmented by low-level processes, which exploit the basic acoustic properties of each component to group together sounds that share common characteristics such as harmonicity, periodicity, and common onset. The second stage, (schema-driven grouping) employs high-level processes, which take advantage of the lis-

tener's knowledge and experience of their environment, built up over time, to further organise and classify each component sound. Within this framework, the target and interference
are both presented to the 'recogniser' in a partially organised form and perceptual organisation is completed during the 'recognition' process; i.e., by the action of schemas. This
stands in contrast to feature compensation techniques that require the intrusions to be effectively eliminated from the signal prior to its presentation to the recogniser. Such an
approach allows for the treatment of the intrusion as a stream (or a number of separate
streams) that can be attended to or disregarded as the listener wishes.

One will notice that in the synopsis provided in the previous paragraph there was no
specific mention of speech. The reason for this is that the principles of ASA are meant
to be universal; applicable to all categories of sound, speech included. This makes ASA
an extremely attractive framework within which to draft an approach to noise robust ASR.
Consider some of the potential benefits of attacking the problem of noise robust ASR using
ASA principles: 1) Primitive ASA holds the promise of clearly identifying each component
of a sound scene in the absence of complex models for each sound; 2) All sounds are treated
equally - as long as the fundamental characteristics of a sound are understood, it may be
possible to isolate it from an acoustic scene.

The early studies of perceptual organisation that contributed to the auditory scene analysis account focused on simple sounds. Even though it was meant to be a general account
of perceptual organisation, the fact that complex signals were not investigated meant that it
could not justifiably be considered an overarching theory, which would mean that there is
no rationale for its deployment in ASR. Following on from this, several studies were performed which employed complex speech-like signals, as well as re-synthesised speech to
test whether or not ASA could account for speech perception in humans. The overwhelming majority of these studies have drawn the conclusion that the explanations offered by
ASA go a long way to explain human speech perception (see Barker (2006) for a survey of
the relevant studies supporting and critiquing the use of ASA to explain human speech perception). Experiments have been conducted which show that the ASA account can explain
the grouping of spectral elements that overlap – simultaneous grouping. ASA can account
for grouping by harmonicity (Scheffers, 1983; Zwicker, 1984) and by common onset and,
or, offset (Darwin, 1981). ASA can also account for sequential grouping where cues such
as fundamental frequency continuity (Darwin and Bethell-Fox, 1977), and spectral continuity (Darwin and Hukin, 2000) are employed. These findings offered a great boost to
the effort to link ASA and ASR, however, there remained a significant issue. Perceptual
effects are generally quite difficult to model computationally, and even where they can be
realised, they are often computationally expensive. The challenge was then to find methods of transforming this qualitative insight gained from perceptual studies into models of
speech perception.

2.4.2. Computational Auditory Scene Analysis

Computational auditory scene analysis (CASA) (Brown and Cooke, 1994a) is an approach
that has steadily been gaining acceptance as a computational method for segmenting sound
sources. What CASA systems aim to do is to emulate human performance in sound scene
analysis by developing and implementing algorithms motivated by studies of human per-

ception. In the majority of these algorithms sound scene analysis takes the form of segmentation. A certain amount of flexibility is afforded to CASA researchers because of the lack of requirement for their systems to directly model the properties of the auditory system they attempt to mimic. This freedom has led to the development of myriad speech segmentation systems, which use one or more cues motivated by ASA.

One approach is to use purely primitive techniques to identify and group related components in a mixture of sounds (Mellinger, 1991; Brown, 1992; Cooke, 1993), while another employs a combination of primitive and schema-driven knowledge to perform the segmentation (Ellis, 1996, 1999a; Godsmark and Brown, 1999). Regardless of the approach taken, CASA algorithms will typically involve the use of spectral features which are based on models of the peripheral auditory system. The sound mixture is first passed through a filterbank populated with bandpass filters, simulating the pattern of frequency response of the basilar membrane. The next stage is the sampling and compression of the output of the filterbank to produce a time-frequency representation that is suitable for the identification and extraction of low-level cues. The time-frequency representation is ideal for the task of sound scene analysis because it takes into account the fact that sounds vary in both time and frequency. This suggests that both dimensions should be given equal emphasis in the symbolic representations of sound used in CASA systems (Brown and Cooke, 1994b). The sampling of the filterbank output leads to a frame-based representation of the acoustic mixture. This belies the true nature of sound, by assuming that there is little variation within the time span of a frame (typically 10 – 30 ms). The use of frame-based representations is a concession to ASR systems, which currently employ them. However, they are not well suited to source segmentation using CASA. CASA-based systems work best with representations that employ temporal integration, for example, the stabilised auditory image (Patterson et al., 1995). Another such representation is the *auditory ratemap* proposed by Cooke (1993) – see Figure 2.2. The acoustic signal is passed through a bank of gammatone filters with centre frequencies equally spaced on an *equivalent rectangular bandwidth* (ERB) scale. The instantaneous Hilbert envelope of the filterbank output is smoothed using a first order filter with an appropriate time constant (typically 8 ms). The smoothed envelope in each channel is then sampled. Non-linear compression is then applied to the envelope values.[4] Auditory representations, such as the ratemap, are information rich and retain the correlation between consecutive frames that is so crucial to many CASA-based algorithms. This poses a problem when spectral representations come to be used for ASR; this is discussed in Section 2.4.3..

It can be seen from Figure 2.2 that the auditory representation provides access to several low-level cues; for example, the signal's harmonicity is clearly visible. Onsets and offsets are also easily identifiable. Importantly, the relationships between temporally separate occurrences are also apparent. This makes it possible for segmentation algorithms to exploit the low-level cues present in a sound scene in the absence of detailed knowledge of the components. This sums up the appeal of CASA and the auditory representations it employs. An auditory scene can be decomposed by applying algorithms which model the physics of sound. This does not by any means suggest that such modelling is simple, but it does provide a framework for developing truly general sound scene analysis tools. Whereas

---

[4]Cube-root or log compression are sometimes used as they approximately model the energy-to-loudness mapping of the ear.

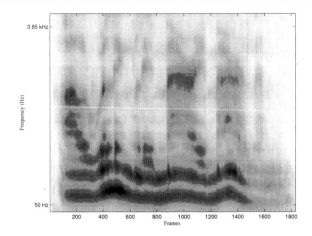

Figure 2.2. Ratemap of the utterance 'I'll willingly marry Marylin'.

the previously mentioned methods of dealing with noise intrusions rely on devices such as prior exposure to noise, and strong assumptions about the type and quality of the competing sources, the use of unconditional cues for source segmentation makes CASA seem, in theory, quite a useful front-end for speech recognisers (Green et al., 1995; Morris et al., 1998).

2.4.3. Missing Data Automatic Speech Recognition

Let us for the moment take the stance that CASA can effectively segment individual components of a sound scene. There is still the issue of how to implement ASR using the output from a CASA-based segmentation system. When sounds are mixed, the resulting overlap will lead to the distortion and partial occlusion of each source. Thus, when CASA is applied, only portions of each source will be recovered from the mixture, that is, the segmentation procedure produces incomplete spectral data. Consider Figure 2.3: In the upper panel (**A**) a ratemap of the utterance 'I'll willingly marry Marylin' is presented.

When that signal is mixed in the time domain, at 0 *dB*, with another speaker's utterance, the distortions are immediately obvious (panel **B**). The role of CASA is then to extract the regions of the mixture that can be reliably attributed to one or other source. Panel **C** shows the regions of the original utterance that a CASA-based scheme, employing knowledge of the unmixed signals to detect the regions where the spectro-temporal energy of the first source is greater than that of the interfering speech, could recover from the mixture. It is evident that some spectro-temporal regions of the first utterance have been masked and can no longer be unambiguously attributed to the original source. This illustrates the typical output of a CASA-based sound segmentation system.

Given that conventional speech recognition systems use models that are trained using undistorted feature vectors it would seem that in order to successfully implement CASA as a front end for ASR, some adjustments would have to be made. There are two alternatives, one is to train the speech models using feature vectors with missing data, the other is to alter the recognition process to accommodate these incomplete data. Training with partial

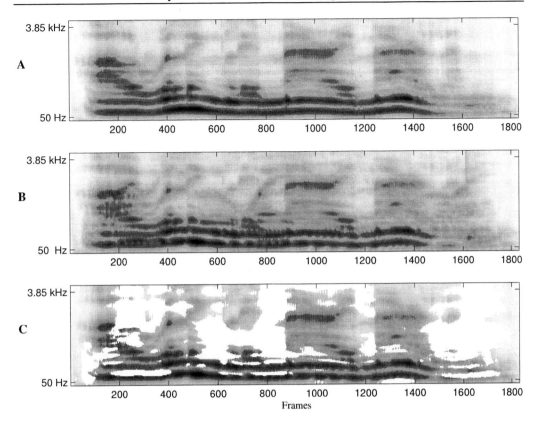

Figure 2.3. Illustration of the masking effect of interfering speech. **A**) Ratemap of the utterance 'I'll willingly marry Marylin'. **B**) The utterance illustrated in **A** is mixed at 0 dB with another speech signal, leading to the partial masking of both utterances. **C**) The regions of **A** that are undisturbed by the introduction of the second utterance.

data is clearly infeasible for the simple reason that a given feature vector can be distorted in innumerable ways, all of which would have to be accounted for in the training data. The solution proposed by Cooke et al. (1997) is encapsulated in an approach referred to as *missing data automatic speech recognition* (MDASR).

The problem of visual occlusion has received more attention than its analogue in audition (Marr, 1982; Witkin and Tenenbaum, 1983). Thus, many of the studies of audition and ASR (for example Bregman (1990); Green et al. (2001)) have taken inspiration from techniques employed in the field of computer vision. Following that trend, a leading study dealing with the missing data (MD) problem in vision (Ahmad and Tresp, 1993), paved the way and provided some insight for the development of MDASR.

The reasons for applying missing data theory (MDT) are well laid out in previous studies (Green et al., 2001; Cooke et al., 2001b). Some of them will be outlined here:

- Humans can adapt to, and recognise, speech that has undergone severe distortion from natural (Lippmann and Carlson, 1997), and artificial sources (Barker and Cooke, 1997). The typical ASR systems on the other hand, show a marked decrease in performance (an order of magnitude greater than humans) when recognising the same distorted speech (Lippmann, 1997). In order to emulate the performance of humans on speech recognition tasks using partial spectra, the typical ASR system must be able to handle these incomplete spectral features – this is where MDT plays a role.

- Missing data occurs in everyday circumstances. Thus, the use of ASR in daily life would be facilitated by improving its performance in noisy conditions where it is likely that parts of the signal will be obscured.

- Masked data are effectively missing data. When a region of the spectrum of one speech source is masked by a more energetic source, that region will be dominated by the contribution of the masking source; the other source is treated as missing. This has been shown to be true in human neural responses (Moore, 1997) and is reflected in the *max approximation* employed by some approaches to ASR (Varga and Moore, 1990).

Within a noisy signal, some spectro-temporal regions are dominated by speech and others by noise. In MDASR, the speech dominated portions are considered to be reliable (present) and all others, unreliable (missing). Thus, a feature vector, x, is effectively partitioned into sub-vectors x_r (reliable features) and x_u (unreliable features). The likelihood calculation, outlined in Section 2.2., $P(x \mid q)$ cannot be evaluated in the regular manner, as it requires a full set of feature vectors. This can be addressed in one of two ways, either by *imputation* or by *marginalisation*. Imputation strategies aim to produce estimates for the unreliable components and thus reconstruct the feature vector, obviating the need to modify the likelihood calculation. Marginalisation, on the other hand, allows recognition to be performed with the incomplete feature vector consisting of the reliable features only. This is achieved by considering all possible values of the unreliable features. Data imputation is attractive because it allows for the construction of cepstra and the attendant gains that confers.

Data Imputation

Imputation strategies take one of two forms: *feature-based imputation*, or *state-based imputation*. Feature-based solutions reconstruct the noisy signal prior to recognition, producing a new feature vector for further processing. State-based imputation schemes work at recognition time to estimate values for the unreliable components within each state of the HMM.

A simple imputation strategy involves the replacement of unreliable spectral components with values estimated by interpolating between the two closest reliable components (Raj, 2000). However, this approach does not exploit the full potential of the technique. More recent implementations replace unreliable components by drawing from a distribution which models the relationship between the elements of each individual vector. For example, in Raj et al. (2004) a *cluster-based reconstruction* procedure was proposed, which replaced unreliable features with values estimated from a distribution which modelled clean speech features using Gaussian mixture models.

An alternative way to approach feature-based imputation is to take long-term feature correlations into account (Raj et al., 2004). First, a model of clean speech is estimated from clean training data. The feature vectors of the training data are considered to be the output of a Gaussian wide-sense stationary (WSS) random process (Papoulis, 1991). What this assumption allows for is the position-independence of the means of, and covariance matrices between, spectral vectors (Raj et al., 2004). The means and covariances are, however, dependent on the temporal distance between the components of the feature vectors. The means and covariances fully describe the process. If the correlations of reliable features within a neighbourhood of the unreliable ones exceed a certain threshold, they are used in the reconstruction. Initial estimates are continually re-estimated using the masked observations as an upper bound. The correlation method produced disappointing results when compared to the cluster-based method, but was considered attractive due to its simplicity and ease of implementation.

Feature-based data imputation offers two significant benefits: Firstly, the entire feature set is available for further processing; the second advantage involves the use of the features for recognition. It has already been established that cepstral features give significantly better recognition performance than spectral features.

State-based imputation makes use of the incomplete feature vectors for recognition and reconstruct features within each state of the HMM. The most basic approach is to replace the unreliable values within a state by the means of all the feature vectors for the state; this was shown to produce poor results (Cooke et al., 1997). Cooke et al. (2001b) replaced unreliable features with the expected value of the distribution of unreliable values conditioned on the reliable values and the state. Recall that a feature vector x is decomposed into sub-vectors of reliable speech, x_r, and unreliable speech x_u. The values of x_u can be estimated from the distribution, $P(x_u \mid x_r, q)$. Cooke et al. (2001b) chose the expected value of this distribution:

$$x'_u = E_{x_u \mid x_r, q} = \int P(x_u \mid x_r, q) \tag{2.7}$$

Though the features are not reconstructed prior to recognition, the state sequence can be recovered after recognition, making the imputed values available for further processing.

Marginalisation

Marginalisation seeks to use the unmodified feature vectors, this requires a slight modification of the recognition procedure. As is the case with imputation, the feature vector is split into reliable and unreliable features. The difference is that the state emission likelihood is calculated using the marginal distribution of reliable features formed by integrating over the unreliable features. Formally,

$$P(x \mid q) = P(x_r \mid q) = \int P(x_r, x_u \mid q) dx_u = \int P(x \mid q) dx_u \tag{2.8}$$

The computation of Equation 2.8 can be quite expensive, depending on the form of $P(x \mid q)$. Some studies modelled the speech data using multivariate Gaussians with full covariance matrices owing to the high level of correlation between the features of the spectral representation they employed (Cooke et al., 1997). An alternative to this is to model the data using Gaussian mixture models with diagonal covariance. That is,

$$P(x \mid q) = \sum_{k=1}^{M} P(k \mid q) P(x \mid k, q), \tag{2.9}$$

where $P(k \mid q)$ are the mixture weights.

Cooke and his co-workers (2001b) expanded upon work done in earlier MD studies (Ahmad and Tresp, 1993; Lippmann and Carlson, 1997; Green et al., 1995). Formerly, the unreliable data was ignored; this was extended so that information about the maximum value of the unreliable data is used as a *bound* for the likelihood calculation.[5] this was shown to significantly improve recognition performance. It has been found that marginalisation consistently gives better recognition results than imputation when spectral features are used (Morris et al., 1998; Cooke et al., 2001b; Raj and Stern, 2005)

Raj et al., (2000; 2001) have highlighted the benefit (over marginalisation) of using imputation to reconstruct the signal, generating cepstral features from the reconstructed signal and using the cepstra for recognition. The study carried out experiments on the Resource Management database (Price et al., 1988) using the SPHINX-III HMM-based speech recognition system (Placeway et al., 1997). The models employed were context-dependent HMMs with 2000 tied states, each modelled by a single Gaussian. The means of the features were normalised except where marginalisation is employed. Test utterances were corrupted with white noise and music at several SNRs. They point out that although marginalisation is more robust to errors, there is a cost of increased complexity that comes with the technique. Their recognition results for a system using cepstra derived from reconstructed signals show superior performance at most SNRs.

At this point in the discussion, the use of a spectral representation of the speech signal is again brought into question. Features obtained through the linear transformation of spectra (cepstra for example) tend to spread uncertainty throughout the representation (Cooke et al., 2001b; Barker et al., 2001b), this renders them unsuitable for MD ASR. For this reason, several researchers (Lippmann and Carlson, 1997; Cooke et al., 2001b; Morris et al., 2001) have put forward the spectral representation as the most suitable one for use within the MD framework. One objection to the use of spectral representations is the obvious redundancy they contain. However, this redundancy is welcome in MD ASR. As already pointed out, there is useful information available in a speech signal that has been distorted; this implies that there are more grouping cues available in a clean signal than are strictly necessary for recognition. Redundant representations therefore, lessen the reliance on a single cue and can be exploited in MD ASR by employing several grouping mechanisms. Morris et al. (2001) pointed out, however, that the drawback to using these highly correlated features is the fact that the current framework - HMM - precludes taking the full advantage afforded by the modelling of these features. This liability is somewhat overcome by representing the correlated features by a number of uncorrelated mixtures; the greater the number of mixtures, the better the fit to the data. This calls for significant amounts of training data to reliably estimate all the parameters required for these more detailed models; this is less than is needed for training full covariance matrices. Others however, have attempted to apply MDT in the cepstral domain (Häkkinen and Haverinen, 2001; Van hamme, 2003; Jun et al., 2004). Van hamme (2003) estimates the unreliable cepstral vectors by solving a nonnegative least squares problem. The estimated values are bounded by the maximum value of the noisy speech. The approach taken by Häkkinen and Haverinen (2001) is to apply marginalisation to the cepstral features. This is effected by applying a weighting matrix to

---

[5]The fact that the maximum and minimum values are available makes this technique viable. The maximum (and minimum) value is not available in all missing data problems

the cepstral features, minimising the effect of the unreliable components. The weaknesses of this approach are that it does not employ bounds and does not propose a principled approach to estimating the weights (Barker, 2006). The results shown are promising, but computational load and lack of significant improvement have so far made the approach infeasible.

2.4.4. Speech or Not?

This leads to questions about how to decide which time-frequency regions are reliable and which are not. In early systems, spectral subtraction was employed to remove the stationary components of the noise signal. Cooke et al. (2001b) implemented a *negative energy criterion* as an alternative to spectral subtraction. The criterion marks regions as missing if the total energy in a frame falls below the estimated noise threshold. The noise estimate is taken from the first few frames of the signal, which were assumed to be broadly representative of the noise. The obvious drawback to this approach is the assumption of stationarity. The solution proposed by Cooke et al. (2001b) is to use a local SNR criterion to augment the masking provided by the negative energy criterion. The product is the so-called *discrete mask*. Any error in classification made at this stage is irreversible and may lead to incorrect recognition. In order to counter this, the framework was expanded to use a probability of a spectro-temporal point being speech or noise, effectively producing a *soft mask* (see Section 6.4.1.). The technique works well to include a measure of uncertainty in the mask and leads to improvements in recognition performance.

One implementation of CASA was proposed by Barker et al. (2001c). It involved the development of harmonicity masks. The approach was to assume that the speech signal was the only harmonic signal present in the mixture. Therefore, the reliable pixels are determined by grouping regions of harmonicity. Of course, harmonic grouping will fail for unvoiced speech so the harmonicity masks must be combined with SNR masks, which fill in the gaps. The downside is that the method assumes that only the speech has dominant harmonic components and labels all such components as reliable. Reasonable results were achieved and this led the researchers to believe that there was some promise to the technique.

The above segmentation methods work well in limited domains. However, they all have the drawback of making strong assumptions about the corrupting noise. Where these assumptions prove to be incorrect the algorithms will not work. One assumption, often implicitly made, is that the background noise is not speech. Algorithms which make these assumptions will not be able to segment mixtures of monaurally combined speech. One can however, imagine a two-stage segmentation system that closely follows the auditory scene analysis account introduced in Section 2.4.1.: In the first step, all sources in the mixture are treated as generalised sounds and segmentation is performed by exploiting the physical properties of each constituent. This avoids potentially harmful assumptions and presents a partially segmented scene containing both noise and target to a second stage. For a truly general CASA system, there should be no strong assumptions about the noise and segmentation should be based on knowledge of the target source only. The second stage envisioned would exploit this knowledge to select regions of the segmented signal that relate to the target. An algorithm following such an approach would work equally well for speech corrupted with stationary or non-stationary sources, speech included.

2.5. Summary

Despite the many significant advances made in ASR, state-of-the-art systems are still susceptible to even slight noise intrusions. Many sophisticated techniques have been proposed for making ASR systems robust, ranging from the development of features insensitive to noise intrusions, to the development of detailed models of the environment. However, surprisingly few have made it into mainstream applications. Feature compensation techniques are somewhat limited because of the assumptions they tend to make about the operating environment. These compensation measures can be quite useful if the domain in which the ASR system is to be used is known beforehand; for a general purpose ASR application this is difficult to achieve.

Feature compensation methods attempt to 'de-noise' the signal prior to recognition, whereas model compensation involves the use of statistical models of both the noise and speech source at recognition time. Model compensation suffers from some of the same drawbacks that hamper feature compensation. Namely, the need to have detailed knowledge of each noise source that has to be compensated for, a requirement that cannot be met in natural environments, where noises tend to be varied and unpredictable. Nevertheless, where the pre-conditions are satisfied, the resulting performance can be impressive.

Since the corruption of speech is unpredictable, it would seem that a general noise compensation approach would take advantage of the power of simple heuristics developed from knowledge about the human auditory system and the environment in which it operates. This is the domain of ASA, which has been advanced as a general theory of sound organisation in humans. By studying how complex mixtures of sounds are organised by the human auditory system, researchers can develop models that either directly emulate the auditory system, or simply incorporate the principles learnt. The benefit of approaching the robustness problem from this perspective is that fewer assumptions need to be made and a wider cross-section of noises can be handled.

With the introduction of CASA, algorithms have been developed that model many of the principles of ASA. This has led to the advancement of several procedures for sound segmentation in which the constituents of an acoustic mixture can be segmented and grouped as isolated events. The potential for the use of CASA in research into noise robustness is immediately obvious. CASA-based algorithms have employed either primitive or schema-driven processes to perform speech segmentation. Primitive CASA uses primitive grouping rules to decide which sections of the mixed acoustic scene belong together. With primitive processes there is usually no knowledge of the nature of each segment. The power of schema-driven processes is that they can use *a priori* knowledge about speech to determine which regions of the mixed signal are speech. A significant drawback is that the output of most CASA systems is a spectral time-frequency representation with missing components, which is generally unsuitable for ASR.

Missing data theory was introduced as a method of harnessing the power of CASA and making the adjustments to the recognition process that were necessary for CASA to be used as a suitable front-end for ASR. Through the processes of marginalisation and imputation, it has been shown that the incomplete spectral representations can be successfully used for ASR with reasonably good results.

The combination of CASA and MD ASR is a potentially powerful one for improving the robustness of ASR. The difficulties faced by the typical MD ASR system could possibly be overcome by combining the power of primitive, data driven CASA with statistically trained schema-driven processes to give better performance than systems based on either taken in isolation. The following chapter proposes one such system.

Chapter 3

Speech Fragment Decoding

3.1. Introduction

The human auditory system is adept at recognising speech that has been corrupted with noise intrusions, even if those intrusions are also speech. Despite the many advances made in automatic speech recognition (ASR) none has led to the development of an automatic recogniser that can match human performance for accuracy or flexibility. This disparity in human and machine speech recognition performance has been receiving much attention in recent years (Huckvale, 1998; ten Bosch, 2001) – for a review see Scharenborg (2007). The general consensus of these studies is that, in the effort to increase machine recognition performance, there is something to be learnt from human speech recognition (HSR) – exactly what that is, and how to implement it in a computational model remains unclear.

The robustness and flexibility of the human auditory system is highlighted when one considers the ability of listeners to recognise the speech of some target speaker in a noisy environment. Evidence from psycho-acoustic studies (see Bregman, 1990, for a comprehensive review) have shown that humans possess mechanisms for segmenting the sound scene, creating from the apparent 'jumble' of noise and speech, related perceptual objects that have some common characteristic. Using a combination of signal-driven and schema-driven processes, isolated elements emanating from individual sound sources are placed in perceptually incongruent groupings, which can be separately organised, greatly assisting in the recognition of individual components of the acoustic mixture. This auditory scene analysis (ASA) (Bregman, 1990) is far different to the approach taken by typical ASR systems when dealing with noise corrupted speech.

This chapter introduces the *speech fragment decoder* (SFD), which is a speech recognition system that attempts to perform speech recognition in a manner inspired by the human auditory system. The novelty of the SFD is that it couples signal-driven and schema-driven components in a principled manner, whereas related systems treat them as separate. In Section 3.2. schema-driven and signal-driven processes are defined, highlighting the interpretation of these terms that motivates their use in this work. Sections 3.3. and 3.4. give overviews of signal-driven and schema-driven auditory scene analysis, respectively. Section 3.5. introduces the idea of a coupled system and goes on to outline, briefly, one possible instantiation of such a system, while Section 3.6. describes the SFD in detail. In Section 3.7. some of the issues surrounding the implementation of the decoder are highlighted. The chapter concludes with a summary in Section 3.8..

3.2.   Signal-driven or Schema-driven Scene Analysis

In the scene analysis account of auditory perception it is hypothesised that there are two types of processes that work to organise the auditory scene (Bregman, 1990). *Signal-driven* (or primitive) processes are defined as unconditioned grouping mechanisms that serve to organise the scene using very basic rules that take advantage of the physical characteristics of sound, grouping related objects based on their similarity and regularity. Such processes occur in the auditory periphery and are thought to be immune to the effect of higher-level of processing.[6] *Schema-driven* (or model-driven) processes on the other hand, are defined by Bregman (1990) as processes which call upon the knowledge stored in representations of individual objects in the auditory scene.

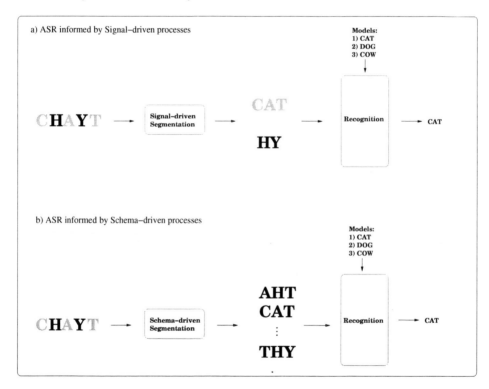

Figure 3.1. Illustration of the difference between automatic speech recognition informed by signal-driven processes and those informed by schema-driven processes - See text for details.

As a visual illustration of the different modes of action of signal- and schema-driven processes, consider Figure 3.1. The signal – 'CHAYT' – can be interpreted, based on

---

[6]This assumption has been shown to be too strong, given that primitive processes can be influenced by factors such as the attention of the listener (Alain and Izenberg, 2003; Carlyon et al., 2001; Carlyon, 2004). The simplification is employed here to highlight the innate nature of primitive processes.

visual clues, to be a mixture of the words 'CAT', and 'HY'. The illustration at the top of Figure 3.1, a), shows an ASR system informed by signal-driven processes. The signal is first segmented, based on the auditory equivalent of the visible colour-similarity of each element, forming two separate objects. The recognition grammar consists of three-letter animal names, 'COW', 'DOG' and 'CAT'. During recognition each object is considered separately and the model with the highest likelihood is chosen. The same signal is subject to a purely schema-driven segmentation (Figure 3.1, b), that is, the segmentation processes do not take advantage of any of the primitive cues available for segmentation. What results is a set of segmentations consisting of all combinations, as informed by the schemas. The recognition proceeds as before.

While this simple illustration serves to highlight the basic differences betwen scema- and signal driven ASR, referring to an ASR system as schema-driven or signal-driven can be misleading, as all ASR systems have some aspect of both schema- and signal-driven processing in them. For instance, the feature extraction in many systems employs 'primitive' knowledge of the frequency response of the human auditory system to design the spacing of the frequency bands during pre-processing – employing either the Mel-scale (Stevens et al., 1937) or bark-scale (Zwicker, 1961) in the design of the filterbank used for frequency analysis.[7] The reason for making this distinction is to direct attention to the different mechanisms employed for auditory scene segmentation in both methods of processing. A more detailed discussion is presented in the following sections.

3.3. ASR Informed by Signal-Driven Auditory Scene Analysis

The basic principle of a 'primitive' (or signal-driven) ASA system is the grouping of regions of regularity within a non-stationary auditory scene (Bregman, 1995). What this suggests is that there are related auditory objects within a sound signal that can be identified, given their general acoustic characteristics, and isolated from surrounding units. Identification of these objects follows from the application of certain *rules* (or *cues*) that are derived from the observation of the 'behaviour' of sounds in the natural world. If for instance a signal is composed of two sources originating from different locations, it is likely that those sources would form separate objects. Differences in fundamental frequency, temporal onset and offset also allow for the segmentation of a signal into discrete objects. This type of processing derives all its information from the input signal itself and does not rely on knowledge gained from experience or specific knowledge of particular sound sources (schema-driven information).

Weintraub (1985) recognised the power of signal-driven ASA and the promise it offered for addressing the problem of recognising the speech of overlapping speakers – the so-called *cocktail party problem* discussed by Cherry (1953), (see Bronkhorst (2000); Haykin and Chen (2005) for reviews). Weintraub first employed computational models of some of the signal-driven principles suggested by ASA, to segment the overlapping speech of two speakers in an acoustic signal. By employing pitch detection and tracking, the signal-driven

---

[7](See Hermansky, 1998, for a discussion of the ways in which modern ASR systems incorporate knowledge of human hearing.)

algorithm was able to recover partial descriptions of each component in the mixture. These were then separately re-synthesised to give recovered signals representing each speaker's utterance. Listening tests and ASR were then performed on the individual signals. This early attempt at a fusion between the two techniques did not produce very good recognition results, however, it provided a framework within which to perform ASA inspired ASR.

The majority of CASA systems were developed for speech enhancement purposes, given that CASA algorithms could extract unmasked portions of the signal from the noisy background, thereby increasing the SNR of the recovered portions of the signal. This partial recovery process was deemed incapable of producing output to be used by statistical ASR systems, since the models used for recognition were trained using representations of the complete signal. Missing data (MD) systems (as introduced in Chapter 2) were developed to overcome this weakness by exploiting the fact that spectral representations of speech are highly redundant, to the point where the deletion of significant portions of the data does not necessarily lead to correspondingly poor recognition performance (Cooke et al., 2001b).

The missing data approach typically employs a variety of procedures to segment a noisy speech signal into reliable and unreliable regions; it treats signal-driven ASA as a pre-processing *front-end* to the ASR *back-end*. This approach does not recouple the segmentation and recognition processes as is envisioned in the ASA account; the front-end produces a single foreground/background (reliable/unreliable) segmentation and passes it on to the recogniser, which assumes that the signal-driven segmentation decisions were error free.

3.4. ASR Informed by Schema-driven Auditory Scene Analysis

Whereas signal-driven systems interpret the evidence provided to the sensor to segment the sound scene, schema-driven systems combine statistical models of each acoustic source in the scene so as to provide the best possible explanation of the observed signal. In order to work, schema-driven systems must have models of sound sources that are likely to be found in the environment. In certain circumstances it is possible to develop detailed statistical models of all the sources in an acoustic mixture. By carefully manipulating these models it is possible to obtain a combination which 'reconstructs' the mixture. This reconstruction will serve as an explanation of the sound scene which can be reconciled with the observed data. Thus, by utilising the information contained in stochastic models of the elements in the environment, a schema-driven system can be more flexible than a signal-driven one. This flexibility comes about because the particular schema-driven system does not attempt to recover the 'interference-free' regions of the mixture by employing rules derived from interference-free signals. Because the *environmental models* employed by schema-driven systems encode a wide range of variation, such systems are less affected by the impact of intrusions on the target signal.

Take for instance the *HMM decomposition* system of Varga and Moore (1990), which is described in Section 2.3.2.. This involves creating models for the target source as well as a noise model that captures all the variability expressed in the noise. Decoding takes place in the joint noise/source state-space where a Viterbi search is performed to find the optimal path through the expanded state-space. As such, both components of the mixture can be recognised simultaneously.

While the model combination approach works well within a limited domain, its potential for application to a wider range of problems is restricted, not least because of the requirement that all sources in the mixture need to be known *a priori*. One way to overcome this is to develop a system, which employs generic models of elemental environmental sound sources which can be combined, with the aid of some control mechanism, to fully describe the acoustic environment. The *blackboard architecture* is well suited to this. The blackboard architecture was originally developed to tackle problems in the domain of speech understanding (Lesser et al., 1975; Erman et al., 1980). Blackboard systems are ideal for dealing with problems characterised by a large search space, incomplete data and partial knowledge. Essentially, the blackboard acts as a structure within which data and (preferably) independent *knowledge sources* modify or create hypotheses based on the state of the blackboard. Integral to the framework is the ability to adapt its strategies to the particular situation. However this has to be performed in a manner that allows for the search to be focused and orderly; thus the need for some *control mechanism*. Given these characteristics, and the incremental approach to search, the blackboard architecture is useful for tackling CASA-based problems.

Several CASA systems based on the blackboard architecture have been proposed (see Cooke et al., 1993; Godsmark and Brown, 1999; Ellis, 1996, for example). Ellis proposes a somewhat generalised solution to the limitations of signal-driven CASA systems with his *prediction-driven* approach (Ellis, 1996). This technique advocates a schema-driven approach to sound segmentation with the introduction of a *world model* which is defined as a grouping of individual items that explain and predict the sound scene. The prediction-driven model reconciles the predictions made by the world model with the input signal through the use of a feed-back loop, which modifies the world model based on an error signal encoding the difference between the prediction and observation. The observations of the system are acoustic representations of the sound signal such as the smoothed spectral envelope and summary autocorrelogram. These are matched against the internal representations of the world model, which are *noise clouds*, *wefts* and *transients*. The noise cloud represents all environmental signals whose fine structure can safely be ignored as they carry little perceptually relevant information. The weft is a depiction of real-world events that have a discernible periodicity. Transients cover the range of sounds with short, impulsive energy bursts.

A major criticism levelled at signal-driven (data-driven) systems, such as those outlined in Section 3.3. is their inability to emulate the human auditory system's capacity to restore obscured regions of a mixed signal (Ellis, 1996; Srinivasan, 2006). The prediction-driven approach allows for the inference of missing data through the predictions of the world model. If the prediction is deemed consistent with the input signal, within some range of uncertainty, the absence of a cue in the acoustic representation does not preclude its acceptance by the model. Ellis attributes this to the flexibility of the system that is afforded it by the non-specific nature of the internal representations of the world model.

Although the prediction-driven approach was designed to produce a reconstruction of the sources in a sound mixture and was not evaluated using automatic speech recognition, it did provide several useful insights that can be incorporated into ASR systems that deal with occluded speech.[8] While signal-driven systems rely on the detection of low-level cues, which can be absent in occluded speech, schema-driven systems employ *a priori* information about the structure of sources making them less susceptible to cue obstruction. Ellis also recommended that source segmentation algorithms ought to be flexible in the way they handle the modification of existing cues or the introduction of new ones. Schema-driven systems such as the prediction-driven approach can selectively modify the running hypotheses based on the dictates of the observations. This would be one way to overcome the limitation faced by MD ASR systems that produce foreground/background segmentations, but lack the ability to alter these segmentations.

While schema-driven segmentation systems have some clear advantages over signal-driven systems, there are also some constraints. Schema-driven processing is more successful if there are specific models of all elements in the environment. However, there is a limit on the number of models that can be incorporated in the system, while maintaining some level of computational efficiency. It would then seem infeasible to have a single generalised schema-driven segmentation scheme. Ellis' prediction-driven system attempted to overcome this by employing a hierarchy of models, from the general to the more specific. However, a weakness of this approach is that the generalised noise models do not provide a great level of discrimination, leading to similar treatment for most noise sources. A problem occurs if the recovery of more than one component of the sound scene is necessary. If more than one noise source is present with the target, it is likely that all the noise will be treated as a single source. This could be overcome with the introduction of noise models with more structure, that is, by not simply modelling the general properties of the noise, but by modelling the fine structure of each noise. However, the difficulty of creating complex models for each possible source emerges.

As the number of elemental models increases, a second shortcoming becomes evident, namely, the computational complexity of performing a search over the entire model space. With creative and aggressive pruning mechanisms it is possible to reduce the search space to some degree, but there are still significant limitations on the number and complexity of the models that can be used in a schema-driven search (see Ellis (2006) for an analysis of schema-driven source segmentation techniques).

3.5.   Coupling Schema-driven and Signal-driven Auditory Processing

Both schema-driven and signal-driven processing have advantages, however, neither approach provides a complete solution to the segmentation problem. The way forward is a deliberate combination of both types of processing into a system that takes advantage of the power of each. Bregman has called for such an approach, suggesting that there is insufficient information in the grouping cues used by signal-driven ASA to produce a complete segmentation of the sound scene prior to recognition (Bregman, 1995). Slaney (1998) also suggested that a combination of the two approaches would serve as a more complete model of auditory processing and would thus help to improve computational models that aim to mimic it, or replicate the recognition performance it produces. While it is acknowl-

---

[8]Ellis (1999b) has suggested how the approach could be modified to perform ASR.

edged that all ASR systems have incorporated aspects of both types of processing (see Section 3.2.), there is some debate about how tightly coupled both processes ought to be – whether signal-driven processing should precede schema-driven, or whether they should be employed simultaneously (Bregman, 1995; Carlyon et al., 2001; Alain and Izenberg, 2003; Carlyon, 2004). While there is no general consensus, studies have shown that the segmentations suggested by signal-driven processes are amendable (and sometimes overridden) by the schema-driven processes if the evidence validates such action (see Alain et al., 2001; Sussman et al., 2002; Davis and Johnsrudeb, 2007, and references therein).

Weintraub (1985) recognised the shortcomings of his attempt to employ perceptually-inspired techniques into an ASR system (see Section 3.3.). He suggested that it was important to follow the ASA paradigm more closely by having a more intimate coupling of the schema-driven and signal-driven analyses. The signal-driven approach to MD ASR can theoretically group the related spectro-temporal regions of a source into separate objects, one of which is the target for recognition. In reality however, signal-driven segmentation algorithms may not be powerful enough to perform the required grouping. They may, however, be able to group related spectro-temporal points of limited extent to form *fragments* which partially describe each source. Through a series of local segmentations, a set of fragments is formed that completely describes the recoverable portions of the acoustic scene. When this occurs there is need for a process that can search the input space and make an intelligent decision about the nature of each fragment, selecting those that are likely to form part of the target stream. In the case where models of the target are available, schema-driven processes can use the knowledge they encode to assist in the decision process.

This fusion of signal-driven and schema-driven processes is closer to Bregman's ASA account, where primitive and schema-driven systems work together to make sense of the auditory scene. Bregman posits that primitive processes, driven by the characteristics of the incoming signal, sort it into coherent elements; while schema-based processes call into play stored representations of knowledge and accumulated experience of the environment to organise and interpret the scene.

From this definition, a two-stage ASR system can be envisioned, which employs in the first stage, a signal-driven segmentation mechanism that passes on to the second stage a set of coherent fragments. For the purposes of this discussion, a coherent fragment is defined as an aggregation of spectro-temporal points from the acoustic mixture that are energetically dominated by one particular sound source; this definition of coherence will be applied throughout this work. The second stage would consider all the possible foreground/background segmentations that can be achieved by analysing the various foreground/background labellings of individual fragments, where each segmentation is matched against models of clean speech. The outcome of the process is a foreground/background segmentation and a word string that jointly represent the best interpretation of the mixed signal. This differs from the approach of most missing data systems, where the foreground/background segmentation is performed prior to recognition. In contrast, the proposed signal-driven processing does not make a decision as to whether a fragment is representing a region of masking energy (background), or energy due to the target source (foreground); this decision is made as part of the recognition process.

The *speech fragment decoder* (SFD) is one implementation of such a system (Barker et al., 2005). The SFD takes as input the data labelled by signal-driven CASA processes and searches through it for the correct segmentation as well as the correct sequence of words. In contrast to most missing data systems, which employ a single missing data mask (i.e. foreground/background segmentation), the SFD performs an algorithm that is equivalent to running a missing data recognition system using many different masks and then picking the recognition result with the highest overall score. Testing all possible masks (i.e. allowing every possible time-frequency point to be independently labelled as either foreground or background) would clearly be computationally intractable. It would also be undesirable because many of the possible foreground/background segmentations of the data would not be consistent with primitive grouping cues. So, in an initial signal-driven stage, primitive grouping cues are used to segment the spectro-temporal plain into a set of coherent fragments. The spectro-temporal points within these fragments are then grouped together and labelled as either foreground or background as one unit. If the fragments that are found are perfectly coherent, then there will necessarily exist a labelling of the fragments that correctly segments the foreground and background regions. So now, rather than search over all possible combinations of *time-frequency point* labellings, the decoder need only search over the much smaller space of all possible foreground/background *fragment* labellings. With the application of a modified token-passing Viterbi algorithm, the decoder is able to employ the knowledge contained in the statistically trained acoustic models to perform an efficient schema-driven search of the joint segmentation/word-sequence space to find the most likely word-sequence and segmentation hypothesis. The following section will give details of the system and its application.

3.6.   The Speech Fragment Decoder: Theory

Though the theoretical development of the SFD is quite different to that of standard ASR, there are some common elements which will become evident as the discussion progresses. The SFD will first be described as initially implemented by Barker et al. (2005), while the system refinements published in Coy and Barker (2007) will be detailed in Sections 3.6.5., 3.6.6. and 3.6.7..

3.6.1.   From Standard ASR to SFD

The general ASR formulation, described in Chapter 2, must be modified to reflect the operation of the SFD. Firstly, the acoustic vectors representing clean speech must be replaced with those representing occluded speech, $Y = y_1, y_2, \ldots, y_T$. Secondly, the equation must show that the decoder outputs both the word sequence, W, and the foreground/background segmentation, S. Applying these modifications to Equation 2.1 yields the following:

$$W', S' = \operatorname*{argmax}_{W,S} P(W, S \mid Y). \tag{3.1}$$

Given an utterance of speech mixed with a competing sound source, the SFD finds the likelihood that a particular acoustic model, given the segmentation, produced the noisy speech. Since full knowledge of the features of the clean speech is not available, the correct procedure for finding this likelihood is to integrate over all the unobserved clean speech values taking into account the noisy observations and the segmentation. Thus,

$$P(W, S \mid Y) = \int P(W, X, S \mid Y) \, dX \tag{3.2}$$

$$= P(S \mid Y) \cdot \int P(W \mid X, S, Y) \cdot P(X \mid S, Y) \, dX. \tag{3.3}$$

As the segmentation and noisy observation sequence are independent of the word sequence, given the clean speech sequence, Equation 3.3 is reduced to:

$$P(W, S \mid Y) = P(S \mid Y) \cdot \int P(W \mid X) \cdot P(X \mid S, Y) \, dX. \tag{3.4}$$

Applying Bayes' rule and re-arranging:

$$P(W, S \mid Y) = P(W) \cdot P(S \mid Y) \cdot \left(\int P(X \mid W) \cdot \frac{P(X \mid S, Y)}{P(X)} \, dX \right). \tag{3.5}$$

By applying the modifications necessary to reflect the search for the Viterbi path, the aim of the SFD can be stated as:

$$W', S' = \operatorname*{argmax}_{W,S} \max_{Q \in Q_W} P(W) \cdot P(S \mid Y) \cdot P(Q \mid W) \cdot \left(\int P(X \mid Q) \cdot \frac{P(X \mid S, Y)}{P(X)} \, dX \right). \tag{3.6}$$

When Equation 3.6 is compared with Equation 2.4 some clear differences can be identified; Table 3.1 highlights the major distinctions between the two equations:

Table 3.1. A comparison of the terms that differ in Equations 3.6 and 2.4.

	Standard ASR	**Speech Fragment ASR**
Acoustic Model	$P(X \mid Q)$	$\int P(X \mid Q) \cdot \frac{P(X \mid S, Y)}{P(X)} \, dX$
Maximisation	$\operatorname*{argmax}_{W}$	$\operatorname*{argmax}_{W,S}$
Segmentation Model	–	$P(S \mid Y)$

- The acoustic model in the SFD is different in two respects. Firstly, it is evaluated over the possible values of the clean speech, whereas the unmodified decoder employs all speech features. The second difference is that the acoustic model is weighted by the relative likelihood of observing the clean speech values given the occluded speech and the segmentation. The acoustic model will be fully described in Section 3.6.4..

- The SFD searches both the word space and the segmentation space and finds solutions that jointly maximise the likelihood of a particular output. An efficient implementation of this search is described in Section 3.6.3..

- The *segmentation model* gives a measure of the likelihood of a particular segmentation given the observed data. The following section will describe this model.

3.6.2. The SFD Segmentation Model

By parameterising an acoustic source using a spectro-temporal representation, the source can be visualised as a 2-D grid of time-frequency pixels (see Figure 3.2). In an observation with T time frames, each point in the grid represents an observation at time t in one of F frequency channels.

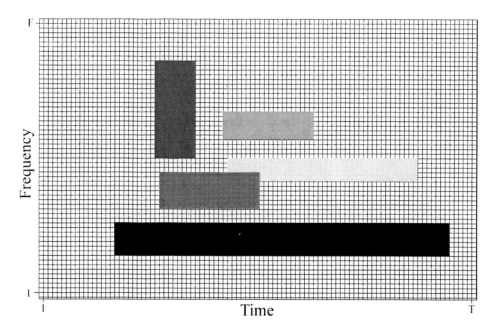

Figure 3.2. Illustration of a time-frequency representation of a mixture of speech sounds. The shaded regions represent coherent fragments of each source.

Each pixel can be labelled with one of two labels, a 1, signifying it belongs to the foreground, or a 0 if it belongs to the background. The segmentation model serves to determine how likely it is that each fragment – grouping of pixels – is either in the foreground or the background. In the case where there are multiple speech sources, each segmentation hypothesis would assign one speech source to the foreground and all others to the background. This requires the segmentation model to consider 2^{TF} possible explanations for the pixels in the grid, which could be too large a search space. One solution is to detect the pixels that share the same label and group them into contiguous regions. The computational savings achieved by this technique can be illustrated by considering Figure 3.2 to be the spectro-temporal representation of a hypothetical mixture of speech sounds with 60 frequency channels and 97 time frames. If every pixel was considered to be part of the segmentation process, this would lead to $2^{60 \times 97}$ hypotheses for the entire utterance. If however, the regions of speech were detected and labelled, there would only be 5 regions (represented by the shaded areas on the grid) and 2^5 possible segmentations of those regions.[9] Thus as

---

[9]The pixels that are recognised as 'silence', that is, containing no energy from any sound source, are not involved in the segmentation process.

a general rule, the segmentation model does not have to evaluate all 2^{TF} hypotheses, but rather, it has to evaluate 2^N hypotheses, where N is the number of contiguous regions of energy. This makes the implicit assumption that the probability of the remaining $2^{TF} - 2^N$ segmentations is 0. Let S' be the 2^N segmentations that can be formed by the fragment set F, then:

$$P(S \mid Y) = \begin{cases} 0 & \text{if } S \notin S' \\ \frac{1}{2^N} & \text{if } S \in S'. \end{cases} \tag{3.7}$$

It is important that the regions defined are coherent, in the sense explained in Section 3.5., otherwise the segmentation model would make irreconcilable errors in assigning a region to a sound source and may label foreground speech energy as background and vice versa.

The formation of these regions, or fragments, is by no means trivial and is the subject of much research (Barker and Coy, 2005; Coy and Barker, 2007; Laidler et al., 2007; Christensen et al., 2007; Ma et al., 2007). Briefly, the segmentation model serves as the signal-driven component of the entire framework. Primitive grouping processes, such as those suggested by ASA, for example: common onset, harmonicity, common fundamental frequency, interaural time difference and interaural level difference, can be used to group regions that belong together. Chapters 6 and 7 give more details of the signal-driven segmentation processes from which fragments can be derived for use with the SFD.

3.6.3. Joint Maximisation of W and S

The searches for the best word sequence and segmentation are carried out simultaneously in the SFD. In order to achieve this, the decoding framework has to be significantly altered. The search of the segmentation space is dependent on the word sequence hypotheses; because each word sequence is associated with a particular subset of fragments, each will potentially have a different most likely segmentation hypothesis. Note that all segmentations are considered in conjunction with all word sequences. This interdependence constrains the form that the search can take and requires that the search be performed as efficiently as possible. The following sections describe the process by which a segmentation hypothesis can evolve before explaining how that evolution can be accomplished within the word-sequence search.

Implementation of a Segmentation Search

Presented with N fragments the decoder has the task of considering all 2^N possible segmentations. For longer words, the value of N is likely to be larger making the required computation quite expensive. Without an efficient implementation, it would be necessary to perform a separate decoding for each possible segmentation of the fragments. Unless N is very small, the cost of implementing this strategy would be prohibitive.

The solution requires a careful observation of the differences between particular pairs of hypotheses. In each segmentation hypothesis the constituent fragments will be labelled as either foreground or background and each segmentation will differ in its labelling of some fragments. Some hypotheses however, differ only in their labelling of a single fragment.

This suggests that up to the point where these segmentations differ, the decoding will be identical and will again become so when the fragment in question has come to an end. While this is true in the case where each segmentation is equally weighted (recall Equation 3.7), it may not be true for more complex segmentation models.

Figure 3.3 illustrates the form of the solution: Both hypotheses share a decoder until the point labelled T_2, at this point a new fragment onsets. One segmentation has this fragment labelled as foreground, while the other labels it as background. To accommodate this divergence, the decodings *split* and there is a separate decoding for each hypothesis. At T_3, when the fragment offsets, the segmentations are again identical and the decoders *merge* so that a single decoder is employed to process the remaining fragments. The merging of decoders is carried out by comparing the likelihoods of the hypotheses and keeping the one with the highest likelihood.[10] Thus, this approach ensures an efficient, fully admissible search that avoids an exponential growth in the number of decoders required to process a given set of fragments.

Implementing a Word Sequence Search

The word-sequence hypothesis search has to take place concurrent with the segmentation search. In order to achieve this a modified Viterbi *token-passing* decoder is employed. With standard token-passing, each state of the model has a token which keeps track of the word hypothesis score at each time frame. In the modified decoder each state of the acoustic model keeps separate tokens for each possible labelling of the active fragments (fragments that have previously onset and have not yet offset); the tokens keep track of the acoustic model score, as well as the labels they have assigned to each fragment. Tokens are duplicated whenever a new fragment begins; one copy has the fragment labelled as foreground while the other labels it as background. This token duplication can be viewed as the development of a separate decoding, which allows for the consideration of all hypotheses regarding the labelling of the fragment. As a fragment ends, the alternate decodings, which differ only in their labelling of the particular fragment, are merged and the token with the most likely fragment label is kept (see Figure 3.3).

The final labelling decision and word model choice is made at the end of the utterance. In this way, no hypothesis pruning occurs and the search is fully admissible (Barker et al., 2005). These modifications allow the search to be more efficient by reducing the number of parallel decoders needed to cope with the separate segmentation hypotheses.

As the tokens are propagated through the states of the HMM, the tokens arriving in the same state, with identical labelling of the active fragments, are compared and the most likely token is passed on. Barker et al. (2005) have shown that the removal of tokens with lower likelihood does not amount to hypothesis pruning and that the efficient implementation leads to the same result as a search which employs separate decoders for each segmentation and chooses the output of the decoding with the highest overall likelihood as the correct one.

---

[10]This hypothesis merging is valid, given that the segmentation model follows the Markov assumption; that is, if each hypothesis is independent of its past (Barker et al., 2005).

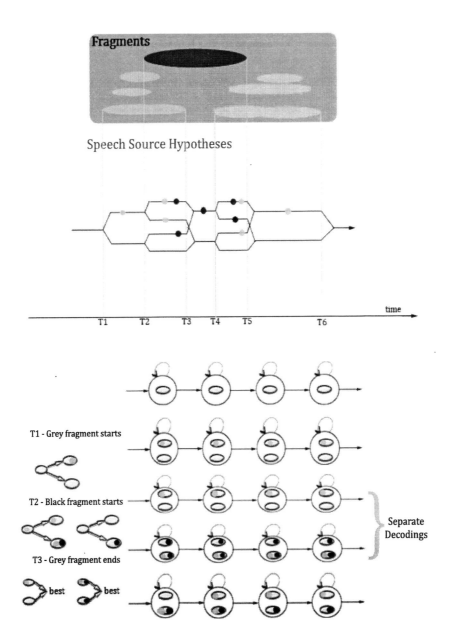

Figure 3.3. An illustration of the implementation of the word sequence search. The solid dots represent hypotheses which label the fragment as speech. The absence of a dot means the fragment is labelled as background. When a new fragment begins, the hypotheses split in order to consider both labellings. When a fragment ends, the hypotheses are merged and the best labellings are propagated.

3.6.4. The Acoustic Model

The operation of the acoustic model developed for use in the SFD differs significantly from that used in a standard ASR system (see Table 3.1). In order to fully explain its implementation the discussion begun in Section 3.6.1. must be further expanded.

Recall that the SFD's acoustic model is a weighted integral over the clean speech features:

$$\int P(X \mid Q) \cdot \frac{P(X \mid S,Y)}{P(X)} \, dX, \tag{3.8}$$

where $P(X \mid Q)$ is the model of the clean speech features that is employed in standard ASR and $\frac{P(X \mid S,Y)}{P(X)}$ is a distribution that expresses the impact of the segmentation and obscured speech features on the decoding.

The first stage of the expansion calls for the use of the *output independence assumption*, which allows the likelihood of a sequence of T time frames to be represented as a product of the likelihoods at each time step, t. The independence of $P(X \mid S,Y)$ and $P(X)$ is also assumed:

$$\int P(X \mid Q) \cdot \frac{P(X \mid S,Y)}{P(X)} \, dX = \prod_j \int P(x_j \mid q_j) \cdot \frac{P(x_j \mid S,Y)}{P(x_j)} \, dx_j. \tag{3.9}$$

In a typical continuous density HMM, $P(x \mid q)$ is modelled as one or more multivariate Gaussians with diagonal covariance matrices, such that

$$P(x \mid q) = \sum_{k=1}^{M} P(k \mid q) \cdot P(x \mid k,q), \tag{3.10}$$

where $P(k \mid q)$ are the mixture weights.

One advantage of modelling the likelihood score as a Gaussian with a diagonal covariance is that the elements of the feature vectors are taken to be independent. Taking advantage of this independence the acoustic model score can be further decomposed with respect to the individual feature vectors x_j:

$$P(x \mid q) = \sum_{k=1}^{M} P(k \mid q) \cdot \prod_j P(x_j \mid k,q). \tag{3.11}$$

Assuming a similar decomposition of the prior $P(X)$:

$$\int P(X \mid W) \cdot \frac{P(X \mid S,Y)}{P(X)} \, dX = \sum_{k=1}^{M} P(k \mid q) \cdot \prod_j \int P(x_j \mid k,q) \cdot \frac{P(x_j \mid S,Y)}{P(x_j)} \, dx_j. \tag{3.12}$$

The Segmentation Weighting

Knowledge of the noisy observations and segmentation is applied in the form of a distribution, which acts as a weight for the clean speech likelihood. Each utterance can be split into a number of sub-bands, which can be categorised as either dominated by speech or dominated by the competing sources. The feature vector is divided into j pixels – some marked as observed, the others as masked. The weighting-distribution then becomes the product of two terms: one for which the speech energy values can be directly calculated and the other where the speech values are occluded by the competing sources.

In the first case, the clean speech values are known and the segmentation weighting is a Dirac delta at the value of sub-band energy, x^*, calculated from the models of clean speech. The integral then turns out to be no more than the likelihood of the value being considered. That is, given:

$$P(x_j \mid S, Y) = \delta(x_j - x^*),\tag{3.13}$$

then,

$$\int P(x_j \mid k, q) \cdot \frac{P(x_j \mid S, Y)}{P(x_j)}\, dx_j = \frac{P(x^* \mid k, q)}{P(x^*)}.\tag{3.14}$$

For the latter case, the clean speech values are unknown, and the weighting-distribution is an integral of what is essentially the likelihood of the clean speech models producing the observed (occluding) energy values. The sub-band energy value, x^*, is then considered to be the value of the more, energetic, masking source(s); the value of the clean speech features is not known, but must have a value less than x^*. Thus,

$$P(x_j \mid S, Y) = \begin{cases} F \cdot P(x_j) & \text{for } x_j \leq x^* \\ 0 & \text{otherwise.} \end{cases}\tag{3.15}$$

The segmentation weighting is assumed to be proportional to the prior distribution of speech values, where the observed energy falls beneath the calculated sub-band spectral energy, and zero elsewhere. The constant of proportionality (F), which is needed to make the distribution sum to 1, takes the form:

$$F = \frac{1}{\int_{-\infty}^{x^*} P(x_j), dx_j}.\tag{3.16}$$

This leads to the following for the segmentation weighting in occluded regions:

$$\int P(x_j \mid k, q) \cdot \frac{P(x_j \mid S, Y)}{P(x_j)} dx_j = \int_{-\infty}^{x^*} P(x_j \mid k, q) \cdot \frac{1}{\int_{-\infty}^{x^*} P(x_j), dx_j} dx_j.\tag{3.17}$$

If the j dimensional feature vector is split into separate sets, those that are present, S_P and those that are missing, S_M, the likelihood over all mixtures is given as:

$$\begin{aligned} &P(x^* \mid q, S_P, S_M) \\ &= \sum_{k=1}^{M} P(k \mid q) \prod_{j \in S_P} \frac{P(x_j^* \mid k, q)}{P(x_j^*)} \prod_{j \in S_M} \frac{1}{\int_{-\infty}^{x^*} P(x_j), dx_j} \cdot \int_{-\infty}^{x_j^*} P(x_j \mid k, q) dx_j. \end{aligned}\tag{3.18}$$

Several improvements have been made to the SFD framework presented in Barker et al. (2005). The most significant of these advancements are highlighted in the sections which follow.[11]

---

[11] These modifications have been published in Coy and Barker (2007)

3.6.5.   The Speech Prior

In Barker et al. (2005) the speech prior $P(x_j)$ is assumed to take on a uniform value of $\frac{1}{x_{max}}$ over the range $0 < x_j < x_{max}$, where x_{max} is a constant chosen to be larger than any observable value in the cube-root compressed energy values used as feature vectors. Equation 3.16 can then be rewritten as:

$$F = \frac{x_{max}}{x^*}. \tag{3.19}$$

The use of a uniform prior leads to a bias in the likelihood calculation towards favouring hypotheses in which either a disproportionate number of fragments have been labelled as background, or too many are labelled as foreground. A correction factor, α, is introduced to scale the likelihood calculation for the occluded regions in order to correct these errors. Thus:

$$F = \alpha \cdot \frac{x_{max}}{x^*}. \tag{3.20}$$

In the current study, a GMM-based speech prior is employed which replaces the uniform prior and removes the need for a tuning parameter. The model can be derived from the clean speech HMMs that have been trained for the schema-driven component of the SFD system. The Gaussian mixtures from all states of all the HMMs are pooled and their mixture weights are rescaled to account for the differing posterior state occupation probabilities. Then, the prior, F would take the following form:

$$F = \frac{1}{\int_{-\infty}^{x^*} P_{sp}(x)dx}, \tag{3.21}$$

where P_{sp} is the speech prior distribution described by the GMM and x^* is the noisy observation in channel j. P_{sp} can be expressed as a sum of mixtures:

$$P_{sp}(x) = \sum_{k=1}^{M} P_{sp}(k) \cdot P_{sp}(x \mid k), \tag{3.22}$$

where $P_{sp}(k)$ are mixture weights.

3.6.6.   Soft Masks

In the original formulation of the SFD, each fragment labelling leads to the production of a discrete missing data mask; one in which a spectro-temporal point is either completely present (indicated by a 1 in the mask), or else, completely missing (indicated by a 0). This implies total confidence in the accuracy of the mask. It has been shown that both missing data systems, and the SFD, work better if they employ 'soft masks' (Barker et al., 2000; Coy and Barker, 2005). In the soft mask the binary decision about a spectro-temporal point's presence is replaced by soft value between 0 and 1 that can be loosely interpreted as the probability that the point is present. To generate competing soft mask hypotheses in the SFD, the fragments act on an underlying spectro-temporal map of confidence scores, c, containing values in the range 0.5 to 1.0. If a fragment is labelled as foreground, the soft mask values, m, in the fragment's region are taken to be the confidence scores, c. Whereas if a fragment is labelled as background, then the mask values, m, are computed as $1 - c$. Hence, the confidence values in the range 0.5 to 1.0 produce soft masks scaled between 0 and 1. Spectro-temporal regions with confidence values of 1 will flip between alternate interpretations of 1 (present) and 0 (missing) (as in the discrete SFD system), whereas regions of low confidence values (i.e. near 0.5) will alternate between less extreme interpretations – a little over 0.5 (most likely present) and a little under 0.5 (most likely missing). This process is made clear by Figure 3.4.

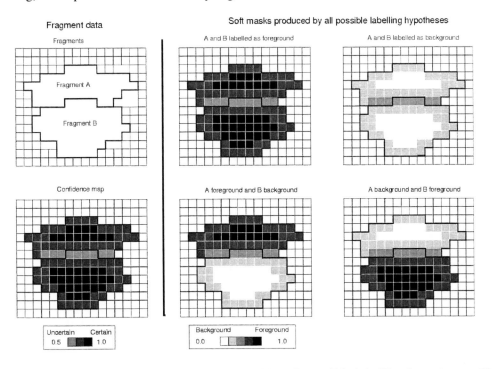

Figure 3.4. Illustrations of soft masks produced by all possible labelling hypotheses. The upper left grid shows spectro-temporal regions defining two example fragments, A and B. Beneath is an example of a *confidence map* on which these fragments operate. Spectro-temporal points in the fragment regions are assigned confidence values ranging from 0.5 (uncertain) to 1.0 (certain). For illustrative purposes the figure employs three discrete levels, (0.5, 0.75, 1.0); in practise the confidence value is continuous. Then, when generating different segmentation hypotheses, fragments may be independently labelled as either foreground or background. With two fragments there are four possible soft masks – shown on the right – that can be generated by considering each possible fragment labelling. Foreground fragments pass the confidence values, x, directly to the soft mask; background fragments pass the values, $1 - x$. The soft mask values will then be spread across the range from 0 (definitely dominated by the background) to 1 (definitely dominated by the foreground). Values closer to 0.5 indicate regions less clearly dominated by either foreground or background. (Reproduced from Coy and Barker (2007)).

Note, any region of the mask with a confidence value of 0.5 will remain at 0.5 under both fragment labellings. So now, during the fragment generation process, spectro-temporal regions in which the energy can be confidently allocated to a fragment can be given values in the mask close to 1.0, and regions that are less confidently grouped – or which are not clearly dominated by any one source – can be given values closer to 0.5. The precise way in which this value is determined depends on the principles underlying the particular fragment generation process (e.g. in the harmonic grouping technique described in Chapter 6, lower values are assigned if there is evidence of multiple pitches within the same frequency channel). When employing soft masks, the acoustic match score is changed so that the contribution of spectro-temporal elements is a weighted interpolation between the present and missing data score (see Barker et al., 2000). Explicitly, Equation 3.18 becomes,

$$P(x^*|q,m) = \sum_{k=1}^{M} P(k|q) \prod_{j=1}^{d} \left(m_j P(x_j^*|k,q) + F \cdot (1-m_j) \int_{-\infty}^{x_j^*} P(x_j|k,q)dx_j \right), \qquad (3.23)$$

where the interpolation weights, m, are taken from the current frame of the soft mask, and d is the dimensionality of the feature vector.

3.6.7.   Delta Features

Temporal difference features, or *deltas*, are common in traditional ASR systems. Typically they are used as additional features that are concatenated to the vector of static features. How are these features best employed in the SFD framework? First, consider the use of static and delta features in missing data systems. In these systems, *reliable* static and delta features are matched to models of clean speech in an identical manner. However, *missing* static and *missing* delta features are handled differently. For missing static features a 'bounds constraint' is applied which uses a bounded integral to consider all values of the speech energy that lie beneath the level of the observed masking energy (i.e. the integral term in Equations 3.18 and 3.23). Missing delta features occur when the underlying static features from which they are computed are judged to be masked. A loose bound on the possible delta values can be computed by considering extreme values of the bounded missing static values. However, for reasons that are not clearly understood, experience with previous missing data systems (see Barker et al., 2000, for example) has shown that this loose bound results in performance that is poorer than that achieved by simply ignoring missing delta features. In the SFD framework missing components are normalised by the integration bound, so not being able to compute an effective missing data bound is problematic.

Experiments have shown that the benefits of deltas can be realised if they are employed in an unconventional manner. In a conventional GMM-based system using diagonal covariance components, given the mixture, the static and delta features are considered to be independent. Each provides a separate additive term in the log-likelihood computation. In contrast, whenever a delta feature is present in the SFD, it is used as though it were completely correlated with the static feature and the observation is just providing a second (perhaps less noisy) view of the same event. If both the static and delta features are judged to be present, the $P(x_j^*|k,q)$ term for the static feature is simply replaced with the average of the static feature, x^*, and corresponding delta feature, $x^{*\prime}$, probabilities, i.e. $\frac{1}{2}(P(x_j^*|k,q) + P(x_j^{*\prime}|k,q))$. The present delta features can be thought of as simply making a correction to the present static feature probabilities. Although somewhat *ad hoc*, this procedure appears to overcome the normalisation problems and allows the delta features to make a significant contribution to recognition performance. However, it is possible that more principled approaches could be developed that would lead to further performance benefits. Now that the theoretical framework for the SFD has been laid down, the following section will provide a more general discussion of the technique.

3.7. Discussion

The SFD provides a framework within which to perform ASA informed ASR. While it is not the first such system, it is novel in the way it attempts to couple both disciplines. ASR with the SFD is a two-stage process: First, there is a source segmentation step, where primitive CASA creates isolated fragments of limited spectro-temporal extent. The second stage, the decoding step, organises these fragments to form the joint, best segmentation and word-sequence hypothesis.

3.7.1. Fragment Size

While the SFD is less reliant on an error-free segmentation process for a full explanation of the auditory scene, it nonetheless requires a relatively accurate fragment generator. This brings into focus the issue of trade-off between fragment coherence and size. Typically, a smaller fragment will be more coherent as it is more likely that regions of uncorrupted energy are presented as *glimpses* of spectro-temporal energy (Cooke, 2006). These glimpses can be loosely defined as gaps in the spectrum of one source, in which the unaltered spectra of a separate source becomes visible. Thus a segmentation algorithm that extracts numerous small accurate fragments would seem to be a good idea. The size of a fragment, however, has implications for both the accuracy and the efficiency of the decoder. Segmenting the scene into many smaller fragments may remove some grouping constraint imposed by the primitive processes. Further, the more numerous the fragments, the more computational power the decoder will require, as there may be several fragments active at the same time. Given the constrained spectro-temporal coverage of the glimpses, related fragments may be spread across time, with the consequence that cues to a relationship between fragments that emerge over time (such as good continuity) could be disrupted. Chapter 7 gives a fuller discussion of the trade-off between fragment coherence and size.

3.7.2. Sequential Integration

When using isolated fragments for recognition, the SFD faces a major challenge – that of sequential organisation of the fragments. When presented a mixture of n sources, segmentation algorithms typically, seek to create n *meta-fragments*. A meta-fragment can be thought of as a fragment that completely describes a source across time and frequency (something akin to a missing data mask). Within the SFD framework, meta-fragments are the exception, it is more likely that there will be several fragments derived from each source, every fragment providing a partial description. Sequential integration is thus performed during the decoding stage, with information for fragment grouping provided by the trained models of speech. Where well trained speaker-dependent models are available, this process of grouping fragments across time is likely to be aided by the discriminatory power of these models. If, however, the models are less well trained, as is the case with speaker-independent models, there is greater difficulty. Sequential integration is also influenced by the perplexity of the task. A small vocabulary task with a highly constrained grammar will provide more sequential grouping constraints than a large vocabulary task.

One simple approach to improving sequential integration within the decoder would be to include a process of fragment grouping, as suggested by Barker et al. (2005). This would involve delaying the decision about the nature of a fragment beyond the frame in which it offsets. By extending a window of say N frames beyond the offset, the relationship between emerging fragments and the one that has most recently offset can be taken into account. The relationship between sets of fragments can be learnt from training and incorporated into the decoding process as part of the hypothesis choosing procedure. This has the potential drawback of increased computation, which would be exponentially proportional to the length of the window; that is, the computation would scale as 2^M, where M is the number of fragments overlapping the window. An implementation of this idea would require careful consideration of the impact of window size on decoding time.

3.8. Summary

This chapter has examined the approaches to auditory-inspired robust speech recognition; both signal-driven and schema-driven systems have been reviewed. The relative merits and drawbacks to each technique have been explored. A re-examination of the early work done in ASA makes it clear that a hybrid approach – one that combines different aspects of both schema-driven and signal-driven processing – is preferred. The speech fragment decoder was proposed as a framework within which such a fusion could take place. It exploits signal-driven procedures, to propose coherent spectro-temporal fragments that are organised by the decoder, which makes a decision as to the combination of fragments that jointly gives the best segmentation and word-sequence hypothesis for the target.

The quality of the fragments derived from the signal-driven processes relies heavily on the exact nature of the CASA algorithm applied to the mixture; this work makes use of pitch as a primitive cue for the segmentation of voiced speech. Thus, the following chapter will investigate the history and recent advances in pitch determination before proposing a novel pitch determination algorithm that will serve as a first step toward the formation of fragments from voiced speech.

Chapter 4

Multi-Pitch Determination

4.1. Introduction

Pitch determination (the detection *and* estimation of pitch[12]) is central to many applications of sound processing; the segmentation of voiced speech is one such application. Many segmentation algorithms employ pitch tracking as an intermediate step on the way to full segmentation (see Weintraub, 1985; Naylor and Porter, 1991; Chazan et al., 1993; Karjalainen and Tolonen, 1999, for example). Determining and tracking the pitch of a single source is a challenging task that has received much attention and yielded several very good algorithms. The problem is far from solved, however, as new more accurate, more efficient algorithms are still being developed especially to deal with the determination of pitch in noise.

The majority of single pitch determination algorithms (PDAs) make the assumption that there is only one harmonic source in the signal. In the scenario where there is more than one simultaneously pitched source, and the aim is to determine them all, a multi-pitch determination algorithm (MPDA) is required. Multi-pitch determination, however, is a significantly more difficult problem than single pitch determination, partly owing to the obscuring of pitch cues through harmonic interaction. One obvious solution is to detect the pitch of one source, remove its influence, and detect the pitch of the remaining source(s). In the simplest implementation, this iterative approach works well, where the pitches of individual sources are not integer multiples of each other. There are other methods that jointly estimate the pitches of all the sources in the mixture. These methods can be computationally expensive and suffer from the same problem as the iterative procedure when sources are harmonically related.

The current chapter explores pitch determination as the first step of a procedure that segments mixtures of speech and present all the segments to the *speech fragment decoder* (see Chapter 3) for decoding. The nature of the decoding process requires that the voiced content of all the sources in the mixture are recovered, thus it is important to implement a multiple-pitch determination algorithm. The algorithm takes as input, a mixture of two

---

[12]Precisely speaking, the chapter is discussing *fundamental frequency* determination. The term *pitch* technically refers to a perceptual characteristic of sound related to fundamental frequency. However, following the standard practice in the literature, this chapter will use the term pitch as a short-hand for fundamental frequency. Instances where it is intended to have its correct technical meaning will be clear from the context.

speech signals and outputs pitch candidates for both signals at each time frame.

This chapter explores the domains of single pitch determination (Section 4.2.) and multiple (simultaneous) pitch determination (Section 4.3.). A novel multiple-pitch determination algorithm is proposed in Section 4.4. and evaluated in Section 4.5.. The chapter is concluded with a summary in Section 4.6..

4.2.   Single Pitch PDAs

PDAs were first developed for the determination of the pitch of a single acoustic source. Given that an exhaustive review of the numerous PDAs is not the aim of this chapter, the reader is referred to the reviews found in Hess (1983), Hermes (1993) and Klapuri (2003).[13] In order to streamline the discussion, PDAs are separated into the logical categories of *time-domain*, *frequency-domain* and *time-frequency* (or *spectro-temporal*) PDAs. This classification is not a strict one and simply serves to highlight the domain in which the pitch candidates were detected.

4.2.1.   Time-Domain PDAs

Time domain PDAs attempt to measure individual period lengths. The basic assumption is that the detector will be applied to periodic (or quasi-periodic) sounds. Such signals exhibit a regularity which can be detected with relatively simple algorithms, which could include calculation of zero-crossings, peak-and-valley determination, and autocorrelation (Rabiner, 1977; Hermes, 1993). The early time-domain methods tend to be particularly susceptible to the detection of the wrong peak, where more than one peak is present in each period. Despite the many pre-processing modifications proposed, the majority of early algorithms have been found to be less than robust (see Hess, 1983, for a review of these early systems).

Of the number of methods that have been proposed for the determination of pitch in the time-domain, those based on autocorrelation seem to be among the most enduring. Autocorrelation is essentially a determination of a signal's similarity to itself. This similarity is determined by summing the product of the windowed signal with time-shifted versions of itself, that is:

$$ACF(\tau) = \sum_{t=1}^{N} x(t) \cdot x(t-\tau), \tag{4.1}$$

where *ACF* is the autocorrelation function at lag τ calculated over a window of length N.

When the autocorrelation function (ACF) is plotted as a function of lag, the periodicity of the signal is reflected by the emergence of relatively large peaks at lags corresponding to the period of the harmonics. The largest peak at non-zero lag is selected as representative of the pitch. The fact that the ACF operates on segments of the signal means it is relatively insensitive to phase distortions, which typically hamper time-domain algorithms (Flego, 2006).

---

[13]The main focus of Klapuri (2003) is multi-pitch determination, but the sections that review single-pitch systems give a good introduction to the established methodologies and explore techniques that have been developed since the reviews of Hess (1983) and Hermes (1993).

There are however, shortcomings to the use of ACF for pitch determination, as pointed out by Rabiner (1977). Among these is the fact that pitch determination based on autocorrelation analysis often leads to the determination of a sub-harmonic instead of the fundamental frequency. The reason this occurs is that there is often a significant peak at twice the pitch period, which is larger than the peak at the pitch period. This often has to be corrected with post-pitch-determination processing. One time-domain algorithm which attempts to overcome these shortcomings is the YIN algorithm (de Cheveigné and Kawahara, 2002). YIN is based on the *squared difference function*:

$$d(\tau) = \sum_{i=1}^{N}(x(i) - x(i+\tau))^2, \tag{4.2}$$

which is shown to be a sum of autocorrelation terms. While autocorrelation analysis searches for maxima, YIN estimates pitch based on the minima of the difference function. Sub-harmonic errors are reduced by implementing the *cumulative mean normalised difference function*:

$$d'(\tau) = \begin{cases} 1 & \text{if } \tau = 0, \\ \dfrac{d(\tau)}{\frac{1}{\tau}\sum_{i=1}^{\tau} d(i)} & \text{otherwise.} \end{cases} \tag{4.3}$$

Among the effects of this normalisation is the de-emphasis of the minima at higher order lags as well as the removal of the minimum at zero lag. The authors then find the smallest lag at which the function falls below an absolute threshold. By normalising the difference function, the algorithm is less likely to choose a minimum related to the sub-harmonic. Other steps (including parabolic interpolation of estimates) are implemented in an effort to refine the pitch estimate. A related algorithm is the *average magnitude difference function* (AMDF), which also exploits the relative computational simplicity of the difference function (Ross et al., 1974).

4.2.2. Frequency-Domain PDAs

The basic difference between time- and frequency-domain PDAs is that frequency-domain PDAs are based on a spectral representation of the signal. This representation is derived using the Fourier transform. This class of PDAs first segments the signal into several frames, containing at least one pitch period, before determining an average pitch for each frame. The majority of these algorithms are based on pattern matching in the spectral domain; where they are not, they use other cues such as inter-partial spacing or instantaneous frequency determination (de Cheveigné, 2006). Some are developed directly from pitch perception theories, while others are developed without specific references to any theory.

Pattern matching pitch perception theories, such as that by Goldstein (1973), have contributed to the development of frequency-domain PDAs. Among these are: the harmonic product spectrum (Schroeder, 1968), the harmonic sum spectrum (Noll, 1970), the harmonic sieve (Duifhuis et al., 1982), the spectral comb (Martin, 1982), and the sub-harmonic summation (Hermes, 1988), (see Hess, 1983; Hermes, 1993; de Cheveigné, 2005, for reviews). Such algorithms are in general agreement with the pitch perception models that serve as the theoretical basis for their development.

The spectral comb method of Martin (1982) passes the signal through a series of comb filters with teeth spacing varied to represent different fundamental frequencies within a particular range. The spacing which gives a maximum output is chosen as representing the pitch of the signal and the spacing taken to be the signal's pitch. The peaks of the comb filter are given decreasing weights so as to avoid the problem of pitch halving.

The algorithm of Duifhuis et al. (1982) utilises a harmonic sieve at successive fundamental frequencies. The spectral components that fall through the sieve are considered harmonic components of the signal. The harmonic patterns from each sieve are compared using a normalised Euclidean distance and the one that produces the minimum distance is chosen as representing the pitch.

One of the most prominent frequency-domain PDAs is the *cepstrum* PDA (Noll, 1967). This PDA follows the source-filter model of speech production, which treats the speech signal as a convolution of a periodic glottal pulse and the filter formed by the buccal cavity (Hermes, 1993). The algorithm requires the application of a Fourier transform and a further transformation into the log domain, which tends to suppress higher order harmonics relative to the pitch. After applying an inverse Fourier transform (yielding the cepstrum) a peak picking technique is applied to choose the highest peak which, most often, yields the pitch of the signal. The use of the cepstrum is attractive because of its intrinsic spectral flattening, computational efficiency and easy implementation. It has been shown, however, that PDAs based on the cepstrum have a tendency to classify frames of voiced speech as being unvoiced (Rabiner et al., 1976; Liu and Lin, 2001). There are also issues with poor 'quefrency' resolution (Morgan et al., 1997).

Frequency domain techniques take advantage of the power and efficiency of the fast Fourier transform (FFT) in transforming the signal into the spectral domain (de Cheveigné, 2006). However, they require extremely good frequency resolution in order to detect spectral patterns and as such, generally use a large number of filters, a constraint that decreases computational efficiency.

4.2.3. Joint Time-frequency domain PDAs

Spectro-temporal PDAs combine frequency- and time-domain processing of the speech signal to detect pitch; these techniques are generally based on the pitch perception model put forward by Licklider (1951). Common among the various implementations of this approach is the decomposition of the windowed signal into several frequency channels by passing it through a bank of bandpass filters. This processing is meant to imitate the physiological filtering performed along the basilar membrane. Filtering is then followed, in most instances, by transduction which includes half-wave rectification and some form of non-linear compression. The output is meant to approximate the output of the inner hair cells that send signals to the auditory nerve fibres.

Time-domain periodicity is then detected by employing a measure of similarity, most often the autocorrelogram (ACG), though other methods such as the AMDF (de Cheveigné, 1991) and Pseudo-Periodic Histogram (Rouat et al., 1997) have been employed. Where the ACG is used, it is usually summed across frequency to produce the summary autocorrelogram (Lyon, 1984; Meddis and Hewitt, 1991a). Since several channels will respond to the fundamental frequency of the signal, there has to be a method of integrating this information across frequency in order to estimate the pitch. Cross-channel summation of the ACG is meant to enhance the peak representing the fundamental frequency by accumulating the peaks in those channels that respond to it. After summation, the pitch is often represented by the largest peak on the lag axis, but this is not always the case. Pre-processing techniques, such as signal-whitening and centre clipping, can be applied to the signal as a method of enhancing the pitch peak and suppressing peaks representing other harmonics. Other methods process the full autocorrelogram, as opposed to the summary, to obtain pitch estimates.

Autocorrelation is not universally accepted as an accurate model of period determination in the auditory system – alternatives include the strobed temporal integration model (Patterson et al., 1995) and recurrent networks (Cariani, 2001). However, there is evidence from computational models, (Licklider, 1951; Meddis and Hewitt, 1991a,b) as well as physiological studies (Cariani and Delgutte, 1996) to support its widespread use (see Hermes (1993) and Klapuri (2003), for discussions). Spectro-temporal PDAs based on the ACF are attractive because they attempt to incorporate knowledge about the physiology of the ear as well as theories of pitch perception. There are issues however, concerning the computational cost of calculating the ACF for each filter channel.

4.3. Multi-Pitch PDAs

This section examines a number of multi-pitch determination algorithms (MPDAs), some of which are simple extensions of single-pitch PDAs, others of which have been developed specifically for the determination of multiple pitch candidates. The scenarios in which multi-pitch determination algorithms are deployed would cause single-pitch algorithms to fail. Consider, for example, the scenario in which both sources, in a two source mixture, are voiced. As there are two voiced signals, there is no guarantee that the single-pitch algorithm will detect the pitch of one particular source across the entire utterance; and as only a single pitch estimate is output by such algorithms, it is unlikely that such errors could be corrected. Thus, not only are single-pitch PDAs unable to detect more than one pitch at a time, they are susceptible to errors where more than one voiced source is present in a mixture. The classification strategy employed in Section 4.2. will also be used here. Good reviews of MPDA development and implementation can be found in Klapuri (2003) and de Cheveigné (2006).

4.3.1. Time-domain MPDAs

Time-domain MPDAs typically apply a method of pitch estimation and cancellation. This is achieved by estimating the pitch of one voice and applying a comb filter with teeth set to match the harmonic series of that voice. The filtering process effectively eliminates the first voice from the mixture, allowing for the easy determination of the pitch of the second voice.

The implementation of this principle with a two-voice mixture allows for the detection and cancellation of the first pitch and the subsequent detection of the second (de Cheveigné and Kawahara, 1999). The initial estimate is found by detecting the minimum in the *squared-difference function* (see Equation 4.2). A comb filter with tooth spacing set to the period of the initial estimate cancels the first voice, a minimum in the residue indicates the pitch of the second source.

A joint estimation-cancellation procedure is also proposed, in which two filters are implemented in cascade (de Cheveigné, 1993; de Cheveigné and Kawahara, 1999). Both pitches are estimated by detecting a minimum in the two-dimensional lag space of the double-difference function. A problem arises if the pitches are harmonically related, as a single filter could cancel the harmonics of both signals, leading to the detection of only one pitch where there should be two. These methods have the advantage over spectral and spectro-temporal detectors of not being tied to the frequency resolution of a filterbank model.

4.3.2. Frequency-domain MPDAs

The work of Parsons (1976) is one of the earliest attempts to detect the pitch of competing speakers. The mixed signal is framed and the short-term magnitude spectrum is calculated for each frame. All the peaks in a particular frame are identified as harmonics of one source or another and placed in a table. The peaks are pooled in a histogram representation loosely based on Schroeder's method (Schroeder, 1968) and the pitch of one speaker is detected by choosing the largest histogram entry. To detect the pitch of the second speaker, the components of the first speaker are eliminated from the histogram - effectively suppressing that speaker's contribution - the remaining harmonic peaks are appropriately weighted and the highest histogram entry chosen as the second speaker's pitch.

A single-voice cepstrum PDA was extended by Stubbs and Summerfield (1990a) to detect the pitch of two simultaneous speakers. The cepstrum was calculated, after which the peaks were normalised and averaged over a three-sample window. The two largest peaks were chosen as the pitch candidates. The benefits and drawbacks of the cepstrum-based approaches, as pointed out in Section 4.2.2., were retained in this approach.

Bach and Jordan (2005) developed a graphical model of speaker characteristics which they used to extract pitch information. Each speaker's characteristics were modelled by an HMM trained using discriminative techniques; multiple speakers were modelled with a factorial HMM. The algorithm modelled the magnitude of the spectrogram as an amplitude modulated comb, thus enabling the iterative determination and cancellation of each pitch in a mixture. This approach effectively coupled pitch determination and tracking.

The drawbacks of frequency-domain methods include the need for very fine frequency resolution to facilitate the determination of individual pitch periods, as well as the need to define the length of the analysis window prior to analysis. A pre-determined window length can be problematic when speakers change from frame to frame, or even when the signal is not strictly periodic. One proposed solution is to vary the window length 'on-the-fly' based on the nature of previously determined pitch periods (Rabiner, 1977)

4.3.3. Joint Time-frequency domain MPDAs

The spectro-temporal approach to multiple-pitch determination first proceeds by passing the windowed signal through a bank of bandpass filters. Several alternatives have been proposed for extracting pitch from this decomposed signal. One such approach is to calculate the ACG from a pre-processed mixture and sum it across frequency to produce the summary ACG. In a two-source mixture, for example, the lags corresponding to the two highest peaks are selected as representing the pitches of the two sources. This technique has been employed in several studies as a first step to signal segmentation (Brown, 1992; Ellis, 1996; Hu and Wang, 2004b). It has been found, however, that the summary ACG is not always ideal for multi-pitch determination. The two highest peaks may in fact represent the pitch of one source and one of its (sub-) harmonics. It is also the case that the process of reducing the ACG into a summary eliminates much, potentially useful, information. This observation has led to efforts aimed at either improving the summary, or using the full ACG.

In Karjalainen and Tolonen (1999) and Tolonen and Karjalainen (2000) an enhanced summary ACG was proposed. It was based on the observation that the spurious peaks in the summary ACG tended to affect the accuracy of multi-pitch determination. After pre-processing the signal, it was passed through two bandpass filters. One filter was used for the high frequency region (frequencies above 1 kHz) and the other for the low-frequency region. The algorithm derived the summary from a combination of two ACGs; one calculated directly from the filter output in the low frequency region, the other calculated from the *envelope* of the filter response in the high frequency region. The enhanced summary was calculated by subtracting integer multiples of the summary ACG from the original summary ACG, which has the effect of removing harmonically related components of the true pitch peaks. The separation of the signal into only two channels reduced the computational requirements for the algorithm when compared to others that utilised multiple filters.

The iterative estimation and cancellation methodology was also employed in Klapuri (2005), where the summary ACG was modified prior to the detection of pitch candidates. A pitch salience function was calculated, from which the pitch of one source was estimated, its harmonics removed and the pitch of the second source estimated from the residual.

Another approach employed for determining multiple pitches from the summary ACG was proposed by Meddis and Hewitt (1992) who introduced the concept of a *residue*. They first computed the summary ACG and selected the highest peak as indicative of the pitch of the stronger source. Frequency channels that responded primarily to the estimated pitch were removed from the representation and the remaining channels summed. From this summary of residual channels, the highest peak was selected to be the pitch of the second source.

This idea of selecting a subset of channels and analysing them for evidence of a single pitch was extended by Wu et al. (2003), who invoked both channel *and* peak selection. After processing the signal through an auditory filterbank, the channels were divided into two categories, namely high frequency ($> 800\,Hz$) and low frequency channels. Autocorrelation was performed on the low frequency channels and on the envelope of the high frequency channels. The separate treatment of high and low frequency regions was similar to the work done by Karjalainen and Tolonen (1999) and Tolonen and Karjalainen (2000). A thresholding process was employed to select low frequency channels with significant peaks. High frequency channels were selected based on the similarity of the shape of the envelope ACG calculated with different frame rates. Peaks were selected from the ACGs if they were deemed to be free from "noise". A noise-free peak was described as one for which a related peak, at twice its lag, could be found. This technique of selecting usable data from the ACG led to improved detection of the more energetic speaker in the mixture; however it has been shown that the other speaker was not always detected (Khurshid and Denham, 2004).

Ma et al. (2007) employs the full ACG in the determination of multiple pitches. When adjacent filter channels respond to the pitch of a signal, a visual inspection of the ACG shows a tree-like structure with its stem, extending across the entire frequency range, centred on the lag corresponding to the pitch of that source (Slaney and Lyon, 1990). When there are multiple sources in a mixture, there will be more than one such structure; each should correspond to the pitch of one source. The stem of these structures (referred to as *dendrites*) will not extend across all frequencies, but will only extend across the subset of frequency channels that respond to the pitch of a particular signal.

Pitch determination proceeds by first computing the normalised cross-correlation between ACG channels with adjacent channels being grouped if the correlation between them exceeds a pre-determined threshold. This grouping produces sub-bands, which are then convolved with Gabor functions producing a strong peak at the stem of the structure and insignificant peaks elsewhere. The full ACG is also convolved with the Gabor function. The output of both convolution processes above are squared and summed to produce an enhanced ACG function where the dendritic structure is highlighted. The largest peak in each sub-band of the enhanced correlogram is selected and a histogram with a 3 Hz bin width is constructed. For a two-source mixture, the two bins with the highest counts are used to mark the positions of two dendrites corresponding to the two sources. Evaluations show that the technique performs significantly better than a system that calculates both pitches from the summary ACG.

Khurshid and Denham (2004) developed a spectro-temporal system that did not employ an ACG. In this system, frequency analysis was performed by a bank of damped harmonic oscillators, which was used as a simple model of the mechanical activity of the basilar membrane. The temporal structure of the output was analysed and a time-frequency energy map was developed. The representation gave improved frequency and temporal resolution, and thus avoided some of the problems faced by ACG-based systems. A harmonic grouping stage was then invoked to derive pitch estimates. Significant spectral peaks and supporting sub-harmonics were extracted from each oscillator. If the sub-harmonics were energetic enough, then the corresponding spectral peak was considered a candidate for the pitch of one of the sources. The technique performed better than previously implemented algorithms, especially in determining the pitch of the masking utterance in two talker mixtures.

4.4. Proposed MPDA

A spectro-temporal approach is employed in the development of the proposed multi-pitch determination algorithm. By so doing, the algorithm exploits the advantages of the spectro-temporal approach that were highlighted in Section 4.2.3.. Autocorrelation is used in the spectral domain to determine the periodicity of all the signals in the mixture. The autocorrelogram is then separated into low and high frequency regions. In a novel approach, only the low frequency regions are summed across frequency in order to enhance the peaks representing the pitches of each source.

The difficulties encountered when employing the summary autocorrelogram for pitch estimation (such as the detection of a harmonic other than the fundamental) are well documented. However, the proposed MPDA seeks to overcome them in a novel way. By retaining multiple peaks from the summary as pitch candidates, the algorithm reduces the probability of missing the fundamental. Retaining multiple peaks from the summary is a strategy employed for minimising the loss of information from the signal that occurs when pitch evidence is pooled across frequency. However, this strategy requires that the pitch determination algorithm be coupled with a robust pitch tracker, so that the pitches of both sources can be tracked across time. The strong statistical framework in which the pitch tracker developed for this purpose (see Chapter 5) is grounded, allows for the implementation of the proposed strategy; in the absence of the pitch tracker there is little justification for the retention of multiple peaks. Another novel aspect of the algorithm is seen in the instance where the fundamental does not appear in the candidates and a harmonic at half, or twice the fundamental is retained; the algorithm treats the harmonic as a valid pitch point. Further support for this approach will be given throughout this section.

The autocorrelogram-based multi-pitch determination algorithm (MPDA) is used to find all pitch periods present in the range between 60 and 400 Hz. The signal is passed through a 64 channel filterbank, which is designed to emulate the mechanical filtering in the cochlea. The filterbank is composed of Gammatone filters with centre frequencies between 50 and 3850 Hz, equally spaced on an equivalent rectangular bandwidth (ERB) rate scale, with gains chosen to reflect the transfer function of the outer and middle ears. The filterbank output is then half-wave rectified. After filtering the signal, it is framed using a 35 ms Hamming window with a 10 ms frame shift. The 35 ms window is long enough to capture at least two complete pitch periods for both female and male speakers, as recommended by Rabiner (1977). The ACG is then calculated as the real part of the inverse Fourier transform of the power spectrum of the rectified filterbank output. Frequency domain compression is realised by taking the square root of the ACG.

ERB-rate spacing of the filters allows for better frequency resolution in the low frequency range, as the filter bandwidths in low frequency channels are relatively narrow and respond, principally, to a single harmonic. As the frequency is increased, the bandwidths become wider and the filters no longer exhibit a primary response to a single harmonic, thus the harmonics in high frequency regions are generally unresolved. Therefore, the algorithm treats resolved and unresolved harmonics in different ways, following the suggestion that the human auditory system functions in a similar manner (Carlyon and Shackleton, 1994). It has also been shown that computational models of speech segmentation are more accurate and efficient if they perform separate processing on high- and low-frequency spectral regions (Gu and van Bokhoven, 1991; Hu and Wang, 2004b).

Autocorrelation is employed for determining the periodicity of each signal in the sound mixtures. For the low frequency channels (those with centre frequencies up to 500 Hz), an autocorrelation of the windowed filter output is computed directly. Performing autocorrelation directly on the filter outputs in high frequency channels may lead to inaccuracies owing to the poor frequency resolution in these channels. While the harmonics are generally unresolved in the high-frequency regions, the amplitude modulation (*beats*) caused by the interaction of several harmonics leads to fluctuations in the envelope response at a rate equal to the fundamental frequency of the signal. To recover the pitch in these channels, autocorrelation is applied to the *envelope* of the filter response. The envelope is obtained by passing the filter output through a lowpass finite impulse response filter with cut-off at 1.2 kHz using a Kaiser window of 18.5 ms. The high-frequency region is not used for pitch determination, but will play a role in voiced speech segmentation (see Chapter 6 for details).

The pitch estimation stage of the algorithm proceeds by computing a normalised summary autocorrelogram (sACG). This is achieved by first summing the autocorrelation functions in the low frequency channels and then normalising the result by the value at lag 0. The motivation for using only these low frequency channels for the determination of pitch is based on studies which appear to show that the auditory system apparently relies heavily on the resolved harmonics of the low-frequency region in its primary mechanism for pitch determination (Houtsma and Smurzynski, 1990; Meddis and O'Mard, 1997). The current technique exploits this by summing only the low-frequency channels of the ACG, as the harmonics are generally resolved in these channels. The peaks from the sACG with amplitudes that exceed an empirically derived threshold, θ_s are ordered by size and the four largest are stored. The value θ_s, which represents the level at which a peak in the sACG is considered significant, is carefully chosen so as to satisfy several aims. One important consideration is how many correct pitch points are retained in the summary. The higher the value of θ_s, the more likely it is that some genuine pitch points will be missed, as the true pitch is not always represented by the highest peak in the summary. However, lowering the threshold introduces more spurious peaks, which has implications for the pitch tracking stage which follows pitch determination. Classification errors occur in pitch tracking, where a voiced segment of speech is marked as unvoiced, often because the peak representing the correct pitch is below the threshold. This type of error often accounts for the majority of errors made by pitch determination algorithms. Thus, a balance has to be struck where both the introduction of erroneous pitch candidates and classification errors are kept to a minimum. Another factor influencing the choice of θ_s is the impact on the overall segmentation process. Briefly, higher values of θ_s will lead to more accurate segmentation with a more sparse output from the segmentation algorithm, and vice-versa (a full description and analysis of this effect is provided in Chapter 6). The level of sparsity further impacts recognition performance when the segmented speech is presented to the automatic speech recogniser. This complex interaction of factors makes the choice of θ_s a non-trivial task. Chapter 6 gives full details of the tuning of θ_s.

Pitch Doubling and Halving

Pitch doubling and halving errors can occur in ACG-based pitch detectors. Owing to the interaction of harmonic components within the overlapping windows of the autocorrelation function, the highest correlation does not always occur at a lag corresponding to the pitch. Doubling is the detection of the harmonic at double the fundamental frequency of the source, while halving errors occur when the detected pitch is half the fundamental. This indicates that there are regions where the signal is found to be periodic but the 'true' pitch is either missing or undetected and the pitch detection algorithm finds a peak, which is a (sub-) multiple, in its place. Different methods have been devised to deal with the occurrence of these phenomena. Liu and Lin (2001) propose a pitch detection algorithm in which they perform a detailed analysis of all harmonically related pitch candidates. They devise a *pitch measure*, based on the relative energy of the harmonics, that attempts to minimise the problem of pitch doubling and halving. However, as they point out, doubling and halving can still occur especially after a break in voicing. Their system includes a stage for correcting such errors by multiplying/dividing any detected halves/doubles by two.

Rouat et al. (1997) compensate for pitch doubling errors by replacing the identified error with the peak representing the closest sub-multiple of the erroneous peak, or in the absence of such a peak, the average values of its neighbours. In the pitch detection algorithm proposed by Wu et al. (2003), the multiples of selected peaks are systematically removed. It is worth noting that these errors can be corrected in the pitch tracking stage, by making use of the temporal context. This is often done by applying post-processing techniques, such as *median smoothing*, to the pitch tracks.

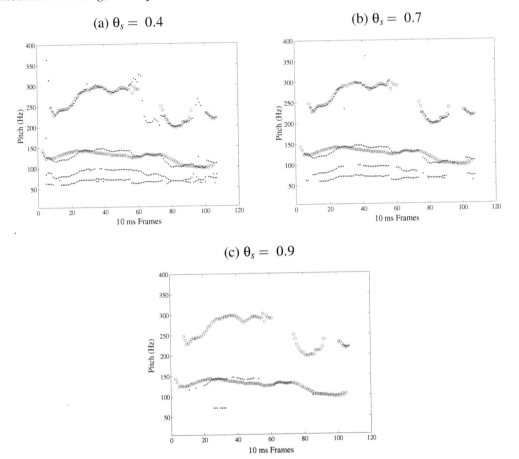

Figure 4.1. Output of the proposed multi-pitch determination algorithm for a mixture of male and female speech. The output at different values of θ_s is shown. Unlabelled pitch data produced by the multi-pitch determination algorithm (marked by '.') overlaid with the pitch tracks derived from the sources prior to mixing (marked by 'o').

Overall, these methods are successful in dealing with doubling and halving, but can cause errors if the sources in the mixture are harmonically related.

Within the current framework, there is less need to correct for such 'errors' as they do not necessarily have a large impact on fragment generation, which is the goal of the primitive segmentation system. In fact, it would be more detrimental to accidentally remove the influence of one of the sources, which is a possibility when the sources are harmonically related. For fragment generation purposes, multiples or sub-multiples of the fundamental can still be used to identify the channels belonging to the fragment.[14] Nevertheless, to take advantage of this, it is still necessary that halved or doubled pitch estimates are not grouped into the wrong pitch track. This can be accomplished by designing the pitch tracker within a statistical framework that models the occurrence of pitch doubling and halving events.

Figure 4.1 shows the typical output of the MPDA for different values of θ_s. It can be seen that the number of pitch points decreases as the value of θ_s increases. At a value of 0.7, some of the correct pitch points are removed, but many of the spurious points are also removed. Setting the value to 0.9 leads to the loss of the majority of the correct pitch points.

4.5. Evaluation

The MPDA is evaluated to determine the accuracy with which it detects and estimates the pitches of the sources in a monaural mixture of speech. Though the algorithm is designed as one stage in a speech recognition system, the true test of which is recognition accuracy, an evaluation is performed at each stage to test the algorithms developed there. The algorithm is tested over a range of conditions and parameter settings, in order to determine the scope of its performance.

The evaluation of the MPDA involves the comparison of detected pitch candidates with the *a priori* (reference) pitch of the sources, calculated before mixing, using Snack (Sjolander, 2002) (an open source version of ESPS/waves+). The toolkit implements an algorithm, in which pitch determination is based on *normalised cross correlation* and tracking is performed using dynamic programming (see Talkin (1995) for full details of the algorithm). The algorithm is set to find pitches between 60 and 400 *Hz*. The window length was 7.5 *ms* and the frame length is set to 10 *ms*.

In order to test the accuracy of the algorithm, a number of evaluation metrics are employed. The method of evaluation employed was proposed by Rabiner et al. (1976) and has been used in evaluations of pitch detectors since then. A *gross estimation error* (GEE) is said to occur if the value of a pitch estimate at time t does not fall within a threshold of a corresponding pitch point in the reference.[15] The threshold is set here to 20%, which is a commonly used value for this type of evaluation (see Wu et al., 2003; Khurshid and Denham, 2004, for example), for example. This error metric essentially measures the estimation accuracy of the algorithm in the frames where both the proposed pitch candidates and reference pitch point agree that voicing is present. There are, however, at most, four pitch candidates in each frame to be compared with, at most, two reference points. In order to calculate GEE, the two pitch candidates that best match the reference must be chosen. This is done by calculating the squared difference between pairs of pitch candidates and the reference pitch points, then selecting the pair of candidate points that gives the minimum distance. Where there are multiple pitch candidates in a time frame, $M = {}_nC_2$, pairs of

---

[14]This approach is supported by the work of Chazan et al. (1993) They propose an estimation-maximisation based PDA, which was developed and implemented as a pre-cursor to a speech segmentation system. The authors recognised that where signal segmentation is the primary goal, and pitch detection is performed as a sub-task, the removal of (sub-)harmonic errors is not a priority as these 'errors' provide useful information about the speech source.

[15]When the double/half is found in the pitch estimates, it is compared to twice/half the reference pitch.

candidates are formed. For each pair, the difference is taken between the reference and the estimated candidate. The differences are squared and summed to give a combined squared distance. The pair that yields the minimum squared distance is selected as the best-matching pair. Where there is only a single reference pitch, the squared difference between each pitch candidate and the reference is computed, and the minimum taken. This calculation is repeated for each frame. The errors reported are the number of gross errors made, expressed as a percentage of the number of pitch points in the reference.

This process of selecting the matching candidates is a reasonable one, which allows only the pitch candidates of interest to be used in the evaluation. As there are only two sources, only a maximum of two candidate points will ever be relevant, regardless of the number output by the algorithm. The MPDA does not stand on its own, it works in tandem with the multiple-pitch tracker (to be discussed in Chapter 5) to select the best matching pitch points, if this were not the case, the proposed MPDA would have had to employ some other method of selecting the relevant pitch points. Thus, the set of pitch candidates which best match the reference will be used throughout the evaluation.

A *fine estimation error* (FEE) is defined as the mean deviation of the estimated pitch from the reference where no gross error has occurred. FEE measures how accurate the estimated pitch points are. The mean deviation of a pitch point is calculated as:

$$\triangle f = \frac{|f_{est} - f_{ref}|}{f_{ref}} \tag{4.4}$$

where f_{ref} is the reference pitch point and f_{est} is the pitch candidate output by the MPDA. This error is reported as a percentage of the times it occurs.

Two other metrics are the *voiced-unvoiced error* (VUE), and the *unvoiced-voiced error* (UVE), which examine the detection accuracy of the algorithm. In the case of the VUE, an error is said to have occurred where the algorithm has failed to detect a valid pitch point[16] The UVE identifies regions where the algorithm detects a pitch point which is not present in the reference. Both these metrics must be modified for use with MPDAs to reflect the fact that more than one source can be active (or inactive) at any one time. Wu et al. (2003) have proposed such an extension, where detection errors are characterised by a set of metrics, the number of which vary based on the number of sources present in the mixture. Adopting their notation: $E_{x \rightarrow y}$ represents a detection error where the reference indicates the presence of x simultaneously voiced sources and the MPDA detects y points. In this way all the relevant detection errors are considered and the algorithm can be evaluated fairly.

Detection errors are also calculated using the best matching pitch candidates, as calculated above. The evaluation of detection errors is concerned with how well the pitch of both sources is detected, not with how many candidates are proposed.

4.5.1. Evaluation Data

The evaluation was designed such that the proposed algorithm was tested in a number of scenarios. It was tested with fully voiced utterances as well as utterances that have breaks

---

[16]A pitch point is considered valid if it appears in the reference. However, the algorithm used to generate the reference points is subject to its own errors; thus, the errors attributed to the algorithm being tested are relative to those errors. Wu et al. (2003) and others have used hand-corrected reference pitches to alleviate this problem.

in voicing. Thus, the algorithm had to deal with situations where there were either two, one, or zero voiced sources.

The fully-voiced data used for the evaluation were a sub-set of the TIMIT corpus (Garofolo et al., 1993). The data set consisted of eight completely voiced utterances spoken by two male (six utterances) and two female speakers (two utterances). The signals were combined such that there were eight matched-gender (but different speaker) mixtures and eight mixed-gender mixtures. Each unmixed utterance was end-pointed (had the silence removed from the beginning and end) by hand, before being additively combined in the time-domain to give 16 mixtures. Differences in signal length were dealt with by truncating the mixture to the length of the shorter utterance.

For the partially-voiced data, the unmixed signals were taken from the clean, test set A of the Aurora 2 corpus (Hirsch and Pearce, 2000). Thirty mixtures (10 mixed-gender and 20 matched-gender) were created from 59 unmixed signals. The signals were produced by 45 speakers (23 female and 22 male). The unmixed signals were end-pointed, matched for length and mixed in the time-domain. Where the signals differed in length, the shorter was zero-padded to match the length of the longer.

Given the importance of θ_s in determining the number of pitch candidates retained, the analysis is performed over a rage of θ_s values from 0.1 to 0.9. The errors made by the MPDA are discussed in relation to the value of θ_s.

4.5.2. The Effect of Target to Masker Ratio

This section considers the effect of *target-to-masker-ratio* (TMR) on the performance of the MPDA. Mixtures are created at seven different TMRs, from $-9dB$ to $9dB$ in $3dB$ steps. The data are mixed at different TMRs in order to assess the performance of the algorithm with different levels of interference. Where there is a difference in TMR, the signal with the lower energy can be completely masked in some time frames; this can lead to errors in pitch determination. By analysing the output of the MPDA at different TMRs it is possible to detect the extent to which these errors occur. The level of one signal, *source1*, is held constant and the other signal, *source2*, is added at a range of SNRs relative to *source1*. Pitch determination performance can be considered separately for each component of the mixture, i.e. when *source2* is added at a relative SNR of 9 *dB*, *source1* can be considered to be the target with a TMR of 9 *dB*, or *source2* can be considered as the target with a TMR of -9 *dB*

Detection errors will now be presented for fully-voiced and partially-voiced utterances, followed by estimation errors for both types of utterance.

Detection Errors – Fully Voiced Utterances

Detection errors for fully voiced utterances are shown in Figure 4.2. As the utterances are fully voiced, the reference will have two pitch points at each frame. Thus, only the under-detection errors, $E_{2\rightarrow0}$ (Panel a) and $E_{2\rightarrow1}$ (Panel b) are considered. Across TMR, there are no $E_{2\rightarrow0}$ errors for values of θ_s up to 0.6. As θ_s values are increased above 0.7, $E_{2\rightarrow0}$ increases and reaches values of more than 50% across TMR. This is consistent with the reduction in the number of pitch candidates found in the summary at higher values of

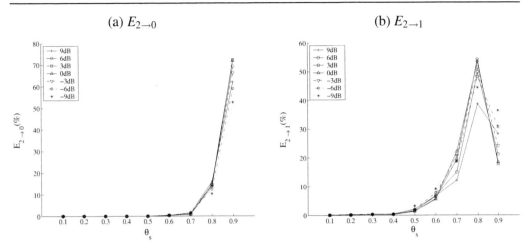

Figure 4.2. Detection errors for fully-voiced utterances. Results are shown for all TMRs and values of θ_s. Panel (a) shows the $E_{2\to0}$ error, while Panel (b) shows the $E_{2\to1}$ errors.

θ_s. For values of θ_s below 0.5, $E_{2\to1}$ errors fall below 1% across TMR. As θ_s is set above 0.6, there emerges some difference in the errors as TMR is varied. At most values of θ_s the error values increase as TMR moves from $-9\ dB$ to $0\ dB$ and fall as TMR increases further. This is unusual, as the expected pattern would be a lower error at $0\ dB$, where both sources have identical global SNR (this pattern is seen when θ_s is set to 0.9). However, it may be this similarity in overall energy that leads to the unusual pattern. At $0\ dB$ there is a possibility that the increase in salience of the harmonics of one source (*source1*, say) comes at the expense of a reduction in the salience of the harmonics of *source2*. As TMR increases further, more of the pitch points of *source1*, that were not significant before, become significant. If there is little further impact on the harmonics of *source2*, then there would be an increase in the number of frames where two pitch points are detected, leading to a reduction in $E_{2\to1}$ errors.

When θ_s is set to 0.9 $E_{2\to1}$ falls. This is likely due to the fact that few pitch candidates will remain at such a high θ_s. This view is supported by the corresponding increase in $E_{2\to0}$ errors at this value of θ_s.

Detection Errors – Utterances with Unvoiced Regions

Detection errors for partially-voiced utterances are shown in Figure 4.3. Panels (a), (c) and (e) show errors relating to the under-detection of pitch points, while the remaining panels show errors of over-detection. For all three under-detection scores, the pattern of errors across TMR and θ_s is very similar. All three show errors of less than 1% across TMR, for values of θ_s up to 0.6. As θ_s is set to higher values, the errors smoothly increase, but remain in single digits. The largest error at high θ_s is $E_{2\to0}$ with a maximum error of 6.5% at the highest value of θ_s. The patterns seen in the detection errors for fully-voiced utterances are not repeated here. This may be related to the fact that there are pitch breaks in these utterances. As there are fewer frames in which both sources are voiced, there are fewer instances where $E_{2\to0}$ and $E_{2\to1}$ errors can occur, thus the patterns seen in Figure 4.2 may

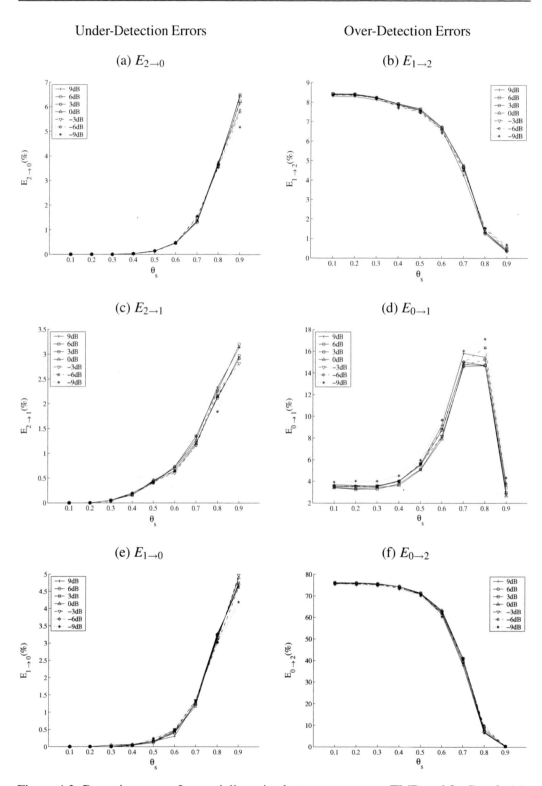

Figure 4.3. Detection errors for partially-voiced utterances across TMR and θ_s. Panels (a), (c) and (e) show under-detection errors, (b) (d) and (f) show over-detection errors.

only become evident where the utterances are completely voiced.

The errors related to over-detection are shown in Panels (b), (d) and (f) of Figure 4.3. The overall pattern of $E_{0\to2}$ and $E_{1\to2}$ errors are similar, in that they fall from high to low as θ_s is increased. They are also similar in having little to no variation in results across TMR. $E_{0\to2}$ errors, however, are much higher in value at low θ_s. This is an indication that, at low values of θ_s, the algorithm detects voicing in regions where the reference algorithm does not. It is important therefore, to carefully choose the value of θ_s in order to reduce the occurrence of these errors. The implications are not just for the pitch determination algorithm, as errors made at this stage could carry through to the segmentation algorithm and even to the recognition stage. For $E_{0\to1}$ there is a constant pattern across TMR. As θ_s increases to 0.8, $E_{0\to1}$ also increases, thereafter it decreases.

Section 4.5.1. referred to the importance of θ_s in determining the number of pitch points retained by the algorithm. While the evaluation performed so far has provided some insight into the behaviour of the algorithm at different values of θ_s, it does not provide clear evidence of which value is likely to yield optimal performance. One way in which this can be addressed is to consider the number of detection errors made for each value of the threshold. The threshold value that leads to the lowest number of errors on the evaluation set is likely to do so on an unseen set of data. The total number of detection errors, both under-detection and over-detection, is calculated for each utterance at each value of θ_s and the average across the data set is taken. Figure 4.4 shows the average number of detection errors plotted at each value of θ_s; a separate plot is shown for each TMR.

The number of errors falls steadily as the threshold value is increased to 0.7. At higher values, the number of errors increases. It is clear from the figure, that the threshold value associated with the lowest number of errors is 0.7. This holds across TMR, except at 9 dB, where there are almost identical numbers of errors for θ_s set to 0.7 and 0.8.

A further consideration when choosing the best threshold value for the MPDA is the trade-off between the number of correct pitch points retained (related to under-detection errors) and the number of spurious pitch points retained (related to over-detection). A desirable threshold value is one that leads to a high retention rate for correct pitch points and low retention rate for spurious pitch points. This trade-off can be visualised using a receiver operating characteristics (ROC) graph, which is used in the evaluation of classification algorithms (Egan, 1975; Swets et al., 2000).One way in which to represent the performance of a particular classifier is to plot *true positive rates* (tp rates) against *false positive rates* (fp rates). The fp rates and tp rates are calculated as follows:

$$fp\ rate = \frac{FP}{FP+TN} \quad and \quad tp\ rate = \frac{TP}{TP+FN}, \tag{4.5}$$

where, FP = *false positives* (over-estimation errors), TN = *true negatives* (pitch breaks correctly detected), TP = *true positives* (pitch points correctly detected), FN = *false negatives* (under-estimation errors). When analysing the output of the proposed MPDA using a ROC graph it must be recognised that there are two events at each time frame. For instance, when two pitch points are detected there are three possible explanations: the two pitch points could represent two correctly detected pitch points, or one correctly detected pitch point and a false positive. Finally, both pitch points could be false positives. In the case of discrete classifiers (such as the detection module of the MPDA at different values of θ_s),

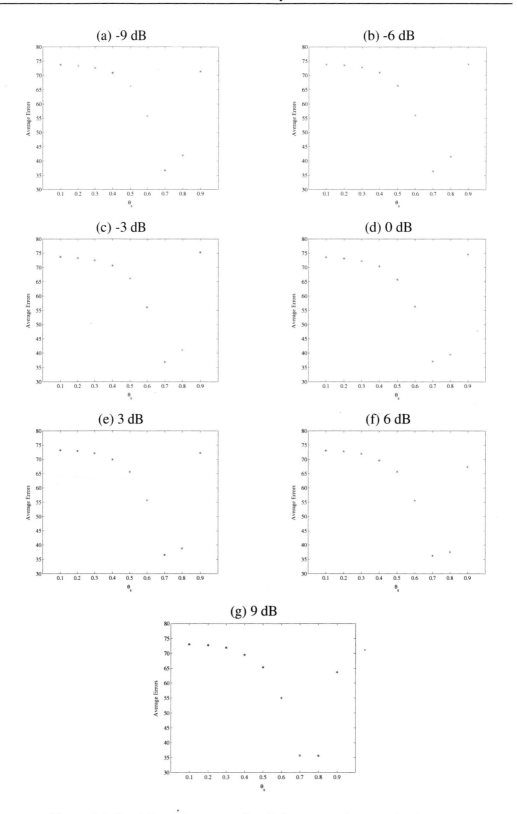

Figure 4.4. Total Detection errors for all θ_s, averaged across the data set.

performance is judged by the position a single point in ROC space representing the (*tp rate, fp rate*) pair (Fawcett, 2006). A good classifier gives a point close to the upper left hand quadrant of the graph (high tp rate and low fp rate), while a poor classifier gives a point close to the lower right hand quadrant (low tp rate, high fp rate). Random performance is represented by a point on the line $y = x$. Figure 4.5 shows ROC graphs for the proposed MPDA at each TMR, for different values of θ_s.

Analysis of the graphs shows consistent performance across TMR with low values of θ_s yielding high tp rates and correspondingly high fp rates. As θ_s is increased the fp rate falls off, as does the tp rate. When the threshold is set to 0.6 there is a very high tp rate (0.99) as well as a high fp rate (0.68). In contrast, with θ_s set to 0.7 gives a tp rate of 0.95 and a fp rate of 0.39. The decision to be made is whether the sharp reduction in the fp rate compensates for the reduction in tp rate. While the majority of false positives will not lead to spurious fragments (and the attendant negative impact on recognition accuracy) some do. Thus, the general rule when tuning the MPDA is to chose a threshold value that yields a low fp rate without dramatically lowering the tp rate.

Estimation Errors – Fully Voiced Utterances

Figure 4.6 (a), shows the gross errors made by the MPDA when estimating the pitches in fully-voiced mixtures. TMR does not seem to have much impact on the resulting GEE except at higher values of θ_s. At a value of $\theta_s = 0.9$, GEE is low for high TMRs and vice versa. The sharp increase in GEE at values of θ_s between 0.6 and 0.8 is likely due to the fact that there are some spurious peaks in the summary ACG that are larger than the true pitch peaks. As θ_s is increased, initially, more correct pitch candidates are removed, leading to an increase in GEE. However, as θ_s is increased further, the number of spurious peaks is also reduced leading to the reduction seen at the highest value of θ_s.

Fine estimation errors are shown in Figure 4.6 (b). It can be seen that, higher TMR corresponds to lower FEE; this holds as θ_s is varied. The fine errors show a similar pattern to that seen for GEE as θ_s is increased.

Estimation Errors – Utterances with Unvoiced Regions

Figure 4.7 (a), shows the GEE for utterances with unvoiced regions. The overall pattern of results across TMR is very similar. GEE increases as θ_s is increased to 0.8. As θ_s is set to 0.9, marked differences can be seen at different TMRs. At the extremes of the range, GEE is lower, which points to increased harmonic interaction between the sources when their global SNRs are similar.

Fine errors, shown in Figure 4.7 (b), also show a pattern of similarity across TMR in the overall result. FEE decreases as θ_s increases.

Discussion of the Effect of TMR

From the results shown, it appears that the effect of TMR on the proposed pitch determination algorithm is minimal. This is somewhat surprising, as it might be expected that the differences in signal levels would provide some benefit for the source with the higher level.

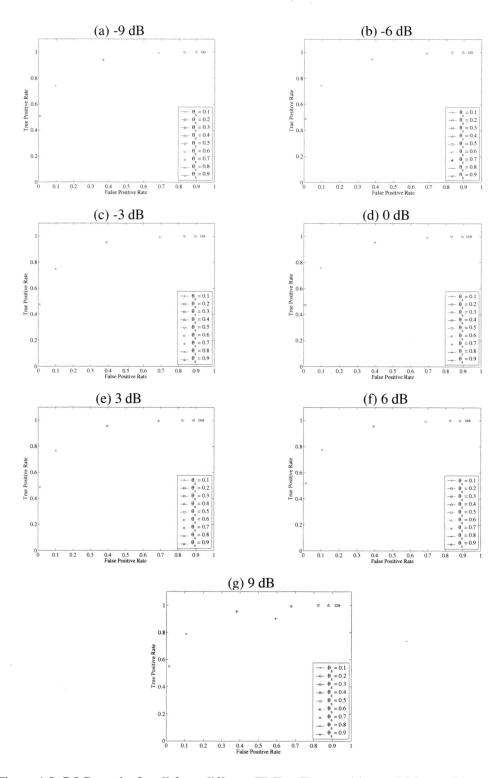

Figure 4.5. ROC graphs for all θ_s at different TMRs. True positive and false positive rates are averaged across the data set.

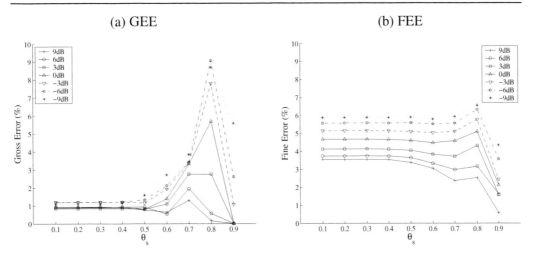

Figure 4.6. Estimation errors for fully-voiced utterances. Results are shown for all TMRs and values of θ_s. Panel (a) shows the GEE while Panel (b) shows the FEE.

It would seem however, that the fully-voiced results are somewhat more TMR dependent, though not significantly so.

The limited impact of TMR on the MPDA suggests that it is robust to differences in overall signal level. It is important to note, however, that the local (within a frame) SNR is likely to have a greater influence on the performance than does the global SNR, as the spread of local SNR values around the global TMR is quite wide for speech mixtures (Barker, 2006). Thus, as mentioned earlier, the source that has the higher global SNR may not have the higher local SNR for all time frames, making the weaker source more 'visible' in that frame. The MPDA is then able to detect strong evidence of the pitch of the weaker source. This may help to explain why there is little spread in the results at different TMRs.

It must also be noted that the error metrics are not designed to fully expose some of the effects of TMR. The calculation of the detection errors, for instance, involves the combination of the detection errors of both sources. However, the weaker source will likely have higher under-detection errors, while the stronger source will likely suffer more over-detection errors. Given the nature of the metrics, these effects will be masked.

4.5.3. A Comparison of Errors in Mixed-Gender and Matched-Gender Utterances

The separate effect of matched- and mixed-gender utterances on the MPDA is considered in this section. As the pattern of errors across TMR have been discussed in the previous section, the results for different gender conditions are only shown at 0 *dB*.

Detection Errors – Fully Voiced Utterances

The detection errors are shown in Figure 4.8. Panel (a) shows that no errors are made in either condition for values of θ_s below 0.6. Only at high values of θ_s do errors begin to appear, where they are quite high when θ_s is set to 0.9. This is due to the sparsity of very

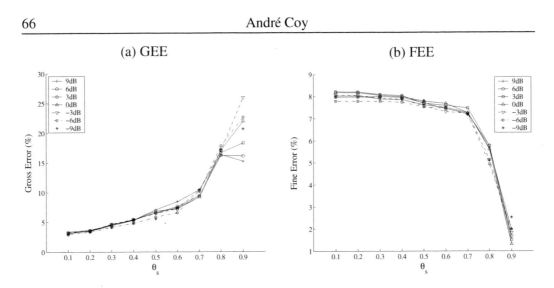

(a) GEE   (b) FEE

Figure 4.7. Estimation errors for partially-voiced utterances. Results are shown for all TMRs and values of θ_s. Panel (a) shows GEE while Panel (b) shows the FEE.

high peaks in the summary ACG. Panel (b) shows a similar pattern for $E_{2\rightarrow1}$, i.e., low errors for values of θ_s below 0.6 and a sharp rise at higher values. The falloff in $E_{2\rightarrow1}$ when θ_s is set to 0.9, combined with the increase in $E_{2\rightarrow0}$, serves to highlight the sparsity of valid pitch points at high θ_s.

Detection Errors – Utterances with Unvoiced Regions

Figure 4.9 shows detection errors for the proposed MPDA, with under-detection errors in Panels (a), (c) and (e) and over-detection errors in Panels (b), (d) and (f). All the under-detection errors show a similar pattern, increasing as the value of θ_s is increased. Matched- and mixed-gender utterances yield similar $E_{2\rightarrow0}$ errors across the range of θ_s. The differences in the errors between the mixture conditions only emerge at high values of θ_s and are confined to $E_{2\rightarrow1}$ and $E_{1\rightarrow0}$ errors. Mixed-gender utterances have higher $E_{1\rightarrow0}$ errors, while matched-gender utterances yield higher $E_{2\rightarrow1}$ errors. Both these patterns can possibly be explained by the fact that each source in the matched-gender mixtures has a similar pitch range. Often, when θ_s is set high, the peaks that remain in the summary represent the pitch of one source and its (sub-)harmonic. This will sometimes cause the algorithm to detect only one source where two are present. For this same reason, the algorithm will make fewer $E_{1\rightarrow0}$ errors for matched-gender sources. Overall the under-detection errors are similar for both gender combinations – 3.7% and 3.1% for mixed- and matched gender, respectively.

For the over-detection errors, $E_{0\rightarrow2}$ and $E_{1\rightarrow2}$ errors show a similar pattern. The errors are reduced as θ_s is increased. The $E_{0\rightarrow1}$ errors increase with increasing θ_s, and fall when it is set to 0.9. Both conditions show identical over-detection errors of (66.5%). The high over-detection errors are not necessarily a problem, as the pitch tracker (see Chapter 5) can play a role in reducing them, by tracking the true pitch points. In fact, within certain limits, it is more desirable to have over-detection errors than under-detection errors, where valid pitch points can be missed.

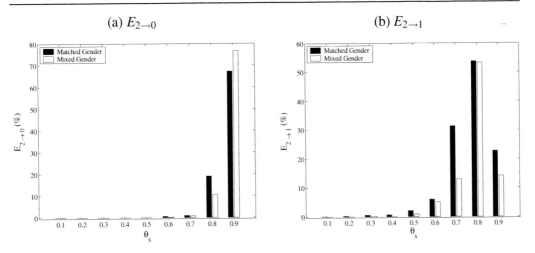

Figure 4.8. Detection errors for fully-voiced utterances. Results are shown for both gender conditions at different values of θ_s. Panel (a) shows the $E_{2\to0}$ error, while Panel (b) shows the $E_{2\to1}$ errors.

Estimation Errors – Fully Voiced Utterances

Figure 4.10 (a) shows the GEE for both matched- and mixed-gender conditions (Panel a). Overall, the mixed-gender condition gives fewer gross estimation errors than the matched-gender condition. When θ_s is set to values below 0.5, there are no errors in the mixed-gender condition, while the errors for the matched gender condition are less than 2%. As the value of θ_s is increased, the error increases in both conditions, with a greater increase in the matched-gender case. When θ_s is set to 0.9, there are no errors in either condition. This is the same pattern seen in Figure 4.6(a).

For the fine errors, shown in Figure 4.10 (b), the matched-gender case accounts for more errors than the mixed-gender case for θ_s below 0.7. This may be because the algorithm is more likely to retain correct pitch points (for at least one source) for high θ_s in the matched-gender case (see Section 4.5.3.). The averages, across θ_s are however, quite similar (4.3% and 4.5% for mixed- and matched gender, respectively).

Estimation Errors – Utterances with Unvoiced Regions

Figure 4.11 (a) shows that, as θ_s is increased, the GEE for the matched-gender case, yields more errors for values of θ_s less than 0.6. The error for the mixed-gender utterances, however, increases at a greater rate than the matched-gender utterances; leading to the scenario where the mixed-gender utterances give a greater error at high values of θ_s. On average the mixed-gender case had more gross errors (10.6%) than the matched-gender case (7.8%)

Figure 4.11 (b) shows that, for partially voiced mixtures, fine errors fall as θ_s is increased, suggesting that the pitch points that are retained at high θ_s tend to be close to the reference. The average values are similar for both conditions – 6.1% and 6.7% for matched and mixed-gender, respectively.

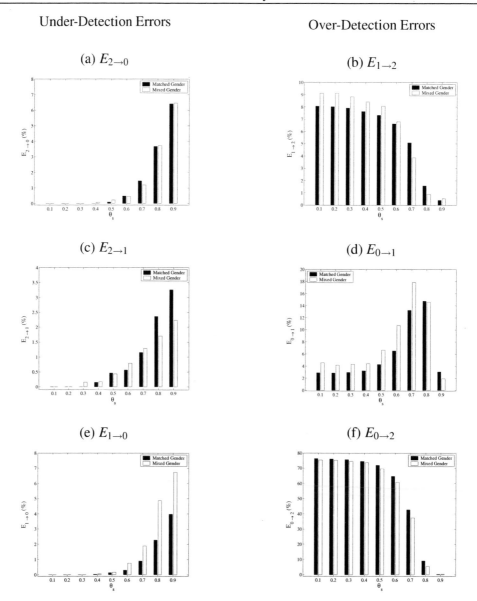

Figure 4.9. Detection errors for partially-voiced utterances. Results are shown for both gender conditions at different values of θ_s. Panels (a), (c) and (e) show errors due to under-detection, while Panels (b), (d) and (f) show errors of over-detection.

Discussion of the Comparison of Mixed-Gender and Matched-Gender Utterances

Overall the algorithm performs well in both conditions. The mixed-gender condition gave fewer estimation errors across the range of θ_s. Detection errors, however were essentially equal in both conditions.

The high $E_{0 \rightarrow 2}$ error for the partially voiced utterances – Figure 4.9 (Panel f) – can be attributed to the detection of harmonic structure in the regions where the reference indicates there should be no voicing. If the MPDA did not link to the pitch tracker, such high errors

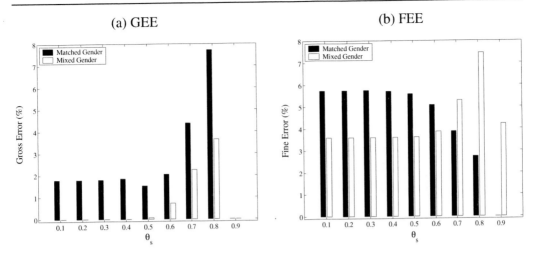

Figure 4.10. Estimation errors for fully-voiced utterances. Results are shown for both gender conditions at different values of θ_s. Panel (a) shows GEE while Panel (b) shows the FEE.

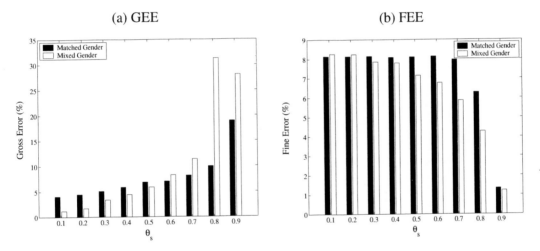

Figure 4.11. Estimation errors for partially-voiced utterances. Results are shown for both gender conditions at different values of θ_s. Panel (a) shows the GEE while Panel (b) shows the FEE.

might be considered a problem. However, the use of the tracker will likely lead to the removal of many of these spurious pitch candidates.

4.6. Summary

For most speech segmentation algorithms, the first step in segmenting voiced regions involves detecting the fundamental frequency of the individual signals that comprise the mixed utterance. Many multi-pitch detection algorithms are extensions of single pitch detection methods, but there are also several techniques that were developed specifically to deal with the multi-pitch detection problem.

The proposed MPDA system employs the autocorrelogram, which is known to highlight the harmonic structure of sound sources. Traditional uses of the ACG rely on the presence of cues for each pitch in the mixture. The cues are often taken to be the two largest peaks in the summary ACG, though there are several, more sophisticated algorithms, that are able to detect pitch of all the sources even where the pitches are not represented by the largest peaks in the summary ACG. The weaknesses of ACG-based pitch detection algorithms include: i) the emergence of spurious peaks owing to the interaction of the sources and ii) the degradation (or removal) of the primary cue to a source's pitch.

Despite the difficulties and shortcomings involved in using the summary ACG, the current system uses it for pitch detection. In recognition of the fact that the primary cues are not always present in the highest two peaks of the summary, four peaks are retained. It is acknowledged, however, that the retention of an arbitrary number of peaks is not an ideal process. Given that this algorithm is meant to be general and extensible to mixtures of more than two sources, one can anticipate the difficulties involved in deciding how many peaks to retain from the summary when handling such a signal.

The experiments performed in the previous section reveal the presence of the correct pitch candidates among the peaks retained from the summary ACG. The challenge remains to track these pitches across time to form a pitch contour for each source. This is an important step on the way to segmentation of the mixture, which has implications for the accuracy of the speech recognition experiments that are performed as a final evaluation of this system. The following chapter examines existing techniques for performing multiple-pitch tracking and presents a novel approach. For the pitch tracking stage, it is necessary to select a value of θ_s for the MPDA. Based on the evaluations of total errors and the ROC graphs, the optimal value of θ_s is chosen to be 0.7. This value represents a balance between retaining the majority of correct pitch points and including too many spurious pitch points.

Chapter 5

Multi-Pitch Tracking

This chapter focuses on the pitch tracking component of the speech segmentation system. When presented with a set of pitch candidates in each frame, it is the task of the pitch tracker to find the optimal path[17] through them and propose a number of tracks corresponding to the number of speakers in the mixture. Given that there may be errors in the initial pitch estimation, the tracker not only links a sequence of estimates through time, but it may also be tasked with correcting initial estimates through the use of the statistics of the sequence. A novel multi-pitch tracker is proposed, which exploits the power and simplicity of the hidden Markov model to model the pitch of male and female speakers. The problem of tracking the pitch of a single source, or that of a single harmonic source mixed with inharmonic noise has been widely addressed. However, little work has been done on tracking speech in multi-source or multi-speaker environments. The proposed tracker is developed in a statistical framework, where the model parameters are derived from data. It is novel in that it systematically models pitch halving and doubling errors, thus allowing for the continuation of a smooth pitch track even in the absence of the fundamental frequency. This approach negates the need for post-processing to smooth the identified tracks. Another novel aspect of the algorithm is the inclusion of a noise model to account for spurious pitch points, i.e. pitch points that do not fit to the track of either source. A thorough evaluation is carried out, with mixtures of male and female speech in mixed- and matched-gender utterances being tested.

The chapter is structured as follows: Section 5.1. gives a general introduction. Section 5.2. reviews multi-pitch tracking, while Section 5.3. details the proposed pitch tracking algorithm. A full evaluation of the proposed algorithm is presented in Section 5.4. after which a summary is given in Section 5.5.

5.1. Introduction

Pitch tracking of speech is a complex and challenging task that has inspired the development of many innovative approaches, some of which are discussed in the following sections. There is still scope, however, for further improvements. Part of the difficulty stems from

---

[17]Optimal in the sense of producing a smooth track that is most likely to correspond to the correct pitch track, given the initial estimates.

factors, such as the proximity of the fundamental frequency to the first formant, which may cause the pitch estimation algorithm to produce candidates that do not follow the smooth trajectory expected of a pitch track. Consider Figure 5.1, which shows the pitch track of a single source: In the region marked **A** there are two pitch points that seem to be inconsistent with the smooth trajectory. These could be due to the pitch determination algorithm detecting a harmonic other than the fundamental frequency, or they could be a part of the track where slight estimation errors have been made. The pitch tracker would need to decide whether to leave them out, creating a break in the final track, or include them at the risk of corrupting the pitch track. A pitch break occurs in the region of **B**; does this signal the end of one source and the beginning of another, or should the pitch track be continued because the frames have been incorrectly labelled as inharmonic? What is the maximum allowable frequency difference, Δf between the pitch point at the beginning of the interruption and that at the end? And further, how long does the break have to be before it counts as a discontinuity in the track? These and other complications make the tracking of pitch in single-source conditions difficult; how much more difficult is it likely to be when there are competing sources (with or without a pitch of their own)?

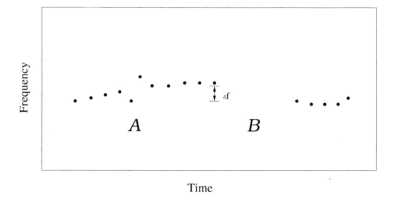

Figure 5.1. Illustration of two of the issues that pitch trackers are likely to face. Firstly, the pitch points at **A** could be part of the track, but it is not always a straight-forward decision as to whether to include them. Secondly, how much deviation, Δf, is allowed between the two points at the beginning and end of the pitch break at **B** before it is judged unlikely that both sections of the track are generated by the same source?

There are some solutions to these problems, however they are not always satisfactory. The following section reviews multi-pitch tracking algorithms in which some of these issues are addressed.

5.2. Multi-Pitch Tracking Algorithms

Multi-pitch tracking algorithms have mainly been developed in the domain of speech segmentation, with the aim of assigning a sequence of pitch candidates to a particular source. These algorithms employ a range of techniques, from dynamic programming (Every and Jackson, 2006) to Kalman filtering (Nishimoto et al., 2004). Along with the development of purpose-built multi-pitch trackers, this emphasis on source segmentation has led investigators to extend single-pitch tracking algorithms to track the pitch of multiple sources (see Gu and van Bokhoven, 1991; Every and Jackson, 2006, for example).

While multi-pitch tracking follows the basic principles of single-pitch trackers, there are additional considerations. Firstly, there is the issue of deciding if and when more than one source is harmonic; if this is not done correctly the algorithm could either track too many sources or too few. This decision is subject to the nature of the pitch determination algorithm used to provide the pitch-track candidates: Some algorithms produce pitch candidates across the entire utterance, regardless of the strength of voicing, leaving the voicing decision to the pitch tracker or to post-processing rules (Weintraub, 1985). Others only produce candidates that have a high likelihood of being part of the final pitch tracks (Rouat et al., 1997; Wu et al., 2003). Another consideration is how to maintain pitch track continuity. This involves a decision of how much frequency deviation should be allowed between adjacent pitch points. The solutions to this are varied, ranging from the use of hand-tuned thresholds (Parsons, 1976; Rouat et al., 1997), to statistical modelling of pitch dynamics (Wu et al., 2003). Finally there is the issue of correctly assigning a pitch track to a source. Difficulties present themselves when there are breaks in the pitch contour, where, depending on the proximity of the restarting tracks, it is possible to make errors in assignment. One proposed solution is to use the average of the pitch candidates in the tracks to decide which source might have generated them (Weintraub, 1985). This approach is problematic, especially where the sources in the mixture have similar pitch ranges. The following paragraphs discuss some of the proposed algorithms for multi-pitch tracking.

A prediction-based multi-pitch tracking algorithm was implemented by Parsons (1976) where pitch predictions were compared with the observed pitch candidates drawn from the spectrum. The predictions were made by fitting a straight line to three consecutive pitch candidates using a least-squares fit. Observations and predictions were compared; a maximum difference of 10 Hz was allowed between them. If the difference was greater than this threshold, an error was thought to have occurred and the mean of adjacent pitches was inserted into the track in place of the observation. A sequence of pitch candidates was only considered to be part of the track if it was more than four frames long. This simple pitch tracking algorithm worked well, especially if the initial pitch determination produced accurate candidates. In fact the initial pitch estimation was deemed to be so accurate, that the pitch tracking algorithm was used by Parsons mainly as a guide to the range in which the observations should fall, that is, a pitch observation was only considered part of the track if it fell within 10 Hz of the predicted value.

A multi-pitch tracker has to detect the subset of several pitch candidates, which form a smooth trajectory for each source in the mixture. Some pitch tracking algorithms accomplish this using rule-based tracking techniques with parameters that are not derived from data (see Parsons, 1976; Rouat et al., 1997, for example). The post-processing performed by Rouat et al. (1997) was applied to "islands" of voiced speech and involved as many as five steps: 1) the median frequency of each island was calculated; 2) pitches that significantly exceeded the median were replaced by the closest sub-multiple; 3) in the absence of such a sub-multiple, median smoothing was applied to the tracklet; 4) segments separated by 40 ms or less were merged and 5) isolated pitch points were removed. While these enhancements may seem reasonable, it is not always advisable to develop systems with hand-tuned parameters, as setting the best values is not always simple, especially if their values are interdependent. Other systems seek to model the distributions of pitch change and implement the tracking in a sound statistical framework.

The Markov model is a candidate for modelling processes involving temporal continuity and several Markov model-based multi-pitch algorithms have thus been proposed to tackle this problem. The pitch tracking algorithm developed by Weintraub (1985) consisted of a number of stages. He first computed a 'coincidence function', based on the cochlear model of Lyon (1984), to highlight the periodicity of the mixed signal. The frequency channels of the coincidence function were then normalised and smoothed, after which, a long-term coincidence function of white noise was subtracted from that of the signal. The output of this process was averaged across frequency to yield a representation that bore some similarity to the summary autocorrelogram used in many pitch estimation algorithms (see Chapter 4). An iterative dynamic programming algorithm was used to track the pitch of both sources across time; the first pitch tracked being that of the 'dominant' source. Pitch tracks were formed across the entire utterance, even where the signals were aperiodic. A Markov model was then used to determine if any sound source (to a maximum of two) was active at each time frame. The model was designed to correctly track the pitch of both sources, as well as, explicitly detect aperiodic sections and assign them to a source. The Viterbi algorithm was employed to make the decision about the best path. One of the major shortcomings of this ground-breaking system was that the weaker source was not tracked as accurately as the dominant one.

In the system described by Gu and van Bokhoven (1991), each pitch track is modelled by a separate hidden Markov model (HMM) (one for male speech and another for female speech), with the transition probabilities trained using Baum-Welch with the hidden states represent decreasing pitch, increasing pitch and constant pitch. For each source, all possible pitch contours are traced and a score calculated using the forward algorithm. The contour that gives the highest score (that is, has the maximum likelihood) for a particular model is chosen as the one generated by that model. This is repeated in order to form the pitch tracks for both sources. This is essentially a single-pitch tracker extended to track multiple pitches.

Wu et al. (2003) also propose an HMM-based pitch tracker. The tracker comprises a number of observation nodes, representing the pitch candidates derived from an ACG-based multi-pitch detection algorithm, and a set of hidden nodes, which represent the number of sources active in a given time frame. Transition probabilities for pitch-change dynamics and transition probabilities for the number of active pitch sources are both estimated from a development set consisting of completely voiced utterances. The transition probabilities concerning the number of sources are estimated given the assumption that two sources are active for half the time, while a single utterance is active for the other half. The Viterbi algorithm is used to find the best state sequence, and thus derive separate pitch tracks for each source. Owing to the high computational cost of the algorithm, pruning is employed to make the algorithm tractable. The tracker was compared to the multi-pitch determination algorithms of Tolonen and Karjalainen (2000) and that of Gu and van Bokhoven (1991). On a set of tasks – which included the tracking of a single speech source in noise, as well as the tracking of both sources[18] in a two source mixture of speech – both these algorithms were

---

[18]Results are only reported for the tracking of the dominant source in the mixture.

found, in general, to make significantly more detection, as well as estimation errors than Wu et al.'s algorithm. However, it has recently been shown that in the case of tracking two speech sources, the algorithm tracks the dominant source well, but often fails to correctly track the secondary source (Khurshid and Denham, 2004).

5.3. Proposed Multi-Pitch Tracker

This section presents an HMM-based pitch tracking algorithm that is novel, in that it systematically models pitch doubling and halving errors, thereby facilitating the identification of smooth pitch segments even in the absence of the fundamental frequency. This approach makes the system less likely to make incorrect source assignment that can occur when sources have similar fundamental frequency or are harmonically related. The algorithm also estimates the distribution of spurious pitch candidates that are generated by the pitch determination algorithm discussed in Chapter 4. By thus modelling the 'noise', the algorithm avoids potential tracking errors.

The section discusses the algorithm as a *generative model* of pitch; initially explaining the model itself in Section 5.3.1., then discussing the *parameter estimation* (Section 5.3.2.) and finally discussing the *inference* in Section 5.3.3..

5.3.1. The Generative Model

Pitch candidates computed from the summary autocorrelogram (sACG) – see Section 4.4. – are passed to the multi-pitch tracker (MPT). The tracker is based on a generative finite state model of the output of the multi-pitch determination algorithm. However, before describing the full generative model, consideration is given to how the model might be constructed from a combination of simpler models. The single-source model (see Figure 5.2) consists of three states and the transitions between them. The source is described by a finite state model that may be in either one of two voiced states (V_1, representing the start of a new voiced segment, or V_2, which indicates the continuation of a voiced segment) or an unvoiced state (U). Possible transitions between states are shown in the figure. In the voiced states, a pitch observation is produced. In voiced state, V_1, this observation is drawn from a distribution $P_s(f_t')$, which is a distribution of pitch frequencies; whereas in state V_2, observations come from the conditional distribution $P_s(f_t'|f_{t-1}')$, which is a distribution modelling the likelihood of pitch values at time t, given the value of the pitch at time $t-1$. In the simplest case, such a model has the potential to produce a single pitch track similar to that shown in Figure 5.3. Where there are two sources present (Figure 5.4) a single-source model cannot simultaneously account for both. The solution proposed employs two independent, single-source models in parallel.

Imagine now, the presence of additional peaks (peaks not accounted for by the pitch models) in the output of the multi-pitch determination algorithm. These peaks could be generated by an interfering source, or even from harmonic components of the individual sources. For simplicity, this noise is presumed to be generated by an independent noise process.[19] At each frame, the number of noisy observations, $\#N_t$, is first selected from a

---

[19]See Section 5.5. for a discussion of the implications of this assumption.

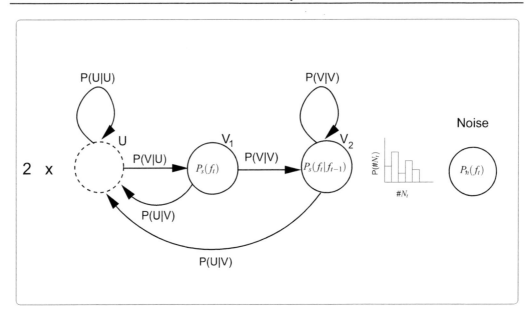

Figure 5.2. Schematic of the generative model used to describe the output of the pitch tracking process. Two speaker-independent models are running independently and in parallel (left); while in each frame, N_t spurious observations are being generated by a noise process (right). See text for details. – [Figure adapted from Coy and Barker (2007)]

discrete distribution. Then, each of the $\#N_t$ observation frequencies is independently drawn from a noise distribution, $P_n(f_t')$. The combination of the single-source models and a noise model allows for pitch tracking in noisy environments. Figure 5.5 shows the type of tracks that can be output by the combined generative model. As can be seen from the figure, more than one pitch candidate can be generated at each time frame.

The full generative model is depicted in Figure 5.2. The problem of tracking can be cast as that of trying to infer the most likely way in which the model may have produced a sequence of observed multiple pitch estimates. The current implementation makes the assumption that a maximum of two sources are active at any instant, however the algorithm is capable of being extended to track more than two sources simply by placing more single source HMMs in parallel. In the current implementation, the number of sources in the mixture is assumed to be known. In the case where this information is not known *a priori*, a model selection mechanism could be developed. Separate models for different numbers of sources could be constructed and a maximum-likelihood or maximum *a posteriori* model selection mechanism could be used to choose between them.

It must be noted that the use of two single-source pitch models for tracking assumes that the output of the multi-pitch determination algorithm for the mixture of sources is the same as the mixture of outputs from two single sources; this is clearly an approximation.

5.3.2. Parameter Estimation

Having described the model, it is now important to discuss the estimation of the model parameters. Parameters for the pitch generation models are estimated using pitch tracks

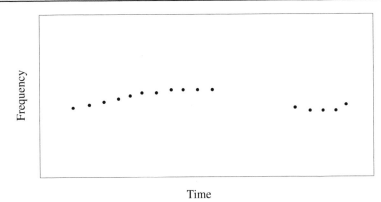

Figure 5.3. Example of a pitch track that could be generated from the single-source generative model.

Figure 5.4. Example of a pitch track that could be generated from the combination of two single-source models.

obtained from training data. The data are selected from the Aurora 2 clean training set (Hirsch and Pearce, 2000). Equal numbers of male and female utterances are used; 3720 utterances are randomly chosen from the 4220 available for each gender. These 3720 digit strings are spoken by 55 male and 55 female speakers. The digit strings range in length from 1 to 7 digits, with the average utterance being approximately 3 digits long. Signal length varies from 213 *ms* to 4.7 *s*, with an average of 1.36 *s*.

In order to develop a corpus of two-speaker utterances, the signals must be processed and mixed. First, an end-point detection algorithm (Rabiner and Sambur, 1975), which uses energy and zero-crossings to detect the boundaries of speech, is used to remove the silences from the beginning and end of the signal. The speech signals are then matched for length and paired (summed in the time domain), yielding 7439 mixed utterances. These mixtures consist of 3449 mixed gender utterances and 3990 matched gender utterances (1995 female and 1995 male). Though the length-matching process is designed to pair together the utterances with the least difference in length, it is important to consider how well the utterances are actually matched for length. Analysis shows that the temporal overlap of the signals is quite good; the maximum difference in length is only 1.9 *ms* and the mean is approximately

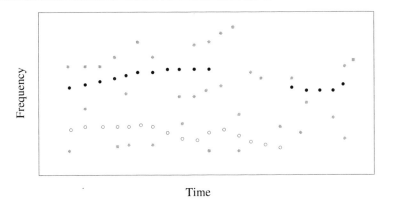

Figure 5.5. Example of a pair of pitch tracks and noisy observations that could be generated from the full generative model.

0.005 *ms*. Where there is a difference in length, zeros are added to the end of the shorter of the two utterances. The sampling rate of the signals is 8 *kHz*.

The tracker works in the log domain, thus an observation, f_t, at time t is transformed to $f'_t = log_2(f_t)$. The distribution $P_s(f'_t)$ used when first entering the voiced state is modelled using a 2-component diagonal covariance GMM trained from the frequencies of the pitches in each voiced segment in the training data – one component to account for the pitches of male utterances and the other for female pitches. The conditional probabilities occurring in successive voiced states, $P_s(f' \mid f'_{t-1})$, are computed by estimating, $P(d|f'_{t-1})$, the conditional distribution of log space pitch differences, $d = log_2(\frac{f_t}{f_{t-1}})$, and then noting that:

$$P_s(f'_t = F'_t \mid f'_{t-1} = F'_{t-1}) = P\left(d = log_2\left(\frac{F_t}{F_{t-1}}\right)\Big| f'_{t-1} = F'_{t-1}\right), \qquad (5.1)$$

where $F' = log_2(F)$, is a set of log-pitch observations. This substitution is made in order to take advantage of the simple form of the distribution of d. The variable d typically has values narrowly spread about a mean of 0 (no pitch change), except where there is pitch doubling or halving. When doubling occurs the values will be narrowly spread about 1; for halving the values are close to -1. The value of d is also approximately independent of the previous pitch. A notable exception is that, for the proposed pitch determination algorithm (Chapter 4), pitch doubling is more likely to occur at low frequencies, while there is more pitch halving at high frequencies. In fact, there is a clear dividing frequency, F_{mid}, separating the regions of low and high frequency behaviour (see Figure 5.6). So $P(d = log_2(\frac{F_t}{F_{t-1}}) \mid f'_{t-1} = F'_{t-1})$ is approximated by the two distributions $P(d = log_2(\frac{F_t}{F_{t-1}}) \mid f'_{t-1} \leq F_{mid})$ and $P(d = log_2(\frac{F_t}{F_{t-1}}) \mid f'_{t-1} > F_{mid})$. These two conditional distributions are modelled by GMMs estimated from the clean pitch track data. The centres of the components are set to -1, 0 and 1, while the variances and weights are estimated using maximum likelihood. Finally, the state transition probabilities are estimated by using the clean speech pitch tracks to estimate the proportion of voiced frames that are followed by a voiced frame, $P(V|V)$ and the proportion of unvoiced frames that are followed by an unvoiced frame, $P(U|U)$. And, trivially, $P(V|U) = 1 - P(V|V)$ and $P(U|V) = 1 - P(U|U)$.

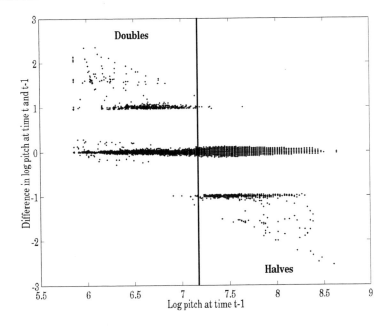

Figure 5.6. An illustration of the threshold for pitch doubling and halving in female speech (the pattern is similar for male speech). The data to the left of the vertical line represent points where the pitch at time t is at least twice the pitch at time $t-1$ (doubles). For the points to the right of the line, the pitch at time t is at most half the pitch at time $t-1$. (Reproduced from Coy and Barker (2006))

The distribution of the peaks produced by the noise model, $P_n(f_t)$, is estimated after first removing the genuine peaks from the output of the multi-pitch determination output. This is done by passing the mixed training utterances through the multi-pitch determination algorithm, taking that output and comparing it to the 'correct' pitch tracks that have been produced by individually tracking the component *clean* sources. Any peaks in the mixed source output that match within three standard deviations of the median value of the single source pitch tracks are removed. Then, $P_n(f_t)$, is estimated by training a Gaussian mixture model (GMM) of the distribution of the log frequencies of the remaining peaks. Two mixture components are used with the centres set by hand, and the variances estimated using maximum likelihood. Also, the number of distractor points per frame, $\#N_t$, is counted and used to estimate the probability of a frame having a given number of distractors, $P_{\#n}(\#n = \#N)$.

5.3.3. Inference

Pitch tracking can now be viewed as an inference problem. Consider the sequence of multiple pitch estimates output by the multi-pitch estimator: At each frame there can be anywhere from 0 to 4 pitch estimates. There are many different ways in which the generative model could have produced the observed data, e.g., any given pitch estimate may have arisen from either the noise model, or one of the voiced states of one of the speech sources. The problem can be considered as that of attaching labels (i.e. *source1*, *source2* or *noise*) to each of the observed pitch estimates. All possible labellings, L, are considered in order to find the one that is most probable given the observed data.

So, formally, given a set of observations, F, we wish to find the labelling, L, for which $P(L|F)$ is greatest,

$$\hat{L} = \underset{L}{\operatorname{argmax}} P(L|F) = \underset{L}{\operatorname{argmax}} P(F|L)P(L). \tag{5.2}$$

Note though, that the generative model (Figure 5.2) is such that the state sequences are totally determined once the labelling, L, is given, i.e. every labelling implies a unique underlying state sequence. So $P(F|L)$ can be expressed as,

$$P(F|L) = \prod_{t=1}^{T} \left(\prod_{i=1}^{\#F_t} P(f = F_{i,t}|q_{i,t}, l_{t-1}) \right), \tag{5.3}$$

where $\#F_t$ is the number of observations in frame t, $F_{i,t}$ is the ith observation, $q_{i,t}$ is the state responsible for having generated it (either one of the speech states or the noise model state), and l_{t-1} is the labelling of the observations in the previous frame (needed because the pitch emission distribution is conditioned on the previous pitch).

The prior probability of any particular set of labels, $P(L)$, can be computed from the transition probabilities of the implied state sequence,

$$P(L) = \prod_{t=1}^{T} P_{\#n}(\#N_t) \prod_{t=2}^{T} P_{s1}(q_{s1,t}|q_{s1,t-1}) P_{s2}(q_{s2,t}|q_{s2,t-1}), \tag{5.4}$$

$\#N_t$ is the number of noise observations at time, t, and $q_{s1,t}$ and $q_{s2,t}$ are the states of the source1 and source2 model components as implied by the labelling, L.

Due to the Markov property of the generative models, Equation 5.2 can be evaluated using the Viterbi algorithm. The two individual 3-state speech pitch models are combined into a single model containing 3×3 composite states. When expanding this model through time each state needs to be further expanded to consider the ways in which it may have generated the observed data for a given frame. For example, when in the composite state modelling *source*1 $= v$ and *source*2 $= v$ and there are 4 observed peaks, then two of the peaks are due to speech and the remaining two are due to noise. So, in this case, there are 4×3 ways of attaching the labels (*source1, source2, noise, noise*) to the 4 peaks. The full set of states is expanded through time to form a trellis of all possible labelling hypotheses. The Viterbi algorithm is then applied to this trellis using the standard token-passing approach.

Once the best labelling has been found, the points that are labelled *source1* and *source2* are taken to make up the two pitch tracks. Examples of the output of the process are shown in Figure 5.7. Note that each pitch track is a sequence of continuously voiced segments divided by unvoiced regions. Each continuously voiced track segment acts as a 'scaffold' which recruits spectro-temporal points to form a voiced fragment as described in Chapter 6. Consider Figure 5.7, the region highlighted with an 'X' shows a typical instance where the pitch at half the fundamental frequency is tracked owing to the absence of the fundamental. At frame 128 the fundamental of the high frequency source is not among the candidates presented to the MPT. A candidate at half this value is however, present so the model tracks it. This track continues to frame 140. At frame 134 the fundamental of the low frequency

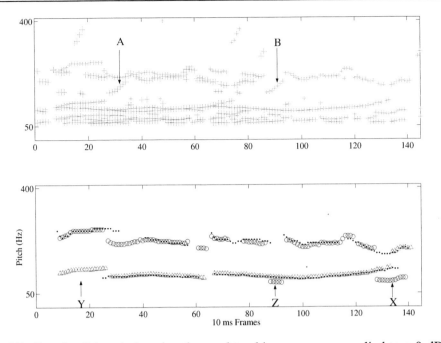

Figure 5.7. Result of the pitch estimation and tracking processes applied to a 0 dB SNR mixture of the utterances, 'four zero one' and 'zero four seven seven two' spoken by a male and a female speaker respectively. (**top**) Unlabelled pitch estimate data produced by the multi-pitch estimation algorithm and (**bottom**) pitch tracks output by the MPT (marked by '△' and 'o') overlaid with the *a priori* pitch tracks (marked by '.'). Note how closely the MPT output matches the *a priori* pitch tracks.

source disappears and the fundamental of the high frequency source re-appears. The model that was tracking the low frequency source then takes over the tracking of the fundamental of the high frequency source. The regions marked Y and Z are where the tracker outputs a pitch where the reference does not. In region Y, the extra track is the harmonic at half the fundamental frequency of the high frequency source. The extra track segment at Z is also related to the high frequency source. In the regions marked by the letters A and B (top panel), it can be seen that there are segments that appear to be reasonable pitch tracks. These however, are not tracked by the proposed MPT. Interestingly, they are not tracked by the reference tracker either, suggesting that they are not valid pitch track segments.

The proposed multi-pitch tracking algorithm is an important component in the overall speech segmentation system developed in this work. It forms the basis of a system that has as its goal the correct segmentation of monaurally-mixed voiced speech. Thus, it is used to track voiced segments separated by unvoiced regions and does not impose temporal continuity across pitch breaks. The reason for this is that the temporal continuity is imposed during decoding in the speech recognition stage (see Chapter 3). Thus it is not necessary to impose strict continuity constraints at this stage. This lessens the possibility that the wrong track, and ultimately the wrong spectro-temporal regions, are assigned to the wrong source. This is a particular risk where the pitch ranges are close and there is a high probability of the pitch tracks crossing.

5.4.   Evaluation

While there is no standard evaluation for multi-pitch trackers, it is important that the performance of the current algorithm be measured in some quantifiable way. The pitch tracking component of the system is critically important for accurate recognition results. The decoding framework requires that the fragments of the mixture that correspond to *both* sources are recovered from the mixture. Thus, the segmentation must be accurate. Accurate pitch tracks will produce accurate voiced-speech segmentation; therefore the pitch tracker must be accurate. The evaluation carried out here not only provides information on the accuracy of the pitch tracking algorithm itself, it also provides insights into how accurate the voiced-speech segmentation, and speech recognition components are likely to be.

The metrics typically employed in the evaluation of the output of a (multiple) pitch tracker are the same as those employed for pitch determination algorithms (Rabiner, 1977). Those metrics measure how closely the pitch tracks correspond to the reference tracks of individual sources. These errors, which have been described in Chapter 4 are outlined here. A *gross estimation error* (GEE) is said to occur if the value of a pitch estimate at time t does not fall within a threshold of a corresponding pitch point in the reference track. When the double/half is found in the pitch track, it is compared to twice/half the value found in the reference pitch track. A *fine estimation error* (FEE) is defined as the mean deviation of the estimated pitch from the reference in the regions where both reference and estimated tracks are present, and no gross error has occurred.

Detection errors, *voiced-unvoiced error* (VUE), and *unvoiced-voiced error* (UVE), are calculated and presented using the notation proposed by Wu et al. (2003). $E_{x \to y}$ represents a detection error where the reference pitch tracker detects x points and the tracker being tested detects y. In this way all possible voicing detection errors are considered based on the number of sources found in the mixture.

The errors are calculated for each track by comparing it to a reference track for the unmixed signal. The reference tracks are obtained using Snack (Sjolander, 2002) (an open source version of ESPS/waves+ – see Chapter 4 for details). The threshold for the GEE calculation is set to 20%.

While the error metrics are the same as those employed in the analysis of the multi-pitch determination algorithm performed in Chapter 4, the resulting errors can differ. It is important to note that the proposed pitch tracker is presented with (a maximum of) four pitch estimates per frame and must reduce that to at most two. This process of removing some of the estimates can lead to a difference in the errors produced by the two processes and motivates the analysis. Based on the analysis performed in Chapter 4, the value of θ_s is chosen to be 0.7. This value represents a trade-off between retaining the majority of correct pitch points and including too many spurious pitch points.

5.4.1.   Evaluation Design

The evaluation is designed such that the proposed algorithm is tested in a number of scenarios. It is tested with fully voiced utterances as well as with utterances that have breaks in voicing. Thus the algorithm has to deal with situations where there are either two, one, or zero voiced sources active in any one frame. The data are the same that were used in

Chapter 4.

The parameters of the proposed MPT are estimated using partially-voiced data. Thus, it may be that the algorithm will not perform well if there are no unvoiced regions in the mixture. The model is, therefore modified to deal with fully-voiced mixtures. All transition probabilities in the pitch tracking HMM (see Section 5.3.2.), except $P(V|V)$ are set to zero. This accounts for the fact that no pitch breaks occur in the mixtures.

In order to judge the relative performance of the algorithm, it is compared to a state-of-the-art multi-pitch tracker, that of Wu et al. (2003) (referred to as WMPT throughout this section); Section 5.2. briefly describes the algorithm. The tracker is chosen for comparison because it tracks estimates derived from an ACG-based pitch determination algorithm using an HMM-based algorithm.

The evaluation proceeds as follows: Section 5.4.2. examines the effect of TMR on the performance of the proposed MPT and the WMPT in tracking fully-voiced utterances as well as partially-voiced utterances. Detection errors are considered first, followed by estimation errors. Section 5.4.3. discusses the effect of TMR. The next stage of the evaluation (Section 5.4.4.) examines the relative performance of both algorithms for tracking matched- and mixed-gender utterances. The tests are carried out on both fully- and partially-voiced utterances and detection and estimation errors are considered. A discussion of the performance differences for matched- and mixed-gender utterances is carried out in Section 5.4.5..

5.4.2. The Effect of TMR

As in Chapter 4, the range of TMRs is chosen to be $-9\ dB$ to $9\ dB$ in $3\ dB$ steps. The results presented show the outcome of tracking the pitch of both signals at each TMR. When one signal is at $9\ dB$, say, the other is effectively at $-9\ dB$ and vice versa; thus the two tracks output from the process of tracking a mixture at $-9\ dB$ TMR correspond to a track for *source1* at $-9\ dB$ and one for *source2* at $9\ dB$. Consequently, the pitch tracker produces tracks for both sources at each TMR.

When the candidate pitch estimates are presented to the tracker, there is no indication of the gender of the sources in the mixture. In the absence of a gender recognition component, the tracker is run with three different model combinations (male/male, male/female and female/female). The Viterbi scores are compared and the combination with the best score is chosen as the correct one.

Detection errors are now be presented for fully-voiced and partially-voiced utterances, followed by estimation errors for both types of utterance.

Detection Errors – Fully Voiced Utterances

Figure 5.8 shows the detection errors for the proposed MPT and the WMPT. As the utterances are fully voiced, only those errors where the tracker did not detect pitches present in the reference are presented. These errors are referred to here as *under-detection* errors.

For the proposed MPT (Panel a), the value of $E_{2\to0}$ varies from 1.7% at $-9\ dB$ to 2.1% at $9\ dB$. Interestingly, it falls to 0.9% at $0\ dB$ before rising again as TMR increases. This suggests that the pitch tracker is more likely, with this type of mixture, to detect both pitches

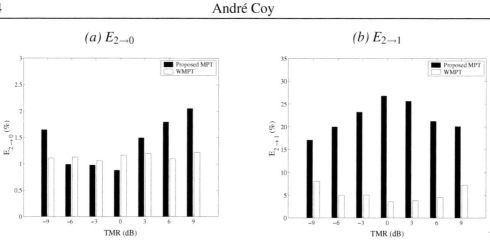

Figure 5.8. Comparison of detection errors for both algorithms with fully-voiced utterances for a range of TMR. Note that the scales are different for both errors.

when both sources have similar global SNR. For the WMPT, the values do not vary a lot across TMR. Overall the WMPT has a lower value of $E_{2\to0}$ (1.1% compared to 1.4%), the differences are greatest at positive TMRs. The values of $E_{2\to1}$ are high (on average four times higher than the WMPT). It is possible that the high proportion of $E_{2\to1}$ arises from single source dominance, rather than poor pitch detection. The $E_{2\to1}$ errors show an initial increase as TMR approaches 0 dB and a falloff as TMR increases further. This seems to run counter to the expectation that a single source will dominate where TMR is either high or low. This will be explored further in Section 5.4.3.. Table 5.1 shows the overall detection errors made by both the proposed MPT (23.6%) and the WMPT (6.5%).

Table 5.1. Average detection errors for fully-voiced utterances for a range of TMR.

	Under-detection Errors
Proposed MPT	23.6%
WMPT	6.5%

Detection Errors – Utterances with Unvoiced Regions

Figure 5.9 shows the various detection errors calculated for both the proposed MPT and the WMPT. These errors can be categorised as either overestimating or underestimating the number of pitch points present in a frame. Panels *(a)*, *(c)* and *(e)* show errors made by the pitch tracking algorithms, where the trackers did not detect all pitches present in the reference and represent *under-detection*. The other three which show errors where the trackers detect more pitches than appear in the reference tracks, are representative of *over-detection*.

In the scenario of underestimating the number of pitch points present in a frame, the error that occurs most often, for both algorithms, is the detection of a single pitch where

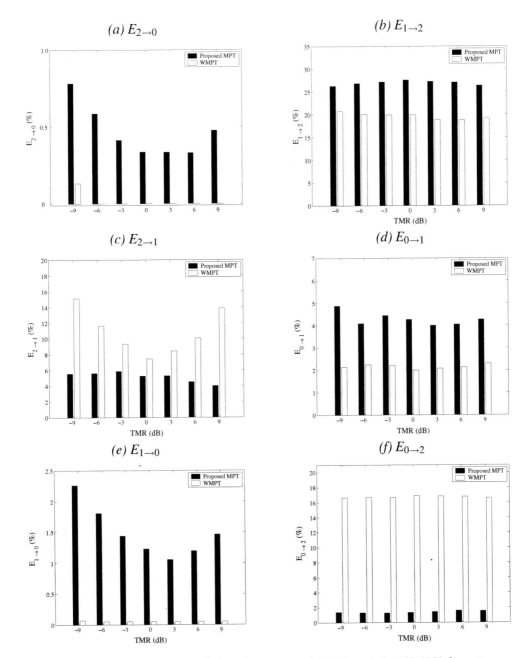

Figure 5.9. Detection errors made by the proposed MPT and the WMPT for utterances with voicing breaks at a range of TMR. Note that the scales are different so as to highlight inter-error differences.

there are two in the reference $E_{2\rightarrow 1}$. The high values of $E_{2\rightarrow 1}$ show that there are many frames in which a single source seems to have been dominant. This could possibly be inherited from the pitch determination algorithm, where two possibilities arise. Either one source was significantly dominant, to the point of completely masking the second source; obliterating evidence for the second source, or the algorithm failed to detect the second pitch, even where there was evidence for it.

The values of $E_{2\rightarrow 1}$ for the proposed MPT (5.2% on average) are half those made by the WMPT (on average, 10.9%). Given that the WMPT employs quite a sophisticated pitch detection algorithm, it seems possible that the high proportion of $E_{2\rightarrow 1}$ in the proposed algorithm arises from single source dominance, rather than from poor pitch detection. The proposed algorithm makes far more $E_{1\rightarrow 0}$ errors than the WMPT (on average, 1.5% compared to 0.1%). The difference is likely due to the fact that the WMPT carefully models the number of sources active at each time step and is thus, less likely to make such errors. This may have some small impact on the fragment generation (see Chapter 6), however the *fragment decoder* can compensate for such small errors in segmentation. The same is true of $E_{2\rightarrow 0}$ errors (on average, 0% compared to 0.5%). On average, the proposed MPT had fewer under-detection errors (7.1% compared to 10.9%).

The detection of two pitches where the reference indicates there was one ($E_{1\rightarrow 2}$) is the most frequently occurring over-detection error for the proposed algorithm (27% compared to 19.7% for the WMPT). As regards the prevalence of $E_{1\rightarrow 2}$ errors, it appears that where there is only one source present in a frame, the proposed algorithm will sometimes track the pitch of a source and, either its half or its double. This is an artifact of the algorithm where generating the source's pitch and its half/double will sometimes be deemed as more likely than generating a single voiced output. A similar explanation can be invoked for the $E_{0\rightarrow 1}$ and $E_{0\rightarrow 2}$ errors. It is interesting to note that the modelling of the number of active sources may have contributed to the higher average $E_{0\rightarrow 2}$ errors made by the WMPT (16.7% compared to 1.4%). Over-detection errors were, on average, lower for the proposed MPT (32.6% compared to 38.5%) – see Table 5.2.

Table 5.2. Average detection errors for partially-voiced utterances for a range of TMR.

	Under-detection Errors	Over-detection Errors
Proposed MPT	32.6%	7.1%
WMPT	38.5%	10.9%

Estimation Errors – Fully Voiced Utterances

Figure 5.10 shows the estimation errors for fully-voiced utterances. For the proposed MPT, GEE decreased as TMR increased toward 3 *dB*, with small increases at 6 *dB* and 9 *dB*. This suggests that when both sources are equally energetic more gross errors occur. This might have been anticipated, as there is likely to be greater harmonic interaction when both signals have similar global SNR. For WMPT the pattern of results is similar. Overall, the proposed MPT had a lower average GEE than the WMPT (4.3% compared to 21.4%). The fine errors made by both algorithms are shown in Figure 5.10 (b). FEE for the proposed algorithm does not show any particular pattern across TMR, with an average error of 4.6%; the errors are lower for the WMPT (3.3%). The overall errors for GEE and FEE are found in Table 5.3.

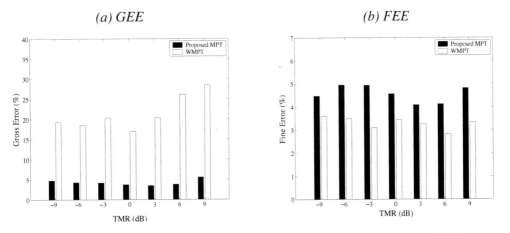

(a) GEE   *(b) FEE*

Figure 5.10. Comparison of the estimation errors made by the proposed MPT and the WMPT for fully-voiced utterances: *(a)*, GEE and *(b)*, FEE. The results are shown at different TMRs, averaged across speaker.

Table 5.3. Average estimation errors made by the proposed MPT and the WMPT for partially-voiced utterances.

	GEE	FEE
Proposed MPT	4.3%	4.6%
WMPT	21.4%	3.3%

It is important to recall that the proposed MPT was modified for the tracking of fully-voiced utterances. However, the unmodified model gives virtually identical performance (within 1%) to the modified one. The modifications were implemented for the sake of rigour and were not required for accurate performance in the fully-voiced condition.

Estimation Errors – Utterances with Unvoiced Regions

Figure 5.11 *(a)* shows the GEE for utterances that were not completely voiced. The pattern of the errors for the proposed MPT shows a small increase in GEE as TMR increases to −3 *dB*, where after, it is effectively constant. The WMPT shows some increase in GEE as TMR increases to 3 *dB* and a small decrease thereafter. The overall GEE for the proposed algorithm (11.3%) is almost a quarter that of the WMPT (39.7%) – see Table 5.4. This is likely due to the fact that the WMPT was trained on fully voiced utterances which might prevent it generalising to the condition where breaks in voicing can occur for both sources throughout the utterance.

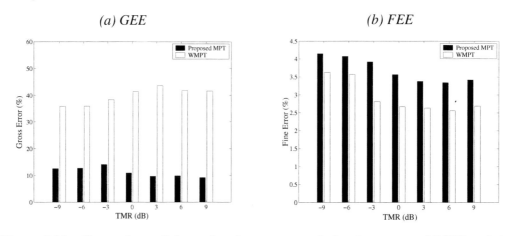

(a) GEE   *(b) FEE*

Figure 5.11. Comparison of the estimation errors made by the proposed MPT and the WMPT for partially-voiced utterances. The results are shown at different TMRs, averaged across speaker.

The fine errors, shown in Figure 5.11 (*b*), show a similar pattern to that of the GEE. The proposed MPT has a higher overall FEE (Table 5.4) than the WMPT (3.7% and 3.0%, respectively).

Table 5.4. Average estimation errors made by the proposed MPT and the WMPT for partially-voiced utterances at a range of TMR.

	GEE	FEE
Proposed MPT	11.3%	3.7%
WMPT	39.7%	3.0%

5.4.3.   Discussion of the Effect of TMR

Most of the effects of TMR can be attributed to the reduction in the number of pitch estimates available at lower TMR values. However, an interesting pattern is seen in the $E_{2\rightarrow1}$ error for the fully-voiced mixtures – an increase as the TMR approaches 0 *dB* and a decrease at lower TMR (See Figure 5.8). The $E_{2\rightarrow1}$ error is one of underestimating the number of pitch candidates present in a frame of speech. This pattern is difficult to explain, but may be due to the complex interaction of harmonics at different TMRs. It is possible that this pattern reflects the nature of the mixtures in the region of 0 *dB*, where both sources are (on average) equally energetic. One possible explanation for the pattern is that the reduced level difference between the sources will lead to greater harmonic interaction and hence degradation of the harmonic structure of both sources. This could lead to significant pitch distortion for both sources; a condition which will not necessarily obtain at other TMRs. The use of the summary ACG for pitch determination could compound these effects, leading to the pattern that is realised. It is worth noting that the results from the WMPT do not show this pattern. This may be because the more sophisticated pitch determination algorithm makes it less susceptible to these effects.

For the proposed algorithm, the pattern of GEE errors showed almost no difference across TMR; decreasing only slightly where the sources have similar overall SNR. For partially-voiced utterances, GEE decreased as TMR increased. The differences are likely due to the differences in the mixtures. Where there are pitch breaks, the algorithm is tracking a single source in aperiodic noise, which could lead to fewer GEE errors.

The overall results in Tables 5.2 and 5.4 show that the proposed MPT outperforms the WMPT in the partially-voiced condition. At first glance it would appear that the WMPT outperforms the proposed MPT in the fully-voiced condition, by virtue of its lower under-detection errors (see Table 5.1), even though it has a higher GEE (see Table 5.3). However, it is instructive to consider the relationship between under-detection errors and GEE. The WMPT has fewer instances of detecting one pitch where the reference indicated that there were two. Nonetheless, the WMPT also has quite high GEE. This suggests that many of the pitch points detected are erroneous. Thus, it may be that the WMPT is not detecting the pitch of both sources, but rather the pitch of one source and an erroneous pitch point. This could explain the difference in $E_{2 \to 1}$ between the two algorithms in the fully-voiced condition.

Analysis of the errors in pitch tracking due to varying TMR has yielded useful insights, which point to strengths and weaknesses of the proposed algorithm. The following section will go further in the analysis of the proposed pitch tracker, to compare the performance of the algorithm on mixed- and matched-gender utterances.

5.4.4. A Comparison of Errors in Mixed-Gender and Matched-Gender Utterances

When performing pitch tracking on mixtures of speech, algorithms generally perform better if the average pitch of one source is different from that of the other; the wider the separation the better. This is related to the ability of the pitch determination algorithm to resolve the harmonics of the individual sources; a task which becomes more difficult as the pitch values become closer. The average pitch values for males and females are widely separated. Thus, when attempting to determine the pitch of both speakers in a mixture of male and female speech this gender-based difference is useful. When applied to matched-gender mixtures, detection algorithms do not benefit from this property. The experiments that are performed in this section are meant to evaluate the relative performance of the proposed algorithm on matched- and mixed-gender utterances.

The experiments performed here are similar to those performed in Section 5.4.2., the difference here is that the results are evaluated separately for each type of mixture (matched and mixed) at a single TMR (0 dB). Note that the scales are different so as to highlight inter-error differences.

Detection Errors – Fully Voiced Utterances

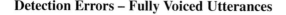

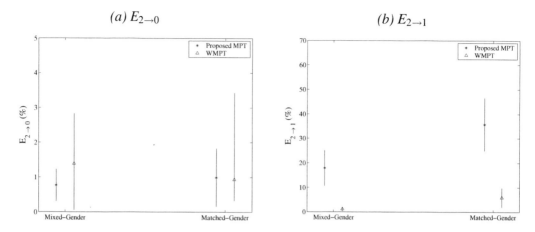

Figure 5.12. Detection errors made by the proposed MPT and the WMPT for fully-voiced mixtures for mixed- and matched-gender utterances.

The results are given in Figure 5.12. Only $E_{2\to0}$ and $E_{2\to1}$ (Panels *(a)* and *(b)*, respectively) are considered as both sources in the mixture are completely voiced. For the mixed-gender condition, the proposed MPT had a lower average $E_{2\to0}$ than the WMPT (0.8% compared to 1.4%); the matched gender performance is similar for both algorithms (1% and 0.9%). The $E_{2\to1}$ errors are much higher for the proposed algorithm in both conditions. While the WMPT makes few errors (1.1% and 5.9% for the mixed- and matched-gender condition, respectively), the proposed algorithm yields a high proportion of $E_{2\to1}$ errors (17.9% and 35.7%). This indicates that, for the fully voiced utterances, the proposed algorithm is more likely than the WMPT to detect only one of the two pitches present in a frame; especially in the matched-gender condition. This may be due to errors made in the pitch determination algorithm. Or it may be due to the WMPT detecting one correct pitch and one erroneous one, as discussed in Section 5.4.3.. The proximity of the pitch contours (and harmonics) of matched-gender speakers generally, makes it more difficult to detect both pitches in the summary ACG.

Detection Errors – Utterances with Unvoiced Regions

Detection errors are shown in Figure 5.13. Neither algorithm makes many $E_{2\to0}$ errors. In fact, the only such error occurs in the proposed algorithm in the matched-gender condition and it is quite small (0.5%). For $E_{2\to1}$, the WMPT makes more errors in the matched-gender condition (9.3% to 5.8%), while the proposed algorithm makes more errors in the mixed-gender condition (4.2% to 3.8%). The proposed algorithm makes $E_{1\to0}$ errors of 1.2% and 1.3% for the matched and mixed-gender conditions, respectively. The WMPT makes no $E_{1\to0}$ errors in the mixed-gender condition and only 0.1% for the matched-gender condition. These three error metrics measure the under-detection errors made by both algorithms. By summing them ($E_{2\to0}+E_{2\to1}+E_{1\to0}$) it is seen that the WMPT makes more under-detection errors for the matched-gender condition (9.3% to 7.5%), but fewer in the mixed-gender condition (3.8% to 5.5%). The proposed algorithm shows consistent performance for the

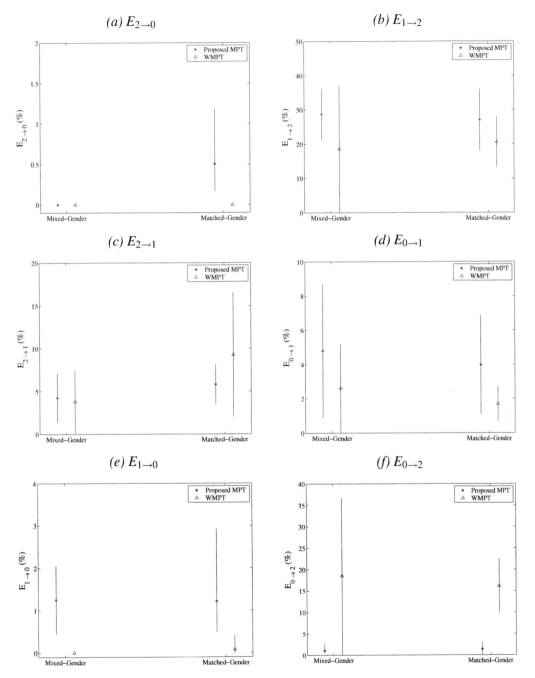

Figure 5.13. Detection errors made by the proposed MPT and the WMPT for partially-voiced mixtures for mixed- and matched-gender utterances.

different conditions.

The proposed algorithm makes fewer total over-detection errors $(E_{1\rightarrow 2} + E_{0\rightarrow 1} + E_{0\rightarrow 2})$ for both conditions: 34.6% compared to 39.7%, for mixed-gender utterances and 32.5% to 38.4%, for matched-gender utterances. The proposed algorithm, however, makes more $E_{1\rightarrow 2}$ and $E_{0\rightarrow 1}$ errors. The WMPT makes more $E_{0\rightarrow 2}$ errors for both conditions.

Estimation Errors – Fully Voiced Utterances

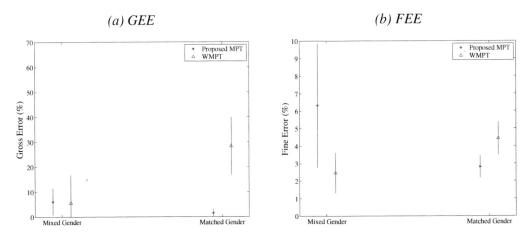

Figure 5.14. Comparison of average estimation errors made by the proposed MPT and the WMPT for fully-voiced mixtures. *(a)* GEE for mixed- and matched-gender utterances. *(b)* FEE for mixed- and matched-gender utterances. Errors are plotted with error bars calculated from the arcsine transformed data.

As seen in Figure 5.14 (Panel *a*) the mixed-gender case has the greater proportion of GEE errors for the proposed MPT (6.1% compared to 1.5% for the matched-gender case). This is somewhat unusual, as tracking in mixed-gender conditions generally yields lower errors. The proposed MPT outperforms the WMPT in the matched-gender condition, but not for the mixed-gender case.

Figure 5.14 (Panel *b*) shows that the proposed MPT has fewer fine errors than the WMPT in the matched-gender case (2.8% compared to 4.4%). The pattern is reversed for the mixed gender case, where the WMPT had the lower errors (2.4% compared to 6.3%).

Estimation Errors – Utterances with Unvoiced Regions

Figure 5.15, Panel *(a)* shows a comparison of average GEE for both algorithms. The proposed algorithm has lower GEE errors for both conditions. The difference in GEE for mixed-gender utterances (7.6% compared to 35.2%) again indicates that the WMPT has difficulty tracking sources that have pitch breaks throughout the utterance (see Section 5.4.2.). For the matched-gender case, the proposed algorithm had GEE of 12.5% compared to 44.4% for the WMPT.

FEE errors (Figure 5.15, Panel *b*) are similar for the proposed MPT, in both conditions (3.1% and 3.8% for the mixed- and matched-gender cases, respectively). For the WMPT the errors are 1.8% and 3.1% in the mixed gender and in the matched-gender cases, respectively. The WMPT outperforms the proposed algorithm in both cases.

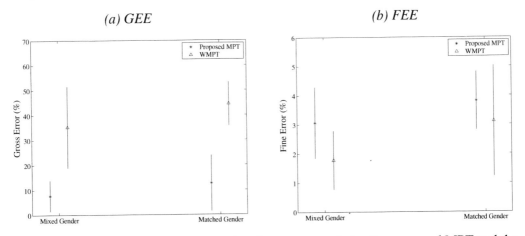

Figure 5.15. Comparison of average estimation errors made by the proposed MPT and the WMPT for partially-voiced mixtures. *(a)* GEE for mixed- and matched-gender utterances. *(b)* FEE for mixed- and matched-gender utterances. Errors are plotted with error bars calculated from the arcsine transformed data.

5.4.5. Discussion of the Comparison of Mixed-Gender and Matched-Gender Utterances

From the results of the experiments performed to test the effect of gender on pitch tracking, it would appear that the tracking of speech mixtures is more difficult for the matched-gender condition. This may not be the case, however, as owing to the similarity of the average pitches of the sources in that condition and the difficulty of resolving such similar pitches, the pitch determination algorithm may not always provide a candidate for each pitch. This is supported by the results of the previous section, where it was seen that the proposed algorithm, applied to mixtures with pitch breaks, made similar percentage detection errors for mixed- and matched-gender utterances. In the fully-voiced condition, the detection error $E_{2 \to 1}$, was much higher for matched-gender utterances than it was for mixed-gender utterances. Again this points to difficulty in detecting the pitch of both sources in a matched-gender utterance. In the fully-voiced condition, it is more likely that one source will dominate across the entire utterance, making it difficult to detect the pitch of the other source. The WMPT, however has a low value of $E_{2 \to 1}$ in this case, which is somewhat misleading. In the matched gender case, there are high GEE errors (higher than that of the proposed MPT), which suggests that at least one of the pitch points detected by the WMPT is erroneous and that the low $E_{2 \to 1}$ errors do not necessarily indicate better tracking of the pitch of both sources. In the mixed-gender case, however, the low $E_{2 \to 1}$ value for the WMPT does seem to be valid, as it is not accompanied by a high GEE. The GEE of the proposed algorithm is lower for mixed-gender utterances in the partially voiced condition, but not for the fully-voiced condition. Generally, however, performance is similar in both conditions.

5.5. Summary

A novel HMM-based multi-pitch tracker has been presented. The tracker employed, in parallel, two separate gender-dependent HMMs – one for each source – which modelled the pitches of male and female speakers, and a noise model to account for spurious pitch points. The tracker was developed and tested with two-source mixtures, however, the framework is readily extensible to the tracking of multi-source mixtures. A number of novel techniques were implemented in this algorithm: among these was the systematic modelling of pitch doubling and halving errors. This facilitated the continuity of smooth pitch segments, even in the absence of the fundamental frequency, and was done to alleviate errors where a pitch point is not tracked owing to the absence of the primary cue supporting its inclusion. The algorithm considered multiple pitch candidates per time frame, however, only a maximum of two could become part of a pitch track. This brings into focus, another unique aspect of the algorithm, which is the inclusion of a noise model to account for spurious pitch points.

The primary purpose of the pitch tracker is the formation of pitch track segments that can be attributed to a single source. It thus functions as one step in the segmentation of voiced speech mixtures. As such, there is no attempt to join pitch track segments across pitch breaks so as to avoid the occurrence of incorrect source assignment. What this means is that the algorithm will output a series of 'tracklets'; regions of voiced speech separated by regions of unvoiced speech. This in no way limits the performance of the tracker; in fact, it has been shown that this constraint significantly improves the segmentation of voiced speech (Coy and Barker, 2006).

Evaluation shows a good performance across a range of TMR, and with mixtures of different gender combinations, tracking both sources with reasonable accuracy. Comparison with a state-of-the-art multi-pitch tracker shows that the proposed algorithm generally outperforms it, especially when employed to track partially-voiced speech. The WMPT may have some advantage in the tracking of fully-voiced speech, but this is not a clear advantage.

Finally, there are some points for consideration. Firstly the halving/doubling threshold F_{mid}. Experiments have shown that its value can be varied within a small range without significantly affecting performance. The assumption that pitch segments are generated by a first order Markov process produces good results, however the framework can readily be extended to model the pitch trajectory using a second order Markov model. Further, using Gaussians to model the pitch dynamics leads to an imperfect fit. However, as a first approximation it provides reasonable results. The assumption that the distractor points are independent-and-identically-distributed noise does not account for the relationship between the distractors and the pitch. There is scope, however for addressing this in the form of a re-estimation of the model parameters. Whilst this will be a further approximation, it may serve to improve the models in a systematic way.

The algorithm presented has been shown to work well in tracking both sources in a two-speaker mixture for a range of signal levels and for different gender combinations. The next stage of the system (Chapter 6) involves the use of these pitch tracks to recruit spectro-temporal regions of the mixed speech signal to form fragments of voiced speech.

Chapter 6

Voiced Speech Segmentation

6.1. Introduction

The general aim of auditory scene analysis (ASA) is the recovery of separate descriptions of each separate sound source in the environment. This, Bregman hypothesises, is achieved by the dual mechanisms of primitive and schema-driven segmentation (Bregman, 1990). Initially, generalised acoustic characteristics (for example, pitch continuity, intensity, location, common onset/offset) of individual sounds are exploited to perform an initial stage of grouping before processes based on learning and experience group related objects and assign each separate sound object to a separate perceptual stream. Through this combination of processes, individual sounds in the acoustic scene are identified. Many primitive cues have been proposed as being useful for the segmentation of co-occurring sound sources. Among these, a difference in fundamental frequency (F0) has been shown to be one of the most powerful cues for the segmentation of monaural speech (Bregman, 1990; Darwin, 2005). Grouping by F0 difference follows a basic principle – the elements within a mixture that have components related to the same fundamental frequency are likely to have arisen from the same source. This ability of humans to segment (and further, to organise) a sound scene based on the harmonicity of its individual components, has inspired many algorithms that attempt to emulate this behaviour, with varying degrees of success. This chapter explores the role of pitch differences in the primitive segmentation component of ASA. It also reviews the relevant speech segmentation algorithms that have been previously implemented. Further, it proposes a novel technique in which pitch is employed to decompose the voiced regions of a monaurally-mixed speech source into coherent fragments that can then be organised by a separate, schema-driven process. The algorithm uniquely outputs a set of fragments as well as a confidence map, which is a measure of the coherence of each fragment. A new measure, which evaluates the fragment quality is proposed.

The chapter is thus organised: Section 6.2. reviews the literature on the role of pitch differences in primitive segmentation. Section 6.3. summarises the major themes of Section 6.2.. Section 6.4. presents the proposed segmentation algorithm, which is evaluated in Section 6.5.. The chapter concludes with a summary in Section 6.6..

6.2. Pitch and Perceptual Sound Segmentation

When presented with an auditory scene populated by harmonic sounds, humans seem to exploit one or more cues found in the acoustic signal to segment the mixture (Bregman, 1990).[20] The results of perceptual, computational and neurological studies seem to suggest that this is a 'primitive' process, that is, it can be achieved without engaging the higher processing centres of the brain (Neisser, 1967; Bregman, 1990; Hartmann and Johnson, 1991; Beauvois and Meddis, 1996; Alain et al., 2001; Sussman, 2005; Alain et al., 2005).

The following sections will divide the review of the role of pitch in segmentation into: i) those studies pertaining to the segmentation of tones and synthetic speech (Section 6.2.1.) and ii) studies with real speech (Section 6.2.2.). The use of tones and synthetic speech for psycho-acoustic studies offers a great level of flexibility, in that the stimuli can be carefully controlled and easily manipulated so that a variety of effects can be studied. Such studies often provide useful insights into human auditory perception, some of which have been employed in the development of automatic speech recognition systems – the use of the Mel scale (Stevens et al., 1937) for frequency analysis, is one such case. While these studies are informative, it is not clear that their findings can be extrapolated to explain the perception of real speech. This distinction is important for many reasons, especially if one aims to develop a computational system that utilises findings from perceptual studies. Hence, several studies have been carried out to test various aspects of the perception of real speech, building upon, and in some cases, refining, the theories proposed as a result of studies with synthetic sounds. This review examines some of the key findings relating to pitch-based segmentation using both synthetic sounds and real speech with a view to developing a pitch-based segmentation system.

6.2.1. Perceptual Segmentation of Tones and Synthetic Speech

Of the cues put forward by Bregman as being useful for the segmentation of auditory scenes composed of harmonic sounds, pitch has generally been shown to be the most effective when the signals are monaurally presented (Brokx and Nooteboom, 1982; Bird and Darwin, 1998; Darwin et al., 2003). The pitch cue is a powerful one for the segmentation of both concurrent sounds – sounds presented at the same time and possibly varying in frequency (Assmann and Summerfield, 1990) and sequential sounds – sounds which have components that are presented at different points in time (Vliegen and Oxenham, 1999).

The early work in ASA concentrated on the segmentation of simple tone sequences because they offered the opportunity to examine separately, the impact of individual properties of each source. It was shown that sequential streaming was more easily achievable if the tones were of different fundamental frequencies; the wider the separation, the better the segmentation. When there was little or no difference in F0, tones were heard to 'fuse' together. In 1975 van Noorden made a detailed study of these effects and found that there were two thresholds that governed the segmentation of tones by F0 difference (van Noorden, 1975). The first, termed the *temporal coherence boundary*, was defined as the smallest F0 difference, at which listeners who were instructed to listen for a single stream, could no longer

---

[20]These cues include, but are not limited to: common onset/offset, periodicity, amplitude modulation and spatial location.

hear alternating tones as such. The *fission boundary* was coined to describe the threshold defining the frequency separation below which alternating tones could not be heard as distinct streams, even though listeners made a concerted effort to do so. The study also found that the tone repetition rate affected the temporal coherence boundary, by making it easier to hear two streams at high repetition rates. The fission boundary however, remained relatively constant. At frequency separations in between the two thresholds, either one or two streams were heard, depending on what the listener was instructed to listen for (van Noorden, 1975). These boundaries are somewhat fluid, as they vary between individuals. There is also experimental evidence to show that familiarity with the sequences, facilitated by 'long term' exposure, can shift the temporal coherence boundary leading to an increase in the perception of two streams (Bregman, 1978; Anstis and Saida, 1985). It must be noted that listeners' familiarity with the patterns of speech, such as the F0 trajectory, can greatly assist them in the task of primitive grouping.

By employing stimuli consisting of pure tones, researchers were able to carefully analyse the perceptual streaming of sound sources. Their results suggested that a difference in fundamental frequency between sound sources allowed listeners to segment them into different streams. While the work with pure tones provides essential information about auditory scene analysis, it does not provide a complete picture, given that the majority of sounds in real listening conditions are not pure tones. It should also be noted that these effects can only be achieved for repeating sequences, and as such may not be applicable to real listening conditions. The next logical step was thus, to study the streaming of complex tones. Bregman pointed out that complex tones will be heard as a separate stream, when alternated with pure tones, if either of the following criteria are met: 1) the tone does not match any of the components of the complex or, 2) the constituents of the complex are tightly packed (1990).

In contrast to the case of pure tones, where pitch difference plays the central role in stream formation, the streaming of complex tones seems to be effected by differences in timbre as well as pitch (Singh, 1987; Dowling, 1973; Vliegen and Oxenham, 1999; Vliegen et al., 1999). McAdams and Bregman (1979) were among the first to note the relationship between timbre and pitch and their interaction in the segmentation of complex tone sequences. The listeners were presented with a cycle of four tones (two high and two low), which they perceived as a single stream. A third harmonic (higher in pitch than the previous two) was then separately combined with the high and low tones before presentation. When the high tones and third harmonic were combined they were perceived as a single coherent stream; the low tones formed a separate stream. A similar, but weaker, effect was found when the low tones and third harmonic were combined (see Figure 6.1). This led to the conclusion that the change in timbre induced perceptual segmentation of the complex tone. As an explanation for the diminishing of the streaming percept observed when the low tone was combined with the third harmonic, the researchers suggested that the addition of the third harmonic raised the pitch of the tones, which brought the low tones closer in pitch to the high tones, diminishing the effect of streaming.

The segmentation of synthetic double-vowels has also been noted to be enhanced as the F0 difference between them is made larger (Zwicker, 1984; Chalikia and Bregman, 1989; Assmann and Summerfield, 1990, 1994; McKeown, 1992; Culling and Darwin, 1993; de Cheveigné et al., 1997; Assmann and Paschall, 1998). When listeners are presented with

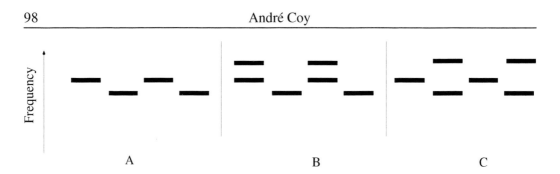

Figure 6.1. Illustration of the Effect of Timbre on Stream Segmentation (**A**) - Cycle of four tones; perceived as a single stream (**B**) Third harmonic combined with high frequency tones; combined tones form a single stream, low frequency tones for a second stream (**C**) Third harmonic combined with low frequency tones; combined tones form a single stream, high frequency tones form a second stream.

vowels having F0 differences of at least two semitones, they typically perceive two separate vowels being produced by different speakers. The computational models that employ this finding to identify each vowel do so in one of two ways. Either they detect the pitch of both vowels (Assmann and Summerfield, 1990; Brown and Wang, 1997) in which case they separately group the channels relating to each pitch; or they detect the pitch of the 'dominant' vowel, group the related channels, and assign the remaining channels to the weaker vowel (Meddis and Hewitt, 1992; de Cheveigné, 1997). McKeown and Patterson (1995) made an observation that seems to suggest that the latter approach may be the more appropriate. Using stimuli that varied in duration from one to eight cycles, they presented listeners with double-vowels in four different F0 combinations, including one where the F0 of both vowels was identical. The results of their experiments showed that there was an increase in vowel identification with increasing duration. However, they found that the increase came about as a result of the identification of the non-dominant vowel, as identification rates for the dominant vowel remained relatively constant across conditions. This led them to suggest that segmentation of the dominant vowels was not guided by F0 differences and that detection of the F0 of the dominant vowel was unnecessary. While the results are certainly intriguing, there are some issues with the conclusions. It has been reported that the assignment of vowel dominance, which is attributed to the differing spectral shapes of each vowel, is not uniform across subjects (McKeown, 1992). Further, McKeown and Patterson (1995) report that there are some vowels that are never dominant, while others are always dominant. These facts suggest that the concept of dominance may be a factor of the stimuli used and may not be an intrinsic property, which could be exploited for generalised source segmentation.

Two interesting issues arise from these studies: The first has to do with the effect of duration on the perception of two vowels, while the second addresses the relationship between pitch identification and vowel identification. Experiments have shown that longer stimuli lend themselves more readily to the perception of two distinct pitches as the difference in F0 is increased (Assmann and Summerfield, 1990, 1994; McKeown and Patterson, 1995; Culling and Darwin, 1994). Results from experiments carried out by Assmann and Paschall (1998) concurred with earlier studies that as the difference in F0 was increased from 0 to 4 semitones, listeners preferentially perceived two pitches when the stimuli were 200 ms as opposed to 50 ms long. The second issue is that vowel identification and pitch detection do not seem to follow the same patterns. Studies have shown that the greatest increase in vowel identification occurred for small differences in F0, while pitch detection seems to be best at large F0 differences (Culling and Darwin, 1994; Assmann and Paschall, 1998). Culling and Darwin (1994) attribute this effect to waveform interactions between the two stimuli. They propose that the beating that occurs provides a cue for vowel segmentation and identification when the difference in their fundamental frequencies is small. While the Culling and Darwin model provides some insight into the processes that fuel the sharp increase in vowel identification at small F0 differences, it does not offer an explanation for the reduction in the rate of increase as the F0 difference increases; in fact, the authors suggest that further research is required to identify the processes that bring about this phenomenon. The experiments reported above were performed on so-called steady-state vowels - vowels with a constant F0. However, it has been shown that a similar pattern of results can be obtained for vowels with dynamic F0 variation (Makin, 2006).

Experiments with double-vowels have provided some insight into the processes employed by listeners to segment sounds. However, it was not clear that the same mechanisms would be employed when the stimuli consisted of longer, sentence-like, utterances. It is possible that many of these mechanisms would become redundant in the presence of more powerful cues, such as prosody, which are more prevalent in longer utterances. Studies of the impact of F0 difference on the segmentation of sentence-like stimuli were performed by Brokx and Nooteboom (1982) as well as Bird and Darwin (1998). Using re-synthesised sentences, they investigated the extent to which listeners used F0 differences to segment two overlapping sentences. Their results were broadly in agreement with studies on double-vowels; they found that the greatest improvement occurred between zero and two semitones F0 separation. However, they found continued improvement in sentence identification at F0 separations where asymptotic double-vowel recognition performance generally occurred. An extension of these studies was carried out by Assmann (1999) who compared the segmentation performance of listeners using monotone sentences and sentences with naturally varying pitch contours. It was expected that the sentences with dynamic F0 would have been more intelligible and thus, contribute to higher identification rates. What was found, however, was that natural intonation did provide an increase in the perceptual *segmentation* of the sentences, but did not provide significant improvement in *identification*.

The studies reviewed have all shown that F0 difference can be a useful cue for the segmentation of synthetic sound sources; however the effect of natural variations have not been examined. The following section will give an overview of the work done in this area.

6.2.2. Pitch-based Segmentation of Speech: Perceptual Studies and Computational Models

Following from the early work done on segmenting synthetic signals, many researchers have studied the segmentation of monaurally presented mixtures of overlapping, natural speech (Miller, 1947; Carhart et al., 1969; Duquesnoy, 1983; Festen and Plomp, 1990). The purpose of these studies was to investigate the effect of masking sounds on the intelligibility of speech. These early studies were, for the most part, interested in the 'disruptiveness' of particular maskers and did not specifically examine the processes that facilitated a release from masking. Carhart et al. (1969) did notice however, that the masking effect produced by mixing two speech sounds was more than could be accounted for by mere spectral interference (or energetic masking). They coined the term *perceptual masking* for this unexplained masking phenomenon and highlighted the fact that it is enhanced when the signals in a mixture have similar characteristics, such as when they are both speech. Drullman and Bronkhorst (1990) also found that it was more difficult to segment speech if the speakers are of the same gender. This was confirmed and elaborated in a study by Brungart (2001). In a comprehensive study of the impact of SNR on listeners' perception of simultaneous speakers, Brungart presented subjects with mixtures at several different SNR values, where the target utterances were masked with utterances spoken by either the same talker, a talker of the same gender, or a talker of differing gender. The results showed a consistent degradation in listener performance when the characteristics of the masking speakers' voice were more similar to those of the target. Thus, maskers of different gender were perceived to be less disruptive than maskers of the same gender. Listener performance was worst when the same talker was used for both target and masker utterances. However, even in the relatively simpler case, where the masker was of the same gender, but a different talker, listeners still found it difficult to segment the two overlapping messages. This was judged to be due to the effect of *informational masking*, which is related to the perceptual masking effect. Informational masking is the inability to assign audible speech energy to a particular source in a mixture of sounds that have similar acoustic energy (Pollack, 1975). Informational masking is thus greater in speech mixtures where the signals have similar global SNR and the speakers have similar speech characteristics. While Brungart concluded that listeners' performance was improved if the voice characteristics of the speakers were different (due to a reduction in informational masking), there was no study to determine which of the myriad properties of the human voice could account for these results.

Darwin et al. (2003) designed a series of experiments to explain the results of Brungart (2001) by determining which properties of the voice could account for the effect found. Three separate experiments were performed: The first of which involved the manipulation of the F0 only, while in the second, only the vocal tract length was modified; the third experiment involved the simultaneous modification of both properties. The results indicate that neither property on its own can account for the difference in performance between the same gender and different gender conditions that was evident in Brungart (2001). When both characteristics were modified, however, the pattern of results was duplicated and it was apparent that changes in these two parameters could account for the majority of the performance difference between the same gender and different gender conditions. These results confirm that, in a monaurally presented mixture, differences in the properties of the voices – in particular differences in F0 and vocal tract length – have a profound effect on the segmentation of voiced speech. It has also been established by Peterson and Barney (1952) as well as by Kuwabara and Takagi (1991) that a perceptual change in gender can be achieved by, artificially, varying the fundamental frequency range and vocal tract length of a speaker.

Some of the earliest attempts at speech segmentation made use of the fact that F0 differences can aid in the segmentation of co-channel speech. (Fraizer et al., 1976) employed *a priori* knowledge of the target speaker's pitch to construct a comb filter to pass only the harmonics of the target utterance. Parsons (1976) examined the Fourier transform of the mixed signal and extracted peaks representing the fundamental frequency (and the corresponding harmonics) of each speaker; a pitch tracker was employed to assign individual pitch streams to different speakers. He then re-synthesised the extracted waveform components and presented the segmented speech to listeners for evaluation.

A number of the speech segmentation algorithms have employed the technique of estimating the pitch of one speaker and using that information to suppress the harmonics of the other (Hanson and Wong, 1984; Naylor and Boll, 1987; Lee and Childers, 1988; Quatieri and Danisewicz, 1990; Stubbs and Summerfield, 1990b). Hanson and Wong (1984) employed a *harmonic magnitude suppression* (HMS) technique that used *a priori* pitch information from the interfering speaker to remove its influence from the magnitude spectrum. The signal was then re-synthesised. Results of listening tests were reported, which showed that there was an improvement in intelligibility at low target-to-masker ratios (TMRs). The study of Naylor and Boll (1987) extended the earlier work of Hanson and Wong (1984), by employing a maximum likelihood pitch estimation algorithm to estimate the pitch of the more dominant source. By so doing, the algorithm was limited to working at negative TMRs. A similar HMS system was employed by Lee and Childers (1988) to make initial estimates of the spectrum of each speaker. They then improved those estimates using a minimum cross-entropy analysis to minimise interference in the recovered target speech. Quatieri and Danisewicz (1990) utilised sinusoidal modelling to estimate the sinusoidal components of each speaker's signal. They employed *a priori* estimates of both speakers' pitch. Stubbs and Summerfield (1990b) implemented a cepstral filtering technique in which, the pitch of both speakers was detected automatically. The algorithm was reported to work well for sentences on a mono-tone, but not as well when the pitch contour was varying.

Some of these algorithms were somewhat rudimentary and either required *a priori* information or were not very robust. The next generation of algorithms employing harmonic estimation and suppression sought to overcome some of these shortcomings (Morgan et al., 1997; Irino et al., 2006). Morgan et al. (1997) utilised a maximum likelihood pitch detector to extract the pitch of the stronger of two talkers in a mixture. After the pitch detection process, a two-stage speaker recovery phase was invoked. In the first stage, the stronger talker's pitch was used to construct a comb filter to extract the spectral components of that talker in each frame, assigning the residual spectral components to the weaker speaker; the weaker speaker's pitch is recovered from the residual spectra. Given these initial estimates, a stage of spectral enhancement augments the components of each talker and refines the output of the initial segmentation phase. A dynamic programming speaker assignment algorithm then examined the pitch and spectral components of both talkers in the frame being analysed, and in the previous four frames, producing two segmented speech signals as a final output. The investigators suggested that the advantages of the system include the ability to segment co-channel speech without *a priori* information and without the need to simultaneously detect and track the pitch of both talkers.

In a further enhancement to the estimation-cancellation paradigm de Cheveigné and Kawahara (1999) suggested a model which jointly estimated and cancelled the pitch of separate mixture components. The model was tested on simple signals which were perfectly periodic and noise free, but it was found to be computationally expensive and no evaluation was performed on more natural speech signals.

Irino et al. (2006) proposed the use of an 'auditory vocoder' for speech segmentation. Using a representation designed to retain fine temporal information, they identified peaks corresponding to the glottal pulses of the target speaker. The glottal pulse detection was not robust to noise and had to be supplemented with F0 information, which was used to refine the auditory image, enhancing the spectral components of the target speech while suppressing those of the interfering speech. The method was compared to one which employed a comb filter and was found to be more robust to noise and F0 estimation errors. This is an example of an algorithm that does not use F0 differences as the only feature for speech segmentation, but rather integrates multiple cues.

The F0 estimation-cancellation formalism has been shown to be effective for co-channel speech segmentation, however there are some drawbacks. One of these is most relevant when recovery of all component signals is required. When the components of the mixture are harmonically related, cancellation of the harmonic components of one signal will also remove those of the other. A potential solution has been supplied by Klapuri (2003) who implemented it for the segmentation of overlapping musical sounds. The method works by first detecting the F0 of the stronger source and applying a psycho-acoustically motivated spectral smoothing prior to subtracting it from the mixed signal. Given that harmonically related sources either amplify or cancel each other, the smoothing of the spectrum reduces the amplitude of the dominant component so that subtraction does not completely remove evidence of the remaining source.

Some segmentation algorithms involve the simultaneous detection of the pitch of all signals in the mixture (Weintraub, 1985; Naylor and Porter, 1991; Chazan et al., 1993; Karjalainen and Tolonen, 1999). Of the many multi-pitch detection algorithms that have been proposed, relatively few have been employed in the direct segmentation of co-channel speech, though, in principle, they could all be used for this purpose. The majority of the algorithms that have been used for speech segmentation have made use of the autocorrelogram representation because of the convenient and effective manner in which it highlights periodicities in the signal as well as the fact that it is inspired by computational models of the auditory system (see Chapter 4 for details). By summing the autocorrelogram across frequency, the dominant pitch components of the signal can be estimated. This property has been exploited by several speech segmentation algorithms (Karjalainen and Tolonen, 1999; Ottaviani and Rocchesso, 2001; Coy and Barker, 2007). These systems generally rely on the detection of peaks in the summary autocorrelogram at lags corresponding to the fundamental frequency of the sources in the mixture. In theory there would be a dominant peak, marked by its height, for each of the sources in the mixture. However, based on the interaction of multiple sources within a single channel, it is not always possible to detect the sources based on peak height alone. Given the richness of the representation, there is a wealth of information in the full autocorrelogram that is lost when the summary is computed. Recognition of this point has led to recent work in which the full autocorrelogram is analysed and pitch candidates for each source in the mixture are extracted based on the dendritic structure formed when different frequency channels respond to the same source (Ma et al., 2007). These candidates are used to drive a robust speech segmentation algorithm.

6.3. Interim Discussion

The previous section has reviewed the segmentation of harmonic sounds by pitch. From the studies reviewed a number of issues have been highlighted. Firstly, the studies have shown that F0 is a useful cue for source segmentation. In longer, sentence-like utterances, the effect of pitch was more pronounced at higher F0 separation. It was found, however, that increases in identification did not occur as a result of increases in segmentation. This suggests that the link between segmentation and intelligibility is not a direct one. The studies showed that source segmentation of sequential, as well as concurrent sounds is facilitated by F0 difference, however, it would appear that timbre also plays a role in the segmentation of concurrent sounds.

For real speech sounds, the major finding from the perceptual studies reviewed was that energetic masking was not the only effect responsible for the degradation in segmentation performance of listeners attempting to disambiguate overlapping sentences. Informational masking was found to be more prevalent in mixtures where the speakers have similar voice characteristics.

These findings have inspired the development of many segmentation algorithms that attempt to take advantage of the difference in F0 for source segmentation. Though the strategies for achieving segmentation varied, they all benefited from the difference in the F0 of the sources in the mixture.

The most obvious question to ask about the segmentation of speech using harmonicity is what to do if the speech is unvoiced. This question is yet to be satisfactorily answered and has only recently begun to receive serious attention (Hu and Wang, 2004a; Seltzer et al., 2004; Coy and Barker, 2007). The lack of research in this area comes about mostly because of the predominance of harmonic speech, and the fact that the majority of segmentation algorithms do not produce output to be employed in large speech recognition experiments involving large vocabulary tasks, where inharmonic speech is more important for discrimination of phonetic units. Chapter 7 previews previous attempts to solve the problem and suggests one approach to unvoiced speech segmentation, which employs the use of image processing techniques.

Another point worth discussing is the accuracy of current pitch detection algorithms. Accurate pitch detection is essential for correct recruitment of spectro-temporal regions of the mixture relevant to each source. While many sophisticated and accurate pitch detectors have been developed, they generally work better in noise-free conditions. With the introduction of time-varying harmonic signals, the task of pitch detection becomes much more difficult, especially if the pitch of all the signals is required (see Chapter 5 for a detailed discussion).

6.4. Proposed Pitch-based Segmentation Algorithm

In the current section a novel pitch-based segmentation algorithm for voiced speech is presented. The focus is on the sub-task of segmenting overlapping speakers, a difficult task, considering that the masker and target have similar characteristics.

There are two outputs produced from the proposed segmentation process. The first is a set of *coherent fragments*, where each fragment is identified by a unique integer label.

The set of fragments is represented as a matrix of time-frequency 'pixels', F_{tf}, where t and f represent the time frame and frequency channel, respectively, where each pixel is found. Each F_{tf} is assigned the integer label L_i, of the fragment to which it is associated. The second output is an identically dimensioned time-frequency matrix, referred to as a *confidence map* C_{tf}. The confidence map contains values between 0.5 and 1.0, reflecting the level of certainty in the coherence of each point. Generally, confidence is low at time-frequency points where there appears to be evidence of significant energy from multiple sources, and high where the point appears to be truly dominated by a single source. The confidence map is employed by the decoder when using the soft version of the missing data mask (see Section 6.4.1.).

6.4.1. Voiced Fragment Generation

Fragments are built using pitch tracks from: i) the multi-pitch tracker (MPT), ii) the auto-correlogram (ACG) and iii) the envelope ACG. Each voiced segment of each pitch track 'recruits' a set of time-frequency points from the ACG representation, to form a single voiced fragment. Grouping the frequency channels of the ACG that show evidence of responding to a similar fundamental frequency follows Bregman's principle of *proximity*, while grouping across time reflects *good continuation*. This recruitment process effectively segments the mixture so that individual sources can be identified and grouped using learnt processes. Recruitment proceeds as follows: In a frame by frame process, each row (i.e. frequency channel) of the ACG is examined for significant peaks along the lag axis that match to either (or both) of the pitch candidates output by the MPT. A peak is considered significant if it has a value equal to, or higher than a threshold, θ_a. This threshold has to be chosen carefully, so as not to exclude pitch points that match to the pitch tracks. The higher the value is set, the greater the risk of removing matching peaks. However, a value that is too low will compound any error made in the pitch track by recruiting spectro-temporal points which have a low value in the ACG in a particular frequency channel (this indicates that there is little evidence for voicing at that time-frequency point). This could lower the coherence of the fragment produced. A match is said to occur if frequency values are within 5% of each other - the value of 5% is chosen to reflect the pitch shift that can occur when sources interact within the speech mixture, and is similar to the value used by Hu and Wang (2004b). Whenever there are multiple peaks within a channel matching a single pitch from the MPT, then the peak that matches most closely is chosen as the representative of that pitch in the channel. This process is repeated for the envelope ACG, as some unresolved peaks in the high frequency regions might be missed if pitch track recruitment is applied to the ACG only.

When performing the above pitch track-to-channel matching, one of three different situations can occur. First, there may be no matches between the pitch track values and the given channel. In this case the time-frequency point (defined by the channel and time frame under consideration) is marked as unvoiced at that time frame. Second, there may be just one pitch track matching the given channel. In this case the pitch track recruits the time-frequency point to its voiced fragment by labelling it with a unique fragment number. Finally, both pitch tracks may find a match in the given channel. In this case the spectro-temporal point is recruited by the pitch track of the source judged to make the largest contribution to the channel.[21]

Discrete Masks

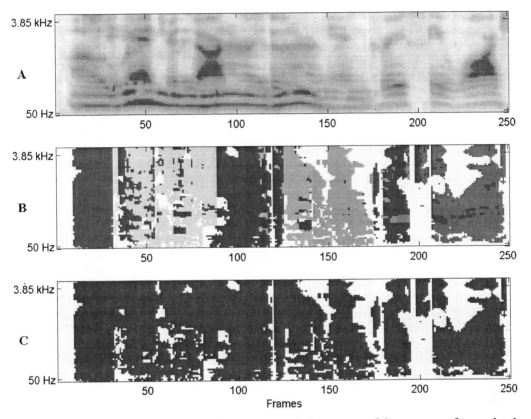

Figure 6.2. Auditory spectrogram, fragments and discrete confidence map of completely voiced utterance and voiced masker. (**A**) - Auditory Spectrogram of completely voiced utterance and voiced masker. Voiced fragments (**B**) and the discrete confidence map (**C**) derived from segmentation process.

A discrete mask is created when all the spectro-temporal points are exclusively allocated to either the background or the foreground. That is, wherever a fragment is defined, the confidence map would contain a 1.0, indicating complete confidence in the coherence of the fragments produced by the above process, where there is no fragment, the confidence map is undefined, thus a '0' is placed in the confidence map as a label, indicating it is part of the background (Figure 6.2). During decoding, the confidence map will act as a discrete mask allowing the decoder to consider a spectro-temporal point as, alternately, being either part of the foreground or as part of the background. As part of the foreground, the point is considered to be completely free of masking, while it is considered to be completely masked if it is part of the background.

---

[21]The size of the contribution of a source is directly related to the height of the peak in the ACG.

The discrete mask has been proposed as suitable for defining the target regions of a mixed speech signal. Early studies such as Weintraub (1985); Brown and Cooke (1994b); Wang and Brown (1999) used the discrete mask to mark regions in a co-channel signal for re-synthesis. Cooke et al. (2001a) found that the discrete mask could be used along with missing data ASR techniques to yield good recognition performance with monaural speech. It has even been argued that an 'ideal binary mask' should be the goal of CASA systems (Wang, 2006). Roman et al. (2003) have shown, through the systematic introduction of errors into the ideal binary mask, that deviations from this mask leads to a reduction in recognition accuracy.

While there is good evidence motivating its use, the strong decisions made in the construction of a discrete mask assumes that the segmentation process is flawless, and makes no provision for potential errors. Should any errors occur, there is no way to recover from them, and recognition performance will be affected. This binary decision of a fragment belonging completely to the background or foreground could be tempered by placing 'soft' values in the confidence map.

Soft Masks

There are two scenarios in which the discrete mask can make source assignment errors. In the first case, the spectro-temporal point is dominated by a single source, but confidence in the evidence supporting the dominance of that source is low. The second case is where the point can be considered a mixture of sources, where there is no overwhelming evidence for the dominance of one. In either of these cases segmentation algorithms may make errors in which spectro-temporal points are assigned to the wrong source. With discrete masks, errors made are irreversible and will have a detrimental impact on the performance of any application in which these masks are used. Where there is evidence of multiple sources in the mixture, it stands to reason that the influence of each should be taken into account at this stage, and that no firm decision should be taken about the dominance of any one source.

Many early missing data systems utilised spectral subtraction as a means of segmenting speech signals corrupted by additive noises (see Cooke et al., 1997; Morris et al., 2001; Renevey and Drygajlo, 2001, for example). By estimating the noise signal's spectrum, the clean signal can be isolated by subtracting the noise from the corrupted signal. Barker et al. (2000) implemented the idea of a soft mask by applying a sigmoid mapping to the estimate of clean speech obtained after spectral subtraction. As a result of the mapping, a mask was derived, which assigned a weight to each spectro-temporal element in the mask. This weight provided the decoder with an estimate of the certainty that an element belonged to the source to which it was assigned. The results they obtained showed that soft masks performed significantly better than discrete masks on a connected-digits task, especially at low SNRs.

Renevey and Drygajlo (2001) also used soft masks to improve the recognition accuracy of their missing data system. In their implementation, they used a Gaussian distribution to model the noise, using a stationary noise estimate to approximate the parameters of the distribution. The probability that the ratio of the noisy speech to the noise exceeded a threshold, was computed and used to create the soft mask. While the technique produced a mask with probabilities, it relied on the assumption that the noise was stationary and followed a Gaussian distribution; assumptions which are not always valid.

By casting the mask estimation problem as a classification task, Seltzer et al. (2004) were able to use Bayesian techniques to produce probabilistic soft masks without making assumptions about the properties of the noise. A two-class classifier was trained to distinguish between reliable (unmasked) and unreliable (masked) spectro-temporal regions. The output probabilities of the classifier were used to populate the mask. Using the Bayesian masks, significant improvements were reported over systems that relied on spectral subtraction for mask estimation.

The soft mask estimation methods described above rely on the assumption that the noise has considerably differing properties to that of the speech signal. In the present study that assumption would not hold and a different approach is required.

Consider once more the track-to-channel matching process described in Section 6.4.1.; the first two scenarios (i.e. where there are 0 or 1 matches between the pitch tracks and ACG channel) would lead to identical confidence maps whether discrete or soft masks were in use. In the third scenario (i.e. where there both pitch tracks match points in the ACG channel) however, the presence of two sources indicates that though one source may dominate, there may be a degree of masking which needs to be accounted for. Consideration is given to the possibility that masking is occurring when two sources are present and a value, less than 1, (that reflects the relative contributions of the sources) is placed in the confidence map. The contribution, c_i, of source i is taken to be $p_i \times h_i$, where h_i is the height of the channel's peak and p_i is the degree of mismatch between the pitch of the channel and that of the pitch track. The contribution of a source is reduced by the degree of mismatch (Note, there may be up to 5% mismatch). Here, p_i is computed as:

$$p_i = \begin{cases} \frac{f_{track}}{f_{channel}} & \text{if } f_{track} < f_{channel} \\ 2 - \frac{f_{track}}{f_{channel}} & \text{otherwise,} \end{cases} \qquad (6.1)$$

where f_{track} and $f_{channel}$ are the pitch of the track and the channel respectively. The value to place in the confidence map is computed by first taking the ratio (x) of the lesser over the greater of the source contributions, and then using a sigmoid mapping to compress the ratio to a value between 0.5 and 1.0. The sigmoid is centred on 1; the point of maximum uncertainty. The mapping function is given by:

$$f(x) = \frac{1}{1 + e^{-\lambda(x-\beta)}}, \qquad (6.2)$$

where λ is the slope of the sigmoid and β is the centre. The value for λ is chosen experimentally and found to be 1. The values derived from this mapping tend toward binary values as λ tends to ∞. The closer the contribution of the two sources, the closer $f(x)$ will be to 0.5, indicating greater uncertainty. By using the confidence map in this way, the contribution of both sources is taken into account and the possibility of fragment incoherence is acknowledged. An example of the soft mask derived from this process is shown in Figure 6.3.

This process results in both, i) a set of fragments that represents the voiced regions of each of the sources in the mixture, and ii) a confidence map indicating the reliability of the points within the fragments. The fragment labels serve only to group spectro-temporal points deemed to belong to a single source; they do not indicate which source that is. The spectro-temporal points that were labelled unvoiced, and thus, not recruited into any voiced fragment, are processed using a separate procedure outlined in Chapter 7.

6.5. Evaluation

Though the final goal of the system being proposed is the recognition of monaurally mixed speech, it is important that a quantitative evaluation is performed at each stage, as the performance of each component of the system has implications for the performance of the final speech recognition system. As the segmentation algorithm aims to produce fragments to be used in recognition, the evaluation must consider the quality of the fragments produced. Section 6.5.1. considers the various evaluation criteria employed for CASA-based systems. A novel evaluation metric for measuring fragment quality is proposed in Section 6.5.2.. Section 6.5.3. explains the experimental setup, while Section 6.5.4. presents the evaluation of the fragments output by the segmentation algorithm.

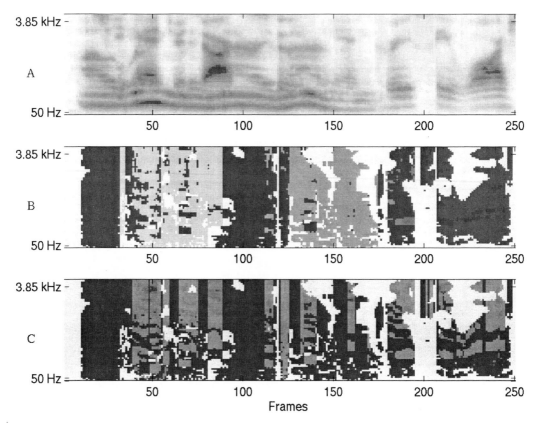

Figure 6.3. (**A**) - Auditory spectrogram of completely voiced utterance and voiced masker. Voiced fragments (**B**) and the soft confidence map (**C**) derived from segmentation process.

6.5.1. Fragment Evaluation Criteria

One of the difficulties faced by individuals involved in CASA research is the lack of consistent evaluation criteria. This deficit has been identified by previous studies, but as yet, no standard procedure has been proposed (Rosenthal and Okuno, 1998; Wang, 2006). Wang gives an outline of the schemes currently employed for CASA evaluation and points to four main areas:

I) Comparison with the pre-mixed target (Cooke, 1993; Brown and Cooke, 1994a; Wang and Brown, 1999; Nakatini and Okuno, 1999), where the segmented speech target is compared with a clean version using metrics ranging from direct comparisons of the two masks, to comparisons of the short term spectra.

II) Improvement in ASR performance gained by using features derived from segmentation as opposed to unsegmented features (Weintraub, 1985; Cooke et al., 2001b; Seltzer et al., 2004).

III) Human listening tests, which judged whether segmentation improved the intelligibility of sounds in a mixture (Ellis, 1996; Moore, 1998).

IV) The fit of the model to perceptual and other biological data (Wang, 1996; Mcabe and Denham, 1997; Wrigley and Brown, 2004) are the other two criteria reported.

Given that the requirements of CASA systems vary, it may be that the evaluation will always be task dependent. For systems that have ASR as the final goal of speech segmentation, it has been suggested that recognition performance is the only meaningful measurement of a mask's usefulness (Seltzer et al., 2004). The authors postulate that the many stages of processing that lie between mask estimation and ASR render comparisons with oracle masks meaningless. However, it has recently been shown that there is a strong correspondence between recognition performance and *coherence* - a measure derived from just such a comparison (Coy and Barker, 2006). Other advantages to employing an evaluation employing oracle masks include: i) they are computationally cheap to compute, and ii) they offer some measure of fragment quality without the need to perform recognition experiments.

Some segmentation algorithms are evaluated based on the improvement in SNR of the target source (Brown and Cooke (1994a); Wang and Brown (1999) and Hu and Wang (2004b) for example). However, it has been suggested that an evaluation criterion based on the improvement of SNR is not always suitable for the evaluation of CASA systems (Hu and Wang, 2004b; Ellis, 2005). This is partly as improved SNR does not indicate increased intelligibility (Wang and Brown, 1999), which is important for speech enhancement algorithms; but further, and more relevant to this study, improving SNR does not necessarily improve recognition accuracy (Gong, 1995). Hence, the current evaluation does not consider SNR improvement; instead, a new metric is developed, which gives a measure of the quality of the fragments.

6.5.2.   The Evaluation Metric

The coherence of a fragment is calculated by comparing it to the *a priori* mask of each unmixed source. *A priori* masks – separately referred to as Oracle Masks (Seltzer et al., 2000) or Ideal Binary Masks (Roman et al., 2001) – are created by comparing the time-frequency representations of the mixed and unmixed signals. For example, consider a two source mixture: the spectro-temporal regions of *source1* that, in the mixture, are observed to have an SNR of 3 dB greater than *source2*, can be assigned to *source1*, and vice versa.[22] In this way, the mixtures are segmented into *a priori* masks representing the regions dominated by *source1* and *source2*; by their nature, *a priori* masks are completely coherent.

   If the fragment fits within the boundaries of a single source, it is fully coherent. However, most fragments will be less than fully coherent, meaning they will have some overlap with the masks of both sources. In this case, the degree of coherence is defined by the following procedure. The two regions defined by the overlap of the fragment with each of the two source masks are separately considered. The confidence map values in these two regions are summed. The source associated with the region producing the higher sum is considered to be the source that has generated the fragment. Fragment coherence is then defined as:

$$coherence = 100 \times \frac{\sum_{i \in R_1} c_{tf}}{\sum_{i \in R_1} c_{tf} + \sum_{i \in R_2} c_{tf}}\%, \qquad (6.3)$$

where c_{tf} are the values from the confidence map, and R_1 is the region where the fragment overlaps the mask of the source which generated it, and R_2 is the region of overlap with the competing source. By definition, the sum over R_1 is greater than that over R_2 so the minimum coherence will be 50%. As the sum over the competing source region (R_2) is reduced, the coherence approaches the maximum value of 100%.

6.5.3.   Experimental Setup

Model Parameters

Owing to the design of the filterbank employed in the frequency analysis of the signals, some filters will respond to several harmonics, leading to the presence of many spurious peaks in the autocorrelogram – see Section 4.4.. In order to reduce the impact of these peaks on the multi-pitch tracker, only significant peaks - those with energy above a certain threshold - are retained for analysis. The summary autocorrelogram is also impacted by the presence of spurious peaks, possibly more so than the autocorrelogram. While many of these unwanted peaks have relatively low energy in each channel, often, more than one frequency channel will respond to them. Thus, as they are summed across frequency, many of them will appear in the summary as significant. The thresholds that define the significance of the peaks in both the autocorrelogram (θ_a, see Section 6.4.1.) and the summary (θ_s, see Section 4.4.) have to be investigated. θ_s determines which peaks from the summary ACG are passed to the MPT, while θ_a indicates which peaks in the autocorrelogram can be considered in the track-to-channel matching process described in Section 6.4.1.. Higher values

---

[22]The SNR criterion for creating *a priori* masks follows that of Cooke et al. (2001a). The value of 3 dB was chosen, however, other values have been used. For example Roman et al. (2001) chose a value of 0 dB for the development of their ideal binary masks.

for these thresholds allow only frequency components with high correlation to be recruited into fragments. The following sections describe a series of experiments used to determine the impact of different values of θ_a and θ_s on the coherence of the fragments produced by the segmentation algorithm.

Test Data

The fully-voiced data employed in Chapters 4 and 5 were used here. The use of completely voiced utterances presents the segmentation algorithm with fewer pitch breaks across the signal and will facilitate a full evaluation of the impact of the tuning parameters.

6.5.4. Experiments

The speech mixtures are segmented using the process outlined in Section 6.4., creating a fragment set and a confidence map for each mixture. The average coherence was calculated across all fragments in the data set for separate values of θ_s and θ_a, ranging from 0.1 to 0.9. Values chosen for θ_s cannot be chosen without consideration of the value that θ_a will take. A high value of θ_s will see highly correlated pitch candidates going through to the pitch-track-to-tracking stage of the system. However, matches found in the individual ACG channels may not be as highly energetic and may not contribute to the overall fragment output. It is thus important to consider the interaction between these two parameters. For each value of θ_s, the impact on coherence of all the values of θ_a is measured - this leads to 81 configurations of the segmentation algorithm.

Figure 6.4 compares average fragment coherence to the number of pitch points retained in the summary ACG at 0 dB.

The figure shows that average fragment coherence increases with θ_s. This may seem to suggest that the choice of θ_s is straight forward - choose the value that produces fragments with the highest coherence. However, it must be noted that the number of true pitch points retained in the summary ACG is directly related to the value of θ_s. As figure 6.4 shows, the percentage of correct pitch points in the summary falls off dramatically when the value of θ_s exceeds 0.7. These two effects are linked: As the threshold is increased, only the frequency components with very high correlation will make it through to be considered as pitch candidates. Many of the spurious peaks in the summary have low correlation and will be removed as the threshold is increased. However, many of the true pitch candidates will also be removed from the summary because they are not significant.. The removal of the incorrect peaks will lead to fewer errors in the pitch tracking stage, and hence fewer erroneous pitch candidates will be involved in the track-to-channel matching. Much of the incoherence of fragments comes from the matching of specious pitch candidates in the summary to peaks in the autocorrelogram; removing these incorrect pitch candidates thus increases the coherence of the fragments.

There is however, an impact on the size of the fragments produced - Figure 6.5 illustrates this effect. Coy and Barker (2006) have shown that, when fragments are generated using the techniques described here, fragment size and coherence are inversely related, with smaller fragments having higher coherence. However, the study used 'optimal' values for both thresholds; fragment sets with differing (average) sizes were derived by applying varied primitive grouping strategies. The grouping method determined the length of the pitch

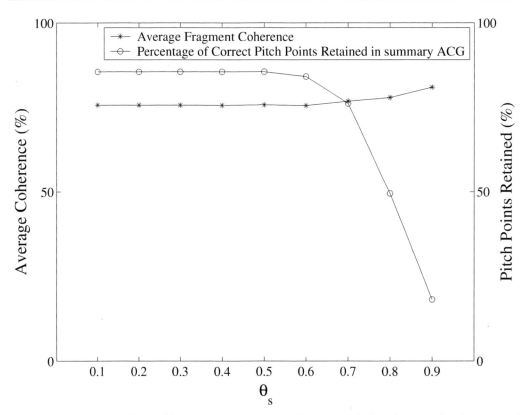

Figure 6.4. A comparison of fragment coherence and correct pitch points retained, averaged across the dataset, and shown on the same axis. The coherence values presented are for a range of θ_s values averaged across θ_a.

tracks formed and would certainly have affected the average size of the fragments formed. The relationship discovered in that study did not consider the impact on coherence of varying tuning parameters. What is emerging here is a more complex picture of the relationship between fragment size and coherence.

Given the interdependence of both thresholds, it is informative to analyse the overall effect on fragment formation of varying one threshold while holding the other constant. Thus, Figure 6.5 shows how average fragment size is affected as either θ_s or θ_a is varied while holding the other constant. Fragment sizes remain relatively constant as θ_a is increased up to a value of 0.8, thereafter they fall off rapidly. This pattern holds across all values of θ_s examined.

Now the consequence of altering θ_s while holding θ_a constant, is a decrease in fragment size above $\theta_s = 0.5$. This can be explained by recalling that increasing this particular threshold reduces the number of incorrect pitch points. The reduction in spurious points allows for the formation of longer pitch segments, which are then formed into larger fragments. This precedent holds until the threshold becomes so high, that very few pitch points (correct or otherwise) survive to the track-to-channel matching stage (see Figure 6.4), giving rise to smaller fragments.

Figure 6.6 shows the change in fragment coherence while varying both θ_a, and θ_s. For

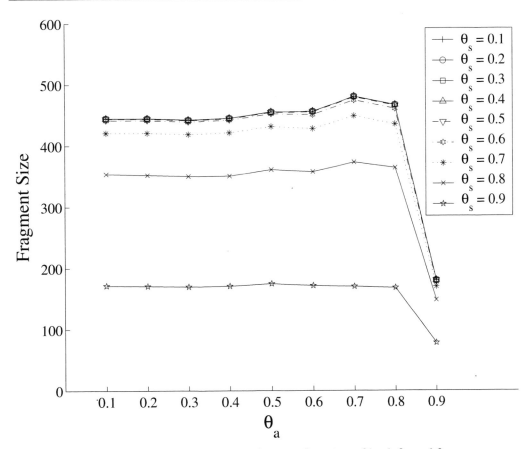

Figure 6.5. Average fragment size as a function of both θ_s and θ_a.

θ_a there is a general downward trend which is more pronounced for high values of θ_s. At the higher values of θ_s, the pitch points that are retained to the fragment generation stage, will likely be spurious points (see Section 5.4.2.), there will be less evidence, in either the ACG or envelope ACG, for those points at high θ_a, thus the fragments formed will be less coherent.

Increasing θ_s causes some slight fluctuation, with an upward trend, in coherence - this trend can be seen in Figure 6.4. Coherence remains basically constant up to values of 0.6, with an increase at higher values. For fully voiced utterances, the pattern of θ_s at values below 0.8 produces fragments with a similar pattern of coherence for the range θ_a.

As is true for θ_s, higher values of θ_a allow only highly energetic pitch candidates to be chosen, leading to a reduction in the number of matches that occur in the track-to-channel matching stage and consequently, a reduction in the spectro-temporal extent of the fragments output. However, the combined effect of varying both thresholds has to be taken into consideration. Part of the increase in coherence that is observed at higher values of θ_s is due to the sparsity of fragments at these values. However smaller fragments are not always more coherent, as is seen when θ_a, is set to high values. A balance has to be found, where fragments of reasonable size and coherence are formed, as both these factors have implications for the ASR performance.

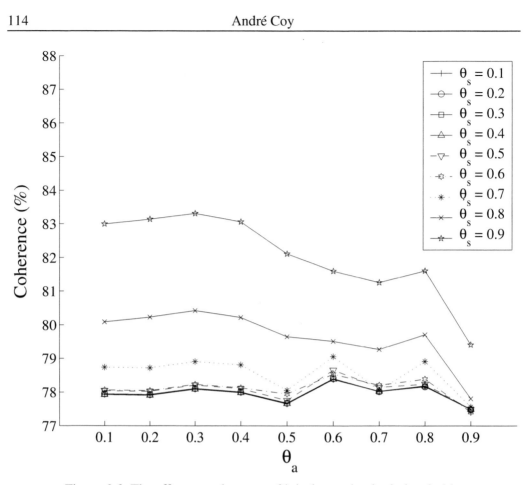

Figure 6.6. The effect on coherence of jointly varying both thresholds.

6.6. Summary

The sources of a monaural mixture of voiced speech can be segmented using cues related to the characteristics of the constituent voices. The extensive research done by Bregman and others in development of the scene analysis account of auditory perception has shown that the pitch of a voice is a very powerful cue for sound scene segmentation. This chapter has reviewed the literature on the role of harmonicity and the perceptual segmentation of sound, from simple tones through to real speech. This early research not only yielded evidence from perceptual and computational experiments, but also provided algorithms useful for the segmentation of mixtures of complex sounds composed of signals with fundamental frequency differences. This gave impetus to work being carried out on segmentation of overlapping speech sources. As a result of these experiments, it has been confirmed that pitch difference can successfully be employed by humans, as well as computational models, to segment one voice from another, even when both are transmitted across a single channel. This does not suggest that there are not still issues that need to be tackled; the limitations of the approach were briefly considered.

The main focus of the chapter was the development of an algorithm for the generation of fragments from voiced speech that was monaurally mixed. Pitch information from each speaker was used to recruit spectro-temporal regions of the mixture that belonged to that speaker. The process considered the contribution of both sources to each spectro-temporal point and thus created a confidence map, which effectively defines how likely it is that each point was derived from each source. This softens the decisions made about the origin of each point; an approach which has yielded improved recognition results in the past. The concept of coherence was introduced and the coherence of each fragment was considered, as a method of evaluating them prior to their use in ASR - the algorithm was shown to yield fragments of high coherence. A consideration of the effect of varying the tuning parameters used in the algorithm provided much insight into the interdependence of fragment size and coherence, which has consequences for the implementation of the speech recogniser employed for decoding the segmented utterances. It must be reiterated that the main goal of this study is speech recognition. Thus, the segmentation algorithm presented here is one step in the entire process, serving as a means of creating a reasonable set of fragments from voiced speech.

Voiced speech makes up the majority of human utterance, however, unvoiced speech plays a role in the perception of speech. Unvoiced speech is also important for ASR systems; especially so for those systems with large vocabularies, where discrimination between models is more difficult. CASA-based ASR systems generally avoid tackling the problem of overlapping unvoiced speech. This provides motivation for the exploration of 1) the role of unvoiced speech in perception and 2) the development of a method of segmenting unvoiced speech mixtures. This is the subject of the following chapter.

Chapter 7

Unvoiced Speech Segmentation

7.1. Introduction

The majority of speech segmentation systems are based, at least partially, on detecting and tracking the voiced content of the sources in the mixture. As such, unvoiced speech is generally ignored. However, as it has been shown that a significant percentage of phones are unvoiced, ignoring them within the current framework is likely to have a negative impact on the final recognition process. In telephone speech, French et al. (1930) found that 24% of spoken phones were unvoiced. For read speech, it was shown that unvoiced speech accounted for 23.1% of all speech in the corpus[23] (Wang and Hu, 2006). The analyses by Wang and Hu (2006) and French et al. (1930) were performed on corpora of American English; an analysis of British English undertaken by Denes (1963) revealed that unvoiced speech made up 23.2% of the speech database they analysed. In English, unvoiced speech is a significant source of linguistic information (Miller, 1951)[24], which if properly segmented, holds the capacity to improve the output of downstream applications - such as automatic speech recognisers - which employ the segmented speech.

7.1.1. Unvoiced Speech

In order to produce unvoiced speech a partial (or in some cases, complete) blockage is formed in the vocal tract. When air from the lungs is forced through this configuration the result is turbulent flow which is characterised as unvoiced speech. Owing to the fact that the vocal cords are held in a configuration that precludes oscillation, there is a lack of periodic excitation. It is this lack of periodicity that differentiates between unvoiced and voiced speech. Only a subset of English consonants are unvoiced, the others, as with vowels are voiced.

The unvoiced consonants of English can be further subdivided based on their place of articulation (see Section 7.2. for more detail). Each subdivision is generally characterised by particular spectral properties precluding a truly general description of the spectral attributes of unvoiced consonants. There are however, some features that they have in common.

---

[23]The TIMIT corpus (Garofolo et al., 1993) was employed in the study.

[24]Miller and others suggest that consonants are more important than vowels for the intelligibility of clean speech, though this view is not universally accepted.

Figure 7.1 shows spectrograms of two telephone quality vowel consonant vowel (VCV) clusters, which can be used to identify some of the general differences between voiced and unvoiced speech sounds. The spectrogram on the right shows the cluster *asa*; that on the left shows the cluster *aza*. It can be clearly seen that the unvoiced consonant [s] has no fundamental frequency (F0) and lacks an organised harmonic structure. The figure also highlights the fact that most of the energy of the unvoiced consonant lies in the high frequency regions. Further, it can be seen that the unvoiced consonant has overall, low energy compared to the vowel and the voiced consonant. Given its low energy, unvoiced speech is more susceptible to masking by more energetic sounds.

(a) VCV cluster with voiced consonant   (b) VCV cluster with unvoiced consonant

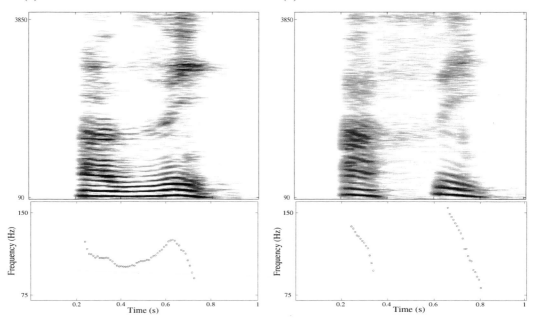

Figure 7.1. Spectrograms and pitch tracks of two VCV clusters, which differ only in the voicing of the consonant. The figures highlight, visually, some of the general differences between voiced and unvoiced speech sounds.

It is well understood that unvoiced speech sounds contribute to the intelligibility of speech in low noise conditions. However, their contribution to the intelligibility of noisy speech is less well understood. Given that vowels are less affected by noise than consonants (especially low energy consonants) one wonders to what extent the loss of intelligibility observed when speech is masked by noise is a result of the masking of low energy consonants, including the unvoiced consonants. In a study by Gordon-Salant (1986) the effect on intelligibility of modifying the consonant portion of VCVs presented in noise at different SNRs was considered. The modifications involved either: increasing the duration of the consonant, increasing the energy of the consonant relative to the vowel, or increasing both the relative energy and the consonant duration. Overall, the latter two modifications produced significant improvement in consonant recognition, while increasing the consonant duration did not yield increased performance. The effect of voicing was among the analyses performed on the consonant recognition results. It was found that unvoiced consonants benefitted more from the modifications than did their voiced cognates. This experiment was repeated, with similar outcome, by Hazan and Simpson (1998) who also found significant improvements for consonants in sentences where co-articulation is likely to play a significant role in intelligibility.

Given the differences between voiced and unvoiced speech it follows that the techniques employed for segmenting voiced speech will have only limited success when applied to unvoiced speech. However, it is not only in speech segmentation that this holds true. Separate treatment of voiced and unvoiced speech has been shown to be beneficial in a variety of applications, including: speech synthesis (Mehta and Quatieri, 2006); speech coding (Shlomot et al., 2001); signal manipulation (Macon and Clements, 1997) and speech recognition (Moreno et al., 2003; Coy and Barker, 2007). This chapter thus presents evidence for, and an approach to, the deliberate segmentation of unvoiced speech from interference.

The rest of the chapter is organised as follows. Section 7.2. reviews the segmentation of unvoiced speech and some of the acoustic cues proposed as being useful in this process. Section 7.3. proposes a novel method for segmenting unvoiced speech. The evaluation of the algorithm on monaurally mixed speech is presented in Section 7.4.. The chapter is concluded in Section 7.5..

7.2. Review of Unvoiced Speech Segmentation

The segmentation of voiced speech is facilitated by the powerful cue of harmonicity. By detecting the fundamental frequency of the signals in a mixture, algorithms that are used to segment voiced speech can often distinguish the individual sources in the amalgam. Unvoiced speech does not have a strong harmonic structure and, therefore, cannot be segmented using cues to harmonicity. The difficulty of the task is compounded by the relatively low energy of unvoiced speech, which makes it susceptible to masking by a more energetic competing source. The published techniques proposed for tackling the problem rely on the assumption that the interference has spectral properties that differ significantly from those of unvoiced speech. This is clearly not always the case when one considers mixtures of competing talkers. Thus, the proposed method makes a more general assumption about the energy distribution of the sources in the mixture. The rest of the paper will explore the methods previously implemented for segmenting unvoiced speech before discussing, in detail, the proposed technique and presenting experiments which appear to support its use.

In the English language, unvoiced speech is represented by the consonants. The consonants can be grouped into three broad phonetic classes, namely, stops, sonorants and obstruents. Of the three classes, only the obstruents (fricatives and affricates) and stops contain regions of unvoiced speech. Obstruents and stops can be further divided into several subclasses defined by characteristic acoustic-phonetic properties, which serve to distinguish them from other sounds, speech-like and otherwise.

In the absence of harmonicity, the cues used for the classification of unvoiced speech are concerned with the characteristic energy distribution of the members of this group. These cues include such things as duration, spectral shape and relative amplitude. The absence of voicing may also be used as a cue to detecting unvoiced speech. It is possible that one, or more, of these cues may also be useful for unvoiced-speech segmentation. The following section will thus examine the use of these cues for the classification of unvoiced speech.

7.2.1. Cues for Classifying Unvoiced Speech

Fricatives

When a partial blockage is formed along the vocal tract, the air passing over it creates turbulence; the sound thus produced is referred to as *frication*. The same configuration of the vocal tract can produce voiced and unvoiced fricatives, where the voicing state is determined by the condition of the vocal folds during frication. How are these sounds distinguished from others? What are the properties that uniquely identify them as fricatives?

Ali and colleagues examined the acoustic-phonetic features of fricatives in an effort to determine which of these cues could be useful for detecting and classifying fricatives in a manner that would be useful for continuous speech recognition systems (Ali et al., 2001a). What they discovered was that some of the cues mentioned in the literature were abstract and qualitative; in the instances where they could be quantified, the results were dependent on the method used to calculate the parameters. This is often the case with purely knowledge-based systems, where the translation of abstract concepts into measurable features varies among researchers and significantly impacts the final system. From this study, the acoustic-phonetic features of fricatives found to be most useful in classifying them were duration, voicing, spectral shape, relative amplitude and the location of the most dominant spectral peak. One important finding was that while particular configurations of each of the parameters were necessary for the identification of fricatives, it was only when used in combination that they could reliably discriminate between voiced and unvoiced fricatives.

Wang exploited the acoustic-phonetic properties of obstruents to segment speech corrupted with non-speech interference (Wang, 2006). Spectral shape, amplitude and duration were used to discriminate between voiced speech, unvoiced speech and non-speech data. The system initially segmented speech, grouping regions of similar intensity by detecting their onsets and offsets. Using a technique referred to as multi-scale integration, the onsets and offsets were iteratively refined, with the dual effect of reducing the number of segments and correctly defining segment boundaries (Hu and Wang, 2004a). After removing all the segments containing voiced speech, they then performed a two stage classification of the remaining energy. Using Gaussian mixture models trained on the spectral information of fricative and non-fricative phones, the first stage removed non-fricative phones in a frame by frame process. The second stage involved removing segments dominated by interference energy. Separate Gaussian mixture models were trained for the interference - using several environmental noises - and the spectrum of unvoiced fricatives. Fricative duration was included as a supplementary feature to the spectral shape and amplitude. A confidence measure was developed to account for the possible mismatch between fricatives and unseen environmental noises. In Wang and Hu (2006) the need for a confidence measure was eliminated by employing multilayer perceptrons to distinguish between fricatives, stops and non-speech sounds. The results reported by the authors showed that their system successfully recruited the majority of the segments that contained fricatives and rejected most of the interference.

Affricates

Affricates are acoustically related to fricatives and the two are at times manipulated using the same techniques (Wang, 2006). Affricates are produced by creating a buildup of pressure behind a constriction formed in the vocal cavity. The configuration of the vocal tract is such that the release of the stricture does not immediately release the pressure built up behind it (Stevens, 1998). After a few milliseconds, the pressure is released resulting in the production of frication. This leads to the affricate being phonetically characterised as a stop followed by a fricative.

While fricatives and affricates have very similar acoustic-phonetic properties, they can be differentiated. Both perceptual and statistical analyses have shown that fricative duration is a useful cue for discriminating between fricatives and affricates with affricates having the shorter duration (Castleman and Diehl, 1996; Mitani et al., 2006; Cohen et al., 1962). It has also been shown that there are systematic differences between the energy onset and decay times of fricatives and affricates, where shorter onsets were perceptually associated with affricates (Cutting and Rosner, 1974). Experiments performed by Mitani et al. (2006) confirmed the use of onset times as a differentiating cue and, furthermore, showed that there is an interaction between the cues of duration and onset time.

The features listed above (duration of frication; absence of voicing; spectral shape; relative amplitude of fricatives to the following vowel; location of the most dominant spectral peak) are useful for classification of obstruents. However, they may not be relevant for segmentation of speech in noise. Fricative duration may be disrupted in noise; the value of frication noise in determining the place of articulation is reduced when high frequency regions are disrupted (Kasturi and Loizou, 2002). When the noise source is harmonic, there will at times be overlap between voiced and unvoiced speech segments, in which case, the absence of voicing will not be a reliable cue. In the instances where two voiceless consonants are mixed, the absence of voicing cannot be effective for segmentation. The cues of spectral shape and relative amplitude are interdependent (Ali et al., 2001a). The spectral shape property employed for fricative classification is useful for determining place of articulation, but it is generally a qualitative measure; further it seems that there is a frequency dependence which makes the cue unreliable (Hedrick and Ohde, 1993). It has also been shown that distortion of relative amplitude features leads to mis-recognition of some fricatives (Hedrick and Ohde, 1993). Even where there is no direct masking of the affricate, the possibility of the following vowel being masked suggests that the relative amplitude cue may not be useful for speech segmentation.

Unvoiced Stops

The other consonant class of interest is the stops. Two of the major differences between stops and obstruents are: 1) stops have a complete closure along the vocal tract rather than a narrow constriction and 2) the obstruents are continuants – they can be prolonged by the speaker. The stops can be further sub-divided based on the place of articulation. The acoustic realisation of a stop is a short, unsustainable burst of noise. Spectrally, stops are characterised by an abrupt increase in spectral amplitude across frequency accompanied by a sudden change in the spectral shape (Stevens, 1980; Ali et al., 2001b). Of the many features derived from the acoustic-phonetic properties of stop consonants, several have been proposed for classification. Of these, the burst spectrum, burst amplitude and formant transitions have been consistently shown to be the most useful (Ali et al., 2001b; Dorman et al., 1977; Stevens, 1998).

The burst spectrum and formant transitions – in particular, the second and third formants – associated with stop consonants are closely related perceptual cues for the recognition of stop consonants. They are highly context dependent and are thus, not necessarily invariant enough to be directly used as a feature for stop classification. Additionally, these two cues have been found to be perceptually equivalent and complementary, i.e., one is significant when the other is not (Dorman et al., 1977).

Burst amplitude, duration and voicing have also been proposed as cues for detection of stop consonants (Ali et al., 2001b). Burst amplitude in and of itself is not sufficiently invariant to serve as a cue for stop classification. However, the relationship between burst amplitude and the amplitude of the following vowel can be modelled (Stevens, 1998). It has been noted that burst amplitude seems to play less of a role than the spectrum (Ali et al., 2001b).

Stop consonants have more than one transition point: There is the point where the initial closure is released, and one where the burst changes to the vowel. The duration of each of these regions has been studied to determine their utility in detecting stops. The analysis of duration performed by Ali et al. (2001b) brought them to the conclusion that the interval between the release and the vowel onset played a significant role in the detection of voicing – the interval in unvoiced stops was longer than that in voiced stops.

Given the complexity and interdependence of these varied cues, it is difficult for any single cue to consistently identify all subgroups of stops. This has led researchers to use different combinations of these cues in their attempts at stop classification. The approach taken by Ali et al. (2001b) is to combine expert knowledge with robust statistical techniques in a knowledge-based system, which they used to successfully classify stops in continuous speech that was free from interference. What they found was that the individual features were not consistently invariant, but their relationships to each other generally were. This interaction of cues was also identified in Section 7.2.1. in reference to affricate discrimination and suggests that combining multiple cues could enhance consonant recognition as a whole.

A Bayesian approach to stop classification was adopted by Hu and Wang, who used spectral amplitude and shape, relative intensity and intensity decay time as features for segmenting stops from non-speech interference (Hu and Wang, 2003; Wang, 2006). First, the voiced portion of speech was removed; the unvoiced region was then segmented based on onset synchrony. Separate distributions were trained for stops and interference and a Bayesian decision rule was used to distinguish a stop burst from interference. The focus was on the burst region of the stop as it was found to be less susceptible to interference and easier to detect than formant transitions.

Of the three main cues proposed for stop identification and classification, burst amplitude may be the most useful for segmentation even though it may not be invariant enough for classification. Duration can be disrupted by the overlap of speech segments, while voicing is known to be susceptible to masking by noise (Parikh and Loizou, 2005). Distortion of relative amplitude features leads to mis-recognition of some unvoiced stops (Ohde and Stevens, 1983; Hedrick and Ohde, 1996) making relative amplitude a poor cue for segmentation. It is accepted, however, that the absolute energy of stop bursts is reasonably high. This may result in the presence of resolvable energy peaks that can be used to segment energy originating from stops from the energy surrounding them, even in noisy conditions.

7.2.2. Cues for Segmenting Unvoiced Speech

From the above discussion it would appear that the majority of cues used for classifying unvoiced speech are unlikely to be robust enough to be useful for segmentation. It is apparent however, that there will be local spectro-temporal regions where the energy of individual signals will be unmasked; this can be exploited to segment the mixtures into isolated regions of coherent energy. Some of these regions will be temporally asynchronous and of limited extent. However, it has been shown that listeners can combine apparently unrelated glimpses of spectral energy to correctly identify speech in noise (Buss et al., 2003, 2004).

Brungart et al. (2006) tested the ability of speakers to segment monaurally-mixed synthetic utterances that lacked many of the features, such as periodicity, used to segment natural speech. The signals assessed were: sine-wave speech (SWS); modulated noise-band (MNB) speech and modulated sine-band (MSB) speech. SWS uses sinusoids to represent the formants in such a way as to remove the spectral fine structure, however, it seems that it retains the pitch differences listeners use to distinguish gender (Fellowes et al., 1997). MNB speech is produced by extracting the spectral envelope in a number of sub-bands and using the envelopes to modulate a broadband noise source, realising an utterance that is acoustically and perceptually similar to whispered speech; MSB speech is similar to MNB except that the extracted spectral envelopes are used to modulate logarithmically spaced sinusoids instead of noise (Brungart et al., 2006). Commands from the Coordinate Resource Measure (CRM) corpus (Bolia et al., 2000) were re-synthesised for the task and listeners were asked to report the colour and number spoken by the talker that spoke the keyword "Baron" (see Brungart et al., 2006, for details). There were three sub-tasks with differing configurations of target and masker: 1) the masker and target were of differing gender; 2) the masker and target were of the same gender; and 3) both utterances were spoken by the same talker.

In the sub-tasks where there was no gender difference, MNB and MSB speech were found to be more intelligible than SWS at positive SNRs; the result was reversed as the SNR became less favourable. The explanation offered for this phenomenon was that the MNB and MSB signals had a greater spectral overlap than SWS signals. At positive SNRs the effect was a reduction in the effect of informational masking – leading to improved target recognition for MNB and MSB speech. With negative SNR values there was an increase in energetic masking and a reduction in recognition performance; this ran counter to experiments with normal speech, where listeners were able to attend to the quieter target and increase recognition accuracy as SNR decreased (Brungart, 2001). For the 'different gender' sub-task, listeners performed better when listening to SWS speech, confirming the postulate that the variations in the formant structure of SWS signals led to the retention of pitch information. The experimental outcomes served to highlight the importance of pitch as a segmentation cue and the difficulty human listeners face with segmenting mixtures of unvoiced speech. The conclusions suggested that listeners use coarse spectral differences to segment speech in the absence of stronger cues, such as pitch differences.

It is generally accepted that segmenting speech mixtures is more difficult if the constituent utterances have the same F0. This has been shown to be true for synthetic double vowels (Assmann and Summerfield, 1990; Meddis and Hewitt, 1992; de Cheveigné, 1993; Summerfield and Culling, 1994; Bird and Darwin, 1998), as well as sentences (Brokx and Nooteboom, 1982; Bird and Darwin, 1998). Brokx and Nooteboom (1982) used mixtures of re-synthesised sentences with monotonous pitch to study the effect of varying the difference in pitch between individual utterances. They took care to remove speaker differences and semantic cues. In general, mixtures with no pitch difference will be devoid of normal periodic and spectral cues and will, in that sense, mimic unvoiced speech; thus only the same pitch condition will be discussed. Brokx and Nooteboom came to the conclusion that when there is little or no difference in the F0 of the sentences, perceptual fusion, caused by the lack of F0 discriminability, could cause listeners to track the wrong message. They further hypothesised that listeners took advantage of the fluctuations in local energy values and recognised target speech through gaps left by the masking sentence. This concept of recognising speech from spectro-temporal glimpses is supported by several studies (Miller and Licklider, 1950; Howard-Jones and Rosen, 1993; Assmann and Summerfield, 1994; Culling and Darwin, 1994; Assmann, 1996; Cooke, 2003; Freyman et al., 2004; Cooke, 2006). Bird and Darwin (1998) repeated these experiments using completely voiced masking sentences. When the number of gaps in the masker is reduced – by making the masker entirely voiced, and reducing the number of stop consonants, thereby reducing the number of onset and offset cues – it is found that recognition rates in the same F0 condition fell significantly.

One implication from the study conducted by Bird and Darwin (1998) is that the sparseness of unvoiced speech makes it possible to exploit glimpses for segmentation. It must be noted though, that for unvoiced speech the glimpses may be small, as more spectral overlap could occur owing to the lack of modulation in the masker (Cooke, 2006). In the context of the current work, the size of the glimpses may be of limited consequence, given that the fragments derived from unvoiced speech will combine with fragments of voiced speech to inform the final recognition hypothesis.

Bird and Darwin (1998) in an analysis of the results of the study by Brokx and Nooteboom (1982), pointed out that common onset and offset cues were a factor influencing the segmentation of the sentences with a common F0. This supports evidence that highlights the utility of these cues for segmentation (Bregman, 1990; Darwin, 1997).

7.3. An Approach for Segmenting Unvoiced Speech

In the previous section, the properties of unvoiced consonants, and techniques for classifying and segmenting them were discussed. These techniques were developed to work for clean speech or speech mixed with non-speech interference. For example, Hu and Wang's algorithms work by assuming that the acoustic-phonetic properties of unvoiced speech remain distinct when speech is mixed with non-speech interference (Wang, 2006). This is not necessarily the case when the interference is speech, especially where it is likely that both voiced and unvoiced speech will overlap. While the research reviewed in the previous section points to cues that discriminate between unvoiced speech and other phone types, there seems to be a sparsity of work that addresses the segmentation of mixtures of unvoiced speech. This may be because many of the cues used for unvoiced speech segmentation are difficult to detect in the presence of interference, this may be compounded when there is speech-like interference. The studies reviewed in Sections 7.2.1. and 7.2.2. suggest that the majority of cues used for the classification of unvoiced speech are not robust enough for segmentation. It is further suggested that segmentation can be achieved by exploiting the coarse spectral differences between the sources in a mixture. The proposed approach will take advantage of this to segment mixtures of unvoiced speech based on a combination of local energy differences and common onset cues.

Different effects can occur given the composition of the overlapped regions – whether they are voiced/voiced; voiced/unvoiced or unvoiced/unvoiced. The first condition involves only voiced speech and is dealt with by a separate process (see Chapter 6). Voiced speech tends to have the majority of its energy focused in the lower frequency regions, while unvoiced speech will have significant energy in high frequencies. Thus, when voiced and unvoiced speech are combined, even though voiced speech will likely be more energetic than unvoiced speech, there will be gaps through which unvoiced speech will be 'visible'. Despite the obvious overlap of energy that can occur when two unvoiced speech sources are mixed, it is unlikely that all the energy arising from one source will be completely masked by the competing source. This may hold true even in the instances where the sources are, temporally, well aligned. In this case, there will be local time-frequency regions where the energy of one or the other source dominates. Thus, even if there was perfect temporal alignment, the sources might be separable across frequency. Despite the synchronicity brought about by the mixing of the sources, each source has the capacity for producing resolvable energy peaks - a property which can be exploited by algorithms that can detect and segment energy maxima into separate regions.

The technique proposed in this work for the segmentation of unvoiced speech takes advantage of the assertions made above. It employs a process known as *marker-controlled watershed segmentation*; which is a standard technique, employed in the image processing literature for image segmentation. The watershed algorithm is used to segment regions surrounding local minima (Meyer and Beucher, 1990). The adoption of image processing techniques to segment spectro-temporal representations is similar in spirit to the work of Hu and Wang (2004a). The current work takes a step forward by applying these techniques to mixtures of speech and non-stationary noise.

7.3.1. The Watershed Algorithm

The watershed algorithm is used for morphological segmentation, which treats images as topographic surfaces (Gonzalez et al., 2004). The inspiration for the name comes from the topographic features of watersheds and catchment basins. Consider a topographic region where two valleys are separated by a single peak; water that falls on the peak will flow into one or other of the valleys. These valleys form two catchment regions which are separated by the peak, or watershed line (see Figure 7.2). Following the analogy, the simple aim of the algorithm is to flood the catchment basins, thus highlighting the connected watershed lines.

In a digital image, the catchment basin represents a minimum intensity value and the watershed line marks the region within which all the pixels are connected. Defining these

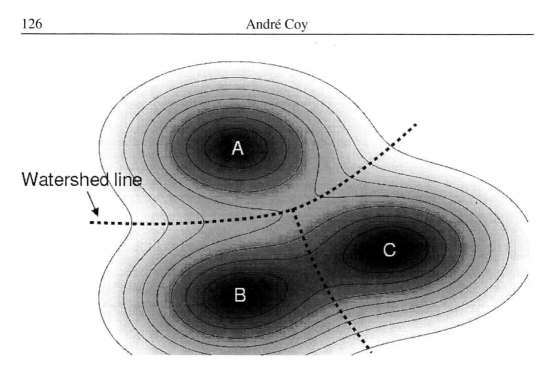

Figure 7.2. The watershed algorithm – commonly used for segmentation in the image processing community (Gonzalez et al., 2004) – segments an intensity map by considering the map as a surface, and then calculating the watershed capture area around each local minima (i.e. consider the region around each minima from which water would be captured if it fell on the surface). In the figure, the minima A, B, and C would be separated by the watershed lines marked. Clearly, the same technique can be employed to segment local maxima by inverting the intensity axis before applying the algorithm. [Figure reproduced from Coy and Barker (2007)]

minima is quite challenging in a digital image and this has led to the development of several algorithms for solving the problem. One of the most practical and efficient of these algorithms was developed by Vincent and Soille (1991). To illustrate their algorithm they proposed a topographic region, with holes at the minima, which was slowly lowered into a body of water. This immersion floods the catchment basins from the bottom up. As the flooding continued, dams were erected around the catchment areas to prevent water spilling out of one into the other - these dams represented·the watershed lines.

The algorithm implemented a two-stage process, where the pixels of an image were first sorted according to their intensity values before the flooding of the catchment basins began. With access to the intensity value of a pixel, it was easier to determine which catchment basin it belonged. A pixel was included in a catchment basin C if its distance to C was smaller than that to any other catchment basin.

Figure 7.3 shows the outcome of applying the watershed algorithm to simple synthetic sounds. Variation in the energy profiles of the signals leads to several fragments being formed from what a listener would perceive as a single continuous sound. The number of fragments formed can be controlled by a tuning parameter described in Section 7.4.

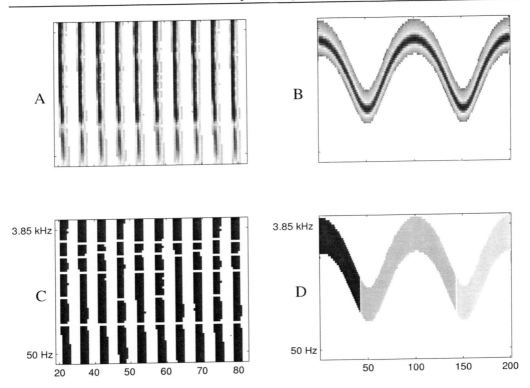

Figure 7.3. Auditory spectrograms of synthetic sounds and the regions defined by the watershed algorithm. *A* – the ringing of a telephone and the output of the watershed algorithm (*C*). The regions of similar energy are grouped together forming several disconnected fragments of energy. *B* – a frequency modulated tone and its fragments (*D*).

7.3.2. Applying Watershed Segmentation to Unvoiced Speech

When segmenting unvoiced speech, the energy regions are negated so that local energy maxima become local energy minima (this is done simply because the aim is to locate maxima, whereas the watershed algorithm finds minima). As the unvoiced regions of speech are inherently noisy, there are likely to be many insignificant local minima, so a direct application of the watershed algorithm would over-segment the image (Figure 7.4 illustrates this). Over-segmentation is undesirable for two reasons: Firstly, because it produces an inordinate number of fragments, which places a large computational burden on the decoder; Secondly, over-segmentation reduces the strength of potentially valuable bottom-up constraints by creating smaller fragments with less temporal extent, thereby erasing temporal cues. The solution – developed within the image processing community – is to use *marker controls* (Meyer and Beucher, 1990): significant local minima are marked and remaining minima are removed using smoothing. The significant local minima are defined as points around which a closed and fully connected boundary can be drawn such that all the points on the boundary exceed the minima defined by a threshold, E_γ. Once significant minima are located, they are highlighted and enhanced by setting the regions outside the boundaries to zero. This technique effectively smooths away all unmarked, insignificant minimum. After smoothing, the watershed algorithm will return one region for each significant minimum.[25]

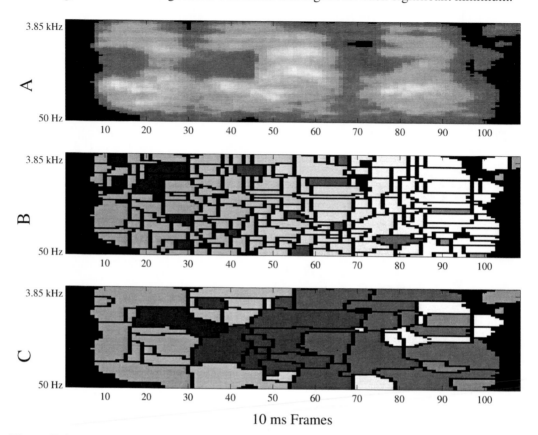

Figure 7.4. (A) - An auditory spectrogram of a whispered speech mixture. When the watershed algorithm is applied without marking the boundaries of significant energy peaks, the signal is over-segmented (B). By applying morphological smoothing, the over-segmentation problem is addressed (C). There are 79 fragments in B and only 41 fragments C.

The threshold E_γ effectively controls the degree of smoothing. An appropriate degree of smoothing is necessary to avoid both over-segmentation and under-segmentation. The problems associated with over-segmentation have already been outlined. Under-segmentation is equally problematic as it results in incoherent fragments that cannot be unambiguously assigned to either foreground or background.

In a final step, the number of fragments are reduced by merging fragments that have a common onset. This follows Bregman's principle of common onset grouping, i.e. acoustic events that onset synchronously are likely to be due to the same acoustic source (Bregman, 1990). This also implements the idea of employing multiple cues to enhance segmentation (see Section 7.2.1.). Grouping by common onset is especially advantageous because, by acting across frequency, it reduces the total number of fragments present within a single 10 ms windowed frame – this reduction in the number of simultaneously active groups, N_a, greatly reduces the search space of the decoder (see Section 3.6.3.).

---

[25]These steps can be implemented using the *imextendedmin*, *imimposemin* and *watershed* functions in the MATLAB image processing toolbox (MathWorks).

Previous studies have taken into account common offset as well as common onset for segmentation (Cooke, 1993; Brown and Cooke, 1994a). However, it is thought that humans employ common offset cues less than they do common onset when segmenting an auditory scene (Carlyon, 2004). Further, this cue is not always consistent (Smaragdis, 2001) and has not been employed in the present work.

7.4.   System Tuning and Evaluation

The effect of the smoothing threshold, E_γ, on segmentation is investigated in this section. As discussed in the previous section, the value of E_γ controls the level of segmentation. As such, it is important that an appropriate value is set for this tuning parameter. An effective way to evaluate the effect of varying its value is to examine the *coherence* of the fragments produced by said variations. The concept of coherence, introduced in the previous chapter as a measure of fragment quality, essentially determines the extent to which the time-frequency regions of a fragment are derived from a single source.

7.4.1.   Unvoiced Data

A test set of monaurally mixed, unvoiced speech data was created to be used for the tuning of E_γ. The digit strings were drawn from the clean training set of the Aurora 2 database; they were end-pointed then matched for length. These utterances consisted of both voiced and unvoiced regions and thus needed to be re-synthesised to remove the harmonic excitation. After the length-matching procedure, a set of one hundred pairs of files of similar length was randomly chosen for re-synthesis. The data were spoken by 26 male and 43 female speakers with an average of 3 digits in each unmixed digit string. Of the 200 utterances there were 58 with the same length – the margin of overlap difference was negligible at 65×10^{-6} ms.

The data were then processed using the high quality vocoder, STRAIGHT (Kawahara et al., 1999), which is based on the source-filter model of speech production. Liu and Kewley-Port (2004b) have found that STRAIGHT provides a reliable method of re-synthesising vowel formants and gives similar results to the Klatt synthesiser (Klatt, 1980). The quality of the algorithm and the simplicity with which parameter manipulation can be accomplished has seen STRAIGHT utilised in a wide range of experiments, in many domains, ranging from the determination of speaker characteristics to musical instrument perception (Saitou et al., 2005; Ives et al., 2005; Smith and Patterson, 2005; Liu and Kewley-Port, 2004a; van Dinther and Patterson, 2006; von Kriegstein et al., 2006).

The processing took the following form: Firstly, the source parameters were extracted from each file. The source parameters consisted of the fundamental frequency and an *aperiodicity index* which is a time-frequency representation of the periodicity of the input signal. The robustness of the F0 extraction is enhanced by using multiple periodicity cues to derive the final contour (Kawahara et al., 2005). The fundamental frequency was employed in the extraction of the spectral envelope. The signal's F0 was used to adaptively smooth the spectral envelope, such that the final output was virtually free from the influence of periodicity. Whispered speech was then produced by exciting the spectral envelope with white noise instead of periodic pulses. Informal listening tests confirmed the quality of the re-synthesised signals. Finally, the 'whispered' speech files were mixed at 0 dB in the time domain to produce 100 mixtures of completely unvoiced speech. An example of the output of the re-synthesis procedure is shown in Figure 7.5.

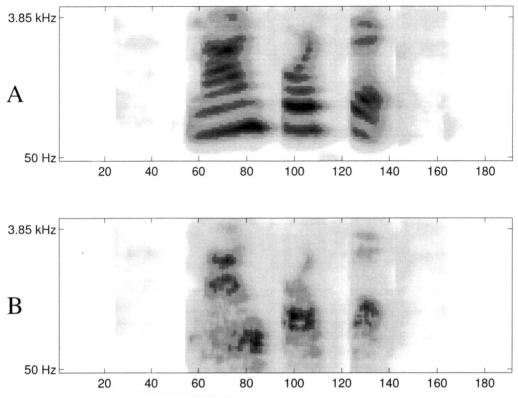

Figure 7.5. Auditory spectrogram of the digit string "nine four six" uttered by a female speaker before (*A*) and after (*B*) re-synthesis. Note the smearing of the formants.

As well as the expected absence of periodicity, other acoustic characteristics of whispered speech are very different to those of phonated speech. Notably, the amplitude of vowels is lower than that of consonants in whispered speech - voiced consonants also have a reduced amplitude, relative to unvoiced consonants (Ito et al., 2005). Ito et al. (2005) also found that the first and second formants (F1 and F2) of whispered speech were shifted upward by an average of 40% and 10%, respectively, compared to their voiced counterparts. The recognition of whispered speech is affected by the difference in parameters, with word accuracy falling by 50% when models trained on regular speech are used to recognise whispered speech.

7.4.2. Experiments

The whispered speech mixtures were segmented using the marker-controlled watershed segmentation, creating a number of fragments from each mixture. The coherence of a fragment was calculated by comparing it to the *a priori* mask of each unmixed source. With access to the unmixed speech files, it is possible to segment the mixture into a set of masks that are totally coherent – *a priori* masks. *A priori* masks were developed for the dataset as described in Chapter 6 (Section 6.5.4..) The average coherence was calculated across all fragments in the data set by weighting each fragment by its size and dividing by the sum of the size of all fragments in the dataset. This was recalculated for 10 separate values of E_γ ranging from 0.1 to 1.0. Figure 7.6 shows that increasing the value of E_γ causes fragment coherence to decrease in a generally linear fashion.

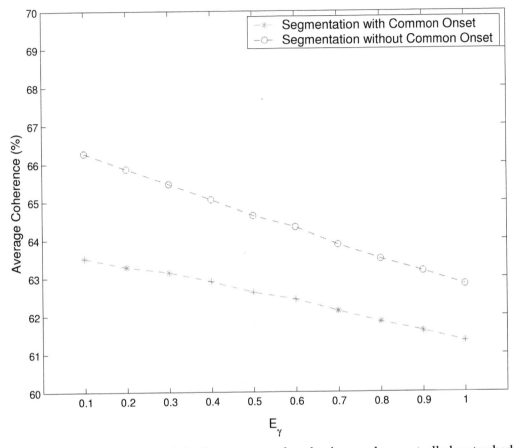

Figure 7.6. The coherence of the fragments produced using marker-controlled watershed segmentation varies with the level of smoothing applied to the unsegmented input. By varying the tuning threshold E_γ, it is possible to investigate how coherence changes with the smoothing threshold. Common onset grouping can be applied to reduce the number of fragments (see the text for details). Coherence of fragments generated, with and without common onset grouping is plotted.

While the grouping of fragments with a common onset reduces the number of fragments, it may have the undesirable effect of reducing coherence by merging fragments from unrelated sources. To test whether this is the case with the fragments derived using the watershed segmentation, a separate set of fragments was created. The new set was created by applying marker-controlled segmentation to the whispered speech data using the same range of values for E_γ. This time however, the algorithm which groups fragments by common onset was not applied. The coherence of these fragments was also calculated. The results (see Figure 7.6) show that the application of common onset grouping causes a small decrease (3%) in average coherence, which is slightly less at values of E_γ above 0.6. This reduction in coherence occurs as a consequence of merging fragments and suggests that the common onset cue may not always be a reliable one.

Coherence gives a measure of the quality of the fragments produced by the proposed segmentation algorithm. There is however, a related property of these fragments that will impact the recognition performance: The size of the derived fragments, which is directly proportional to the number of fragments, has to be considered. Smaller fragments are likely to have a high coherence, however, with smaller, more numerous fragments, some of the primitive grouping cues, such as temporal continuity and common-fate, could be eliminated. Thus, when selecting a value for E_γ, a balance has to be struck between the size and coherence of the fragments produced.

Figure 7.7 shows how fragment size varies with E_γ. Fragment size increases almost linearly with increasing values of E_γ. This is the case whether or not common onset grouping is applied. As expected, common onset grouping – when it is applied – produces fragments that are larger than those produced when this technique is not employed. This holds true across the range of E_γ.

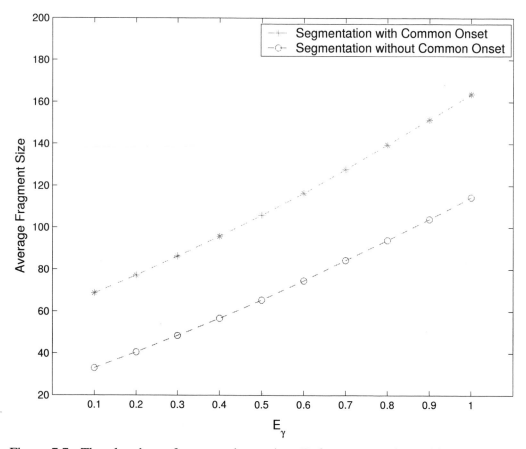

Figure 7.7. The plot shows fragment size against E_γ for a range of E_γ with and without common onset grouping. As E_γ is varied, fragment size is affected.

Taken together, Figures 7.6 and 7.7 suggest that there is an inverse relation between the size and coherence of fragments arising from the segmentation process. This seems to indicate that there are 'islands' of resolvable energy from each source within the mixture. In order to take full advantage of this, it is important to remove the spurious energy peaks that are present in the representation. These peaks have the effect of warping the borders of potential fragments, leading to a drop in the average fragment coherence. By applying an appropriate level of smoothing, the borders can be redefined in such a way as to increase the average fragment coherence. This has the added advantage of reducing the number of fragments that will have to be manipulated when the fragments are processed at a later stage.

7.5. Summary

This chapter has discussed the segmentation of unvoiced speech, a topic that has been largely overlooked in the literature on speech segmentation. However, unvoiced speech segmentation is motivated by the knowledge that unvoiced speech carries much linguistic information, which assists in human speech perception. Further incentive was provided by the fact that some consonant classes (the representatives of unvoiced speech in English) have been shown to be generally more susceptible to noise degradation than voiced speech. There are myriad cues for classifying unvoiced speech sounds. However, it would appear that none of them is robust enough to be used for segmentation. Such susceptibility to noise notwithstanding, the isolated glimpses of coherent spectral energy that occur when different sources overlap are known to be exploitable for source segmentation. The watershed algorithm is utilised to take advantage of the presence of these glimpses. The algorithm groups regions of similar spectral content into isolated fragments. Experiments with mixtures of whispered speech have given rise to fragments with high coherence. However, when the average coherence of these fragments is compared to that of voiced fragments (see Section 6.5.4.) it becomes evident that the cues employed for segmentation of unvoiced speech are not as powerful as those employed for the segmentation of voiced speech.

While the processes used to segment speech in this and the previous chapter have been shown to produce comparatively coherent fragments, it is important to consider how these fragments perform in ASR. The following chapter will explore this.

Chapter 8

Full System Evaluation

A series of speech recognition experiments has been carried out to test the performance of the speech fragment decoder (SFD) with fragments created using the speech segmentation system developed in previous chapters. Section 8.1. introduces and motivates the evaluation. In Section 8.2. speech recognition experiments are carried out with a corpus of monaurally-mixed digit strings. *Alpha-digit* experiments with sentence-length utterances are performed in Section 8.3., while Section 8.4. makes a comparison between the performance of the speech fragment decoder and human speech recognition on the same tasks. The chapter is summarised in Section 8.5..

8.1. Introduction

The aim of the system is to recognise speech in the presence of an interfering speaker using fragments derived from a speech segmentation system exploiting primitive grouping constraints. Thus, the final evaluation of the system must be automatic speech recognition (ASR) experiments.

The grouping constraints are utilised as a method of partially segmenting the acoustic input of each source. This segmentation has been achieved in four stages: Firstly, the multiple-pitch determination algorithm (see Chapter 4) was developed and shown to be able to determine the pitches of both sources in a two-source mixture with a high degree of accuracy. The second stage (Chapter 5) involves the use of a novel multi-pitch tracking algorithm, which outperformed a state-of the-art multi-pitch tracker, being able to form pitch-track segments for both sources from the candidates proposed in the previous stage. Voiced-speech was segmented in the third stage (Chapter 6), which employed the pitch track segments to produce a set of coherent fragments. Finally, unvoiced-speech was segmented (Chapter 7). However, signal segmentation is not an end in itself, but an essential step on the path to recognition; thus, correct segmentation is not a guarantee of accurate recognition performance (see Barker and Coy, 2005, for a discussion). There are a number of reasons for this. Firstly, the partial organisation provided by the primitive segmentation is not enough to provide an unambiguous interpretation of the auditory scene. The schema-driven processes in the recognition engine are thus required to complete the segmentation, which it may not do without errors, even if primitive segmentation is flawless. Secondly, there is no long-term grouping constraint in the fragments proposed by the signal-driven system. Thus, it is the job of the decoder to identify fragments that are related but are separated in time. This can also lead to errors.

A coupling of the segmentation and recognition stages can be introduced within the missing data framework by allowing the recognition stage to search over a set of alternative segmentations. One implementation of this idea is the *speech fragment decoding* (SFD) technique which generates segmentations based on a set of source fragments proposed by the primitive grouping processes. The theory of this technique has been outlined Barker et al. (2005) (see also Chapter 3), but the lack of an adequate model of primitive grouping prevented this earlier work from fully demonstrating the potential of the approach. This current work represents an attempt to exploit that potential.

The experiments performed in this chapter are designed to jointly test the power of the segmentation process and the decoding performed by the SFD. This is achieved by using the fragments and 'fuzzy' confidence map derived from the segmentation component of the system in the decoding (see Chapter 6). The data employed cover a range of signal levels and interference (matched-gender, mixed-gender and same-speaker). In order to provide a thorough evaluation, two separate datasets have been employed: The first is a challenging connected digit task, while the second is a more challenging *alpha-digit recognition* task.

8.2. Experiments with Digit Strings

The speech recognition experiments described in this section employ the fragments developed according to the novel procedures described in Chapters 6 and 7. In conjunction with the speech fragment decoding technique described in Chapter 3.

A set of monaurally mixed digit strings has been constructed for use in these experiments. Digit strings are taken from the clean utterances in the Aurora 2 corpus - test set A (Hirsch and Pearce, 2000). An end-point detection algorithm is used to remove the silences at the beginning and end of the speech files (Rabiner and Sambur, 1975). The 'de-silenced' files are approximately matched for length and artificially mixed in the time domain. The shorter of each pair is padded with zeros (equally at either end) to match the size of the longer signal. From these pairs, 1000 mixed utterances are chosen, with the average difference in length being 0.3%; only 35 pairs have a difference of greater than 1%. Of the 1000, 484 are mixtures of male and female speech; both speakers in the remaining mixtures are of the same gender. Using the same pairs of utterances, the mixing process is repeated for several target-to-masker ratios (TMRs); from -9 *dB* to 9 *dB* in 3 *dB* steps. The TMR is varied by altering the global signal-to-noise ratio (SNR) of one source (the masker) and keeping the global SNR of the other source (the target) constant.

The acoustic data were parameterised using an *auditory spectrogram* representation, which is very similar to the *ratemap* representation employed by Cooke (1993). The acoustic signal was passed through a bank of 64 gammatone filters (centre frequencies equally spaced on an ERB scale from 50 *Hz* to 3850 *Hz*) – this is the same filtering applied in the fragment generation process (see Chapter 4). The instantaneous Hilbert envelope of the filterbank output was smoothed using a first order filter with an 8 *ms* time constant. The smoothed envelope in each channel was then sampled at a 10 *ms* frame rate, producing 64-dimensional feature vectors. Cube root compression was then applied to the envelope values to approximately model the energy-to-loudness mapping of the ear. Finally, delta features were estimated, using a five-frame linear regression, and appended to the feature vector. Whole word, gender-dependent HMMs were trained using the clean speech data in the Aurora 2 training set (8440 utterances). The HMMs had 16 states in a left-to-right, no-skip topology. Each state was modelled with a mixture of seven Gaussian distributions with diagonal covariance matrices. A single-state silence model was constructed to model possible inter-digit pauses.

A baseline system was developed. HMMs with an identical topology were trained on 13 MFCC features (derived from the clean training data) along with their deltas and accelerations.

The parameters for the multi-pitch determination algorithm, voiced and unvoiced-speech segmentation were set to the values shown in Table 8.1. These values were set based on the evaluations performed in the previous chapters, as well as recognition experiments performed on a set of 10 mixtures produced from the training data and prepared as above. The parameters of the multiple-pitch tracker were set during development (see Chapter 5) and are not tuned further.

Table 8.1. Parameters used in the primitive segmentation stage and their values.

Parameter	Algorithm	Chapter	Value
θ_s	Multi-Pitch Determination	4	0.7
θ_a	Voiced-Speech Segmentation	6	0.8
E_γ	Unvoiced-Speech Segmentation	7	0.7

The section proceeds as follows: The statistical significance of recognition results is considered in Section 8.2.1.. Section 8.2.2. discusses the concept of the *a priori* fragments that play an important part in the evaluation process. The results of decoding with the SFD for *mixed-gender* utterances are given in Section 8.2.3. and the results for *matched-gender* utterances in Section 8.2.4.. The digit experiments are concluded with an interim discussion in Section 8.2.5., which raises issues that are further addressed by the alpha-digit experiments that follow.

8.2.1. Statistical Significance

One important issue to consider when comparing the recognition performance of different systems is the significance of the difference in recognition accuracies. Without an analysis of statistical significance it is difficult to know whether performance differences (usually measured in terms of differences in word error rate) are meaningful. While a number of suggestions have been made (see Gillick and Cox, 1989; Strik et al., 2001, for examples) there remains the challenge of determining which significance test is most appropriate for this task.

The test employed for this work is a 'Matched Pairs Test' suggested by Gillick and Cox (1989) (also referred to by Pallet et al. (1990) as the *Matched Pairs Sentence-Segment Word Error* test). The test is a parametric test that compares the numbers of errors made by two models. The errors can be calculated from segments of different sizes, with the single (and quite important) requirement that the segments chosen should be independent. This allows the use of an entire utterance as a segment. Given a large number of utterances, the central limit theorem suggests that the number of errors are, approximately, normally distributed. This test is essentially a t-test for estimating the mean difference of normal distributions with unknown variances. Significance is judged at the $p = 0.05$ level.

8.2.2. *A priori* Fragments

With access to the unmixed target and masker signals it is possible to segment the mixture into a set of fragments that are totally coherent, referred to as *a priori fragments*. Experiments using such fragments provide an approximate upper bound on the performance that can be expected from a high quality fragment generation process. *A priori* results also help to establish which part of the system is responsible for the majority of errors: the fragment generation process or the top-down model matching. *A priori* fragments are developed by comparing the time-frequency representations of the mixed and unmixed signals. For example, consider a two source mixture: the spectro-temporal regions of *source1* that, in the mixture, are observed to be undisturbed by *source2*, can be assigned to *source1*, and vice versa.[26] This step segments the mixture into two *a priori* masks, representing, separately, the regions dominated by *source1* and *source2*. The mask for each source is then segmented into a number of fragments. Here, this is performed by segmenting the masks at time frames corresponding to energy minima in the corresponding source's signal. Any segmentation of the *a priori* mask will produce a set of coherent fragments; this method is chosen in an attempt to model the fragments that might be produced by a robust, signal-driven segmentation process. The approximately, syllable-sized sets of fragments generated for *source1* and *source2* are then combined to form a common set.

8.2.3. Mixed-Gender Mixtures

In the mixed-gender condition the data are prepared in such a way as to make each gender's digit sequence first the target and then the masker. Thus two signals are created from each mixed signal, one where the male is target and the other where the female is target. Recall that the SNR of the target is held constant. In order to compute a recognition score for the female source, the mixture in which the female is the target, is decoded using female gender-dependent models. Decoding the mixture, where the male is target, using male gender-dependent models allows a recognition score to be computed for the male source. Top-down information in the HMM models drives the selection of the appropriate fragments (see Chapter 3).

Voiced Fragments

The first recognition experiments measure the performance achieved using fragments derived solely from the voiced regions of the mixed signal. To measure the performance of

---

[26]For the purpose of creating the masks, a source is considered to be 'undisturbed' if it has a signal-to-noise ratio which is 3 dB greater than the competing source. The value of 3 dB follows the work of Cooke et al. (2001a); however, other values, such as 0 dB have been used (see Roman et al., 2001, for example).

the system with voiced fragments alone, the influence of the unvoiced regions is removed through the process of marginalisation (Cooke et al., 2001b). The probability distributions are marginalised by integrating over all possible values of the unvoiced energy when computing the state likelihoods of the hidden Markov models. This is equivalent to treating the unvoiced regions as missing data with no *bounds constraint* (see Section 2.4.3.).

The results are shown in Figure 8.1 as well as Tables 8.2 and 8.3. Overall, the SFD using voiced fragments, outperforms the baseline decoder using MFCC features for the majority of TMRs. At $-9\ dB$ there is an absolute improvement of 15% over the baseline, while at 9 dB the baseline outperforms the SFD by 1%. On average, across TMR, there is an 8% improvement over the baseline system. Significance testing reveals that the SFD significantly outperformed the baseline system for the female component of the mixture at all TMRs, while for the male component the SFD was only significantly better at $-9\ dB$.

Table 8.2. Results for the mixed-gender condition using voiced fragments only, for a range of TMR. Accuracies significantly better than the baseline are highlighted.

	-9 dB	-6 dB	-3 dB	0 dB	3 dB	6 dB	9 dB	Average
Female	**54**	**60**	**67**	**72**	**75**	**80**	**84**	71
Male	**32**	38	46	55	65	72	80	55
Overall	43	49	57	64	70	76	82	63

Table 8.3. Results for the mixed-gender condition using baseline MFCC-based system. Accuracies significantly better than the SFD are highlighted.

	-9 dB	-6 dB	-3 dB	0 dB	3 dB	6 dB	9 dB	Average
Female	28	35	44	52	62	72	81	53
Male	28	36	47	58	**68**	**79**	**86**	57
Overall	28	35	46	55	65	75	83	55

Performance for the female component of the mixture is significantly higher than that for the male, especially at lower TMRs. This pattern is contrasted to that of the baseline system, where the results for the male speakers are better at high TMR values. Panel a of Figure 8.1 shows that the male utterances are actually recognised with greater accuracy by the baseline system. This is highly unusual, as the male and female fragments have similar average coherence (higher for the male utterances) and size. It may be that the female utterances are obscuring regions of the male utterance that are required for schema-based grouping and recognition. Further study is required to identify the cause of this effect.

The fact that the voiced regions of the mixtures can provide significant performance increase over the baseline is possibly indicative of the nature of the data. The majority of the digits have significant, and distinctive, vowel centres which allow the SFD to recognise them against the background speech. In the following section the unvoiced fragments are incorporated to test whether there is any benefit (in terms of speech recognition accuracy) to including them.

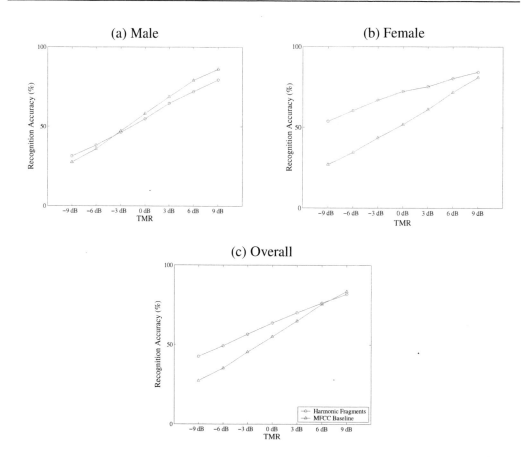

Figure 8.1. Comparison of the baseline decoder and the SFD using voiced fragments.

Combining Voiced and Unvoiced Fragments

In the next experiment, both voiced and unvoiced fragments are employed. The procedure is the same as in the previous experiment, except that the marginalisation, used to remove the effect of the unvoiced fragments, is not performed. Though the majority of speech energy is contained in voiced speech, the extra information in the unvoiced regions has been shown to increase the accuracy of automatic speech recognition systems; even for small-vocabulary tasks (Coy and Barker, 2005). Results for the combined fragments are presented in Table 8.4, while Tables 8.5 and 8.6 present results for the *a priori* fragments and *a priori* masks, respectively. The *a priori* mask results are obtained using a standard missing data decoder. The average overall recognition results show a further absolute improvement of 5% over the results for voiced-only fragments, i.e., an absolute increase of 13%, across TMR, over the baseline system. It should be noted that the performance gain achieved by the SFD is greater at lower TMRs. For negative TMRs the average improvement is 17%, whereas the average improvement at positive TMRs is 8%. At 0 *dB* an improvement of 14% is recorded. As with the voiced-only fragments, the recognition accuracy is higher for female speech at low TMR. Recognition accuracy for the female source with the combined fragments is very similar to that of the *a priori* fragments. This is also seen for the *a priori* fragments (at

−9 *dB* and −6 *dB*, after which the male source dominates) suggesting it may be more to do with the models than the fragments themselves. The overall pattern of improvements is not unexpected, as the baseline system is known to be able to achieve high recognition accuracy with favourable TMR, given the efficiency and power of the MFCC representation in noise-free environments. When the noise levels increase, however, the SFD has the advantage. At lower TMRs, the increasing level of the competing source is reflected in the MFCC by a smearing of the interference across all the cepstral features. This contributes to the reduction in performance. The SFD, on the other hand, is provided with a set of fragments that are largely free from the masking effect of the competing source. Where this is not the case, the confidence map provides a measure of the competing source's impact, which offers the SFD the opportunity of rejecting a 'corrupted' fragment. These factors contribute to the improved performance at low TMR and the robustness of the SFD framework.

Table 8.4. Results for the mixed-gender condition with unvoiced and voiced fragments combined. Percentage accuracy is shown for a range of TMR values. Accuracies that are significantly better than those for the SFD using voiced fragments only are highlighted.

	-9 dB	-6 dB	-3 dB	0 dB	3 dB	6 dB	9 dB	Average
Female	54	60	68	72	**77**	**84**	**89**	72
Male	**39**	**45**	**56**	**66**	75	83	89	65
Overall	46	53	62	69	76	83	89	68

Table 8.5. Results for the mixed-gender condition with *a priori* fragments. Percentage accuracy is shown for a range of TMR values. Accuracies that are significantly better than those for the SFD using both voiced and unvoiced fragments are highlighted.

	-9 dB	-6 dB	-3 dB	0 dB	3 dB	6 dB	9 dB	Average
Female	**59**	62	66	72	**80**	85	**90**	73
Male	38	**52**	**67**	**79**	**87**	**91**	93	72
Overall	48	57	66	75	84	88	91	73

Given that the combined fragments provide a complete description of the utterances, the combined fragment result (Table 8.4 and Figure 8.2 c) is more directly comparable to that achieved with the *a priori* fragments (Table 8.5 and Figure 8.2 c) than is the result obtained using the voiced-only fragments which offer only a partial description. The difference between the combined fragment result and the *a priori* result is presumed to be largely due to the difference in coherence, and size, of the two types of fragment. Overall, the *a priori* fragments outperform the combined fragments by 5% with only 1% difference between the average accuracy at positive and negative TMR values (5% and 4%, respectively). This is a testament to the quality of the fragments formed from the speech segmentation process, as the *a priori* fragments are fully coherent (i.e., they are free from all interference)

Table 8.6. Results for the mixed-gender condition with *a priori* masks. Percentage accuracy is shown for a range of TMR values. Accuracies that are significantly better than those for the SFD using *a priori* fragments are highlighted.

	-9 dB	-6 dB	-3 dB	0 dB	3 dB	6 dB	9 dB	Average
Female	**72**	**79**	**84**	**89**	**92**	**94**	**95**	86
Male	**77**	**84**	**88**	**91**	**94**	**95**	**97**	89
Overall	75	81	86	90	93	95	96	88

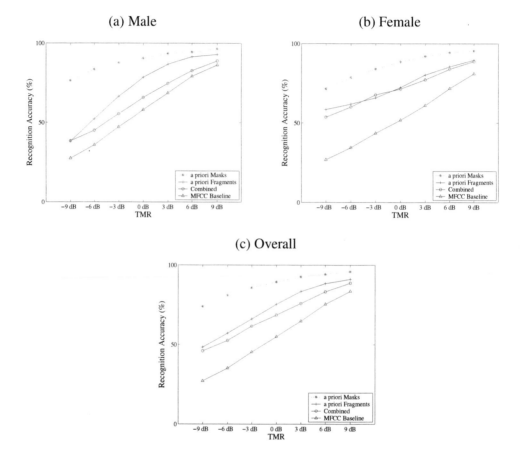

Figure 8.2. Comparison of performance for the baseline MFCC decoder and the SFD, decoding separately, *a priori* fragments and combined fragments.

and the recognition results shown above for these fragments are those that can be achieved with an 'ideal' set of fragments. It is important to note that the *a priori* fragments used in these experiments are only ideal in the sense that there is no intrusion from the competing source; there is no suggestion that these are the best performing fragments that can be derived. The fact that the signals are overlapping means that some regions of each signal will be occluded. Thresholds are used to determine how occluded a spectro-temporal pixel must be before it is excluded from the fragment (see Section 8.2.2.). As different thresholds can be employed, it might be possible, with tuning, to find a threshold that could improve the results for the *a priori* fragments. The *a priori* mask result shows the result that could be achieved if both primitive and schema-driven grouping is error free. The *a priori* mask result gives a 15% improvement (averaged across TMR) over the *a priori* fragments, with the majority of the improvement seen at lower TMR values, where the target is more effectively masked. These results indicate that there is room for improving both the primitive segmentation (for example, through more robust pitch tracking) and the schema-driven segmentation (possibly through better acoustic modelling).

8.2.4. Matched-Gender Mixtures

Experiments involving mixtures of utterances from speakers of the same gender require a different protocol to that used in the experiments of Section 8.2.3.. When the sources in a mixture are of different genders, the selection of the target source can be made by the choice of gender-dependent model (i.e. either male or female). When the two sources are of the same gender, another mechanism is needed to inform the decoder of the identity of the target source. Without instruction, the decoder could arbitrarily return the result for decoding either of the two sources. This would make evaluation problematic. The solution chosen is to provide the decoder with the first few words of the target utterance as a 'key' by which to uniquely identify the target utterance. The decoder is then tasked with returning the remaining words in the utterance. This is an unambiguous task which can also be performed by human listeners, albeit with some difficulty, especially at 0 *dB* (see Section 8.4.). In the following experiment the first two digits of the target utterance are chosen as the key. The key is presented to the decoder through the use of a grammar that describes the target utterance as the key sequence followed by an unknown digit string of unspecified length. Before scoring the result, the key sequence is removed from the start of both the decoder output and the transcripts. This prevents the keys words, which are always recognised correctly, from artificially increasing the recognition score. Male plus male mixtures have been employed.

Some special conditions are required to make the task reasonable: Mixtures of two utterances by the same speaker are not permitted. The target and masker utterance cannot have the same first two digits (otherwise the key would not uniquely identify the target). Target strings are all at least four digits long (since the identity of the first two digits are made known in advance). Given the amount of data in Aurora's *test set A* and the need to match utterances for length, the above conditions reduce the number of usable mixtures to 101. Note that both sequences in the mixture can be alternately considered to be the target simply by changing the key. This effectively creates 202 targets, of which one sequence is omitted from the analysis because the masker was only three digits long. As it has been established (in Section 8.2.3.) that the use of both voiced and unvoiced fragments leads to improved recognition performance, all experiments are performed with the combined fragment set.

Mixed-Gender Recognition with the Reduced Dataset

For comparison, the mixed-gender experiment (Section 8.2.3.) is repeated, but this time using the key sequence methodology. Using the same restrictions on allowable mixtures, a mixed-gender test set containing 199 male targets is constructed. The results are shown in Table 8.7 and Figure 8.3.

Table 8.7. Percentage accuracy for a range of TMR values in the mixed-gender condition using the reduced dataset. A comparison can be made for different sets of features: MFCC, combined fragments, *a priori* fragments and *a priori* masks. Significance testing confirm that the *a priori* masks outperform the *a priori* fragments which outperform the combined fragments, which in turn outperform the baseline system.

	-9 dB	-6 dB	-3 dB	0 dB	3 dB	6 dB	9 dB	Average
MFCC	21	31	44	57	70	79	87	56
Combined	**33**	**43**	**55**	**66**	**75**	**84**	**90**	64
a priori Fragments	**35**	**49**	**63**	**75**	**86**	**91**	**93**	70
a priori Masks	**77**	**84**	**88**	**91**	**94**	**95**	**97**	89

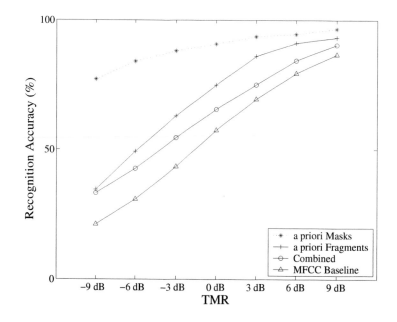

Figure 8.3. Percentage accuracy for a range of TMR values in the mixed-gender condition using the reduced dataset.

Figure 8.3 shows a similar pattern to Figure 8.2 (a), where, in order of increasing accuracy, the performance of the baseline, combined fragments, *a priori* fragments and *a priori* masks are displayed for mixed-gender utterances with the male source as the target. All the differences are statistically significant. The combined fragments give an 8% increase over the baseline, while the *a priori* fragments give a 14% increase over the baseline. While the difference, averaged across TMR, between the performance of the combined and *a priori* fragments is 6%, it is interesting to note that the difference at $-9\ dB$ is approximately 2%

and at 9 *dB* the difference is 3%. This suggests that the two fragment types are most similar at the extremes of the range of TMRs tested.

Matched-Gender Recognition

Figure 8.4 and Table 8.8 show the recognition accuracies for *a priori* masks, combined and *a priori* fragments, as well as the baseline features. Combined fragments outperform the baseline system by (on average) 6.5%. The performance is consistent across TMR, with a slightly wider gap at negative TMR. While the performance relative to the baseline suggests that there is some benefit to using the SFD framework for recognising speech with interfering speakers, the actual recognition accuracy at negative TMR falls below the levels that might be expected, given the performance on mixed-gender utterances.

Table 8.8. Percentage accuracy for a range of TMR values in the matched-gender condition. A comparison can be made for different sets of features: *a priori* masks, *a priori* fragments, MFCC, and Combined fragments. Figures in bold type highlight where each set significantly outperforms the previous one: MFCC is compared to Combined, *a priori* fragments are compared to Combined and *a priori* masks are compared to *a priori* fragments.

	-9 dB	-6 dB	-3 dB	0 dB	3 dB	6 dB	9 dB	Average
MFCC	5	14	25	38	50	64	75	39
Combined	**17**	**22**	**32**	**43**	**54**	**70**	**80**	45
a priori Fragments	5	10	26	44	**63**	**78**	**85**	45
a priori Masks	**69**	**79**	**83**	**89**	**91**	**93**	**95**	86

The pattern appears to be as a result of informational masking effects, i.e., errors that occur in fragment labelling, due to the similarity of target and masker fragments, with respect to the models. In the mixed-gender case, the models for the target source match more readily to the target fragments than to the fragments of the masker. This is not so in the matched-gender case; here the models match just as readily to the masker's fragments as they would to the target's. This acts as an extra source of error and leads to the relatively poor performance at lower TMRs.

Recognition accuracies for the SFD using *a priori* fragments show an intriguing pattern (Figure 8.4). It is expected that these fragments, being perfectly coherent, should provide the decoder with a clear description of the target sequence, which should lead to a performance gain over the combined fragments, as is the case with the mixed-gender fragments. This, however, only holds at positive TMRs. For positive TMRs recognition accuracy for *a priori* fragments is better than combined fragments by an average of 10%. At negative TMRs the pattern is reversed, with combined fragments leading to an average of 8% better recognition accuracy. It would seem that 0 *dB* is a turning point for the performance of the *a priori* fragments, for it is at that level of masker interference that the recognition accuracy begins to dip below that of combined fragments. At the lowest TMRs, −6 *dB* and −9 *dB*, decoding with *a priori* fragments leads to worse performance than the baseline system, this

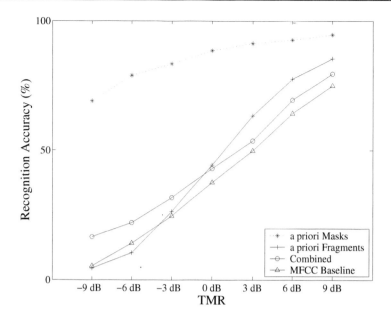

Figure 8.4. Percentage accuracy for a range of TMR values in the matched-gender condition.

is highly unusual. The quality of the fragments that the SFD uses for decoding is critical to its performance; the better the fragment, the better the performance. The results seem anomalous, in light of the fact that the *a priori* fragments are of the highest quality. However, the pattern of results can also be explained by informational masking. Informational masking effects can occur irrespective of the quality of the fragments employed. If there is little evidence to discriminate the target and masker's fragments, then informational masking effects will dominate. It could be that the technique used to segment the *a priori* masks, in the formation of fragments, led to the removal of much of the constraint (such as the temporal continuity) that existed. Again, the *a priori* mask results show what is achievable.

Recognition of the Interfering Sequence

It is entirely possible that the SFD is choosing the fragments that represent the digit sequence of the interfering source. If this is in fact the case, then it would suggest that the SFD is making, what might be considered to be 'reasonable' errors. In order to test this hypothesis, the output of the SFD, for combined and *a priori* fragments is scored against the transcription of the interfering source. For comparison, this is also done for the baseline system. Table 8.9 shows the outcome of the re-scoring procedure.

At negative TMRs, what is immediately obvious is that the decoders (including the baseline decoder) are recognising the interference more often than the target. As the target level is increased, the target is recognised more often than the masker, although interestingly, the MFCC-based decoder has similar performance across TMR. The anomaly noted in Figure 8.4 is explained by analysing Figure 8.5. At negative TMRs, the SFD performs poorly using *a priori* fragments, because it is tracking the interfering source. In fact, it seems that the SFD is choosing the masker's fragments almost exclusively at −9 *dB*.

Table 8.9. Percentage accuracy for a range of TMR values in the matched-gender condition, where the output of the decoding process is scored against the transcription of the interfering digit sequence.

	-9 dB	-6 dB	-3 dB	0 dB	3 dB	6 dB	9 dB	Average
MFCC	40	38	38	37	38	38	40	38
Combined	55	49	44	37	30	22	15	36
a priori Fragments	67	64	50	38	26	15	12	39

(a) MFCC   (b) *A priori* Fragments

(c) Combined Fragments

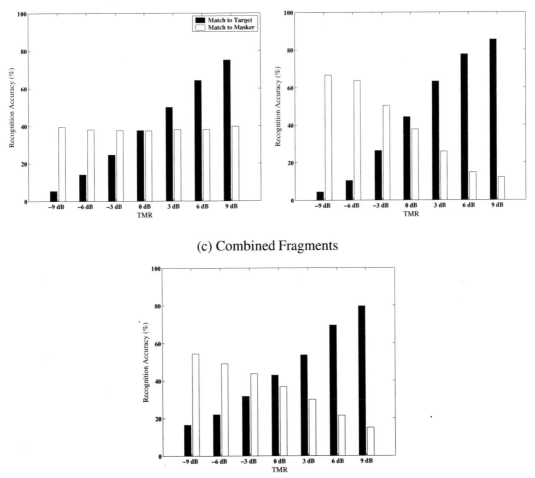

Figure 8.5. Histogram pairs showing the recognition accuracy for all decoder outputs scored first, against the transcription of the target; and then against the transcription of the masker.

Recognition accuracy for the masker is best for the *a priori* fragments. This is made more clear by Figure 8.6. The accuracies shown in the figure are obtained by taking the higher of the two: the decoder output scored against the target transcription, or the decoder output scored against the maker's transcription.

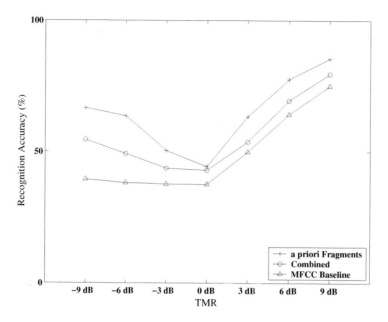

Figure 8.6. Recognition accuracy for matched-gender mixtures. The accuracy shown is the higher of the recognition scores for the decoder's output matched, alternately, against the masker and target transcriptions. Accuracy does not fall steadily with TMR, as in Figure 8.4, but actually increases below 0 *dB*. At negative TMR, the SFD is recognising the masker's utterance more frequently than it does the target's.

The result is a combination of the accuracies from Tables 8.8 and 8.9: At negative TMR values, the masker is recognised more often than the target, while at positive TMRs the target is recognised more often. Recall that the decoder has no access to speaker differences, thus the only cues available for correct fragment labelling come from level differences and within-word continuities. This pattern holds for the baseline decoder as well as the SFD. When the accuracies at negative TMR values are compared it is seen that the decoding employing *a priori* fragments had the largest increase: 58%, more than twice the increase for the baseline system (25%) – while the combined-fragment decoding accuracy improved by 45%. Thus, the *a priori* fragments yield the highest accuracy; re-affirming the link between fragment coherence and recognition accuracy.

8.2.5.   Interim Discussion I

Mixed-Gender Mixtures

For the voiced-only fragments, it is encouraging to see that the accuracy exceeds that of the baseline system at most TMR values. This suggests that the voiced portion of the individual signals of this dataset are enough to provide good performance especially at lower TMR values. As TMR becomes high, the advantage is erased as the target becomes more dominant and the baseline·system then gains access to the unmasked target.

The addition of unvoiced fragments leads to a significant improvement, especially at low TMR, providing justification for including them – the unvoiced energy of speech is often overlooked in source segmentation algorithms. These results suggest that more attention should be paid to segmenting unvoiced speech (especially in systems with speech recognition as the final goal) as it can contribute to the improvement in recognition accuracy. This may be even more important for tasks with larger vocabularies, where unvoiced consonant discrimination plays a greater role. The *a priori* fragment result shows that there is further work to be done in the fragment generation stage.

Matched-Gender Mixtures

In order to trace the source of the unexpected SFD performance in the matched-gender experiments, one must first recall that the experiments employed gender-dependent, but speaker-independent, models of speech (see Section 8.2.4.). It should further be recalled that the grammar used allowed an arbitrary sequence of digits. The use of the key-sequence methodology is meant to give the decoder a hint, in the absence of speaker-dependent models, as to the target speaker's first words and thus, reduce the possibility that the decoder would select fragments corresponding to the interfering source. This potential for the selection of the interferer's fragments is legitimate. The use of gender-dependent models to decode matched-gender utterances does not provide the same advantage that it does with mixed-gender utterances, owing to the fact that there is no way to distinguish the target from the interference. Had there been speaker-dependent models available[27] the key-sequence methodology would have provided the decoder with a measure of the target speakers' spectral characteristics, which would aid it in recruiting the 'correct' fragments. However, the gender-dependent HMMs are insensitive to the spectral characteristics of individual fragments that would differentiate speakers, so the key-sequence approach did not provide them with any incentive to choose the target's fragments. This is akin to the same-speaker case for human listeners, where there is little evidence that allows the listener to segment the two messages spoken by the same speaker. Whereas listeners can employ cues such as co-articulation, speaker identity and pitch continuity to group related words in the message, the models employed in the SFD do not model such effects and thus cannot use these cues.

8.3.   Experiments with Sentence-length Utterances

The experiments in this section are motivated by the fact that the corpus used for testing allows for the use of speaker-dependent models, which should address some of the difficulties faced by the decoder, especially in the matched-gender condition. The other motivating factor relates to the signal-driven segmentation system, which is developed with data from the Aurora digit corpus. By employing it to segment data from a different corpus, the following experiments serve as a rigorous test of the system's generality. Overall, the task is much more challenging than the digit task and should be a good test of the proposed decoding framework.

---

[27]The Aurora 2 database did not have enough utterances per speaker to produce useful speaker-dependent models. Experiments (not reported) showed that adaptation was also infeasible.

Experiments are performed using simultaneous speech data constructed from the GRID corpus (Cooke et al., 2006) in accordance with the rules of the Pascal Speech Separation Challenge.[28] The GRID corpus consists of utterances spoken by 34 native English speakers, including 18 male speakers and 16 female speakers. The utterances are monaurally mixed, short sentences of the form: *<command:4> <colour:4> <preposition:4> <letter:25> <number:10> <adverb:4>*, as indicated in Table 8.10, e.g. 'place white at p 4 now'. The test set consists of 600 pairs of end-pointed utterances which have been artificially added at a range of TMRs. In the test set there are 200 pairs in which target and masker are the same speaker; 200 pairs of the same gender (but different speakers); and 200 pairs of mixed-genders. The 'colour' for the target utterance is always 'white', while the 'colour' of the masking utterance is never 'white'. The task is to recognise the digit and letter spoken by the target.

Table 8.10. Structure of the sentences in the GRID corpus.

VERB	COLOUR	PREP.	LETTER	DIGIT	ADVERB
bin	blue	at	a-z	1-9	again
lay	green	by	(no 'w')	and zero	now
place	red	on			please
set	white	with			soon

8.3.1. Experimental Setup

The same representation is used as in the previous experiments, i.e., a 64-channel 'auditory spectrogram' represented by 128-dimensional feature vectors consisting of 64 energy terms and 64 delta terms. Speaker-dependent word-level HMMs are trained using 500 utterances from each of the 34 Grid speakers. Each word is modelled using a rule of 2 states per phone in a left-to-right model topology with no skips, and with 7 diagonal-covariance Gaussian mixture components per state.

The recogniser employs a grammar representing all allowable grid utterances in which the colour spoken is 'white'. In all experiments it is assumed that the target speaker is one of the speakers encountered in the training set, but two different configurations are employed: i) 'known speaker' - the utterance is decoded using the HMMs corresponding to the target speaker, ii) 'unknown speaker' - the utterance is decoded using HMMs corresponding to each of the 34 speakers and the overall best scoring hypothesis is selected (this can be implemented as an extended grammar in which 34 speaker-dependent grammars are placed in parallel).

A simple adaptive beam-pruning algorithm is employed to reduce the computational cost of decoding the 'unknown speaker' configuration. The algorithm adapted the beam to prune a fixed percentage of partial hypotheses at each time frame. A small development set of 150 mixtures at 0 *dB* is used to select the target percentage of hypotheses to prune. It

[28]http://www.dcs.shef.ac.uk/~martin/SpeechSeparationChallenge.html

was found that this target can be raised to 90% without significant impact on the recognition result, and with a resulting reduction in decoding time of over 75% (Barker et al., 2006).

Results are also obtained for a conventional HMM system using models with an identical topology trained on 13 MFCC features along with their deltas and accelerations. These baseline results are obtained from testing the system using speaker-independent (SI) HMMs employing 32 mixtures per state and trained using the combined training data from all 34 Grid speakers.[29]

The statistical significance of the differences in recognition accuracy for each system is tested using the method described in Section 8.2.1..

8.3.2. Results

The results of the experiments are given in Tables 8.11, 8.12, 8.13, 8.14, as well as Figure 8.7; recognition accuracies represent the percentage of the total number of letter and digit tokens that are recognised correctly. The overall results (Figure 8.7 (a)) show that the SFD gives a higher recognition accuracy than the baseline system across TMR, in both configurations – bold type in the Tables 8.11, 8.12, 8.13 and 8.14 indicate where the performance differences are statistically significant. The benefit is most clearly seen at TMRs below −3 *dB*. The advantage of knowing the identity of the target speaker is manifest in the difference in average recognition accuracy for the two configurations of the SFD; 62% and 42% for the known- and unknown-speaker configurations, respectively. This advantage is virtually erased at 6 *dB*, where the target utterance is highly dominant. For the known-speaker configuration, the decoder's performance decreases steadily with decreasing TMR, while the pattern for the unknown-speaker configuration is somewhat unusual. The accuracy falls as TMR decreases to −3 *dB* and then rises again as TMR decreases further. A more detailed analysis of the individual masker conditions may provide more information about the overall pattern of results.

Table 8.11. Results for the baseline system. All speaker configurations are shown: same speaker (SS), same gender (SG) and mixed-gender (DG). The overall score is also given.

	-9 dB	-6 dB	-3 dB	0 dB	3 dB	6 dB	Average
SS	6	10	18	30	46	62	34
SG	7	15	21	33	44	64	31
DG	8	12	20	34	47	64	31
Overall	7	12	19	32	46	64	30

In the same speaker condition both configurations of the SFD provide only a small, but significant, improvement over the baseline system for all TMR values. As TMR becomes negative, a wider performance gap opens between the baseline system and the SFD. The baseline performance continues to fall off, while that of the SFD begins to increase below

---

[29]This is not a truly speaker-independent system, as the target speaker is represented in the training data.

Table 8.12. Results for the SFD in the unknown-speaker configuration. All speaker configurations are shown: same speaker (SS), matched-gender (SG) and mixed-gender (DG). The overall score is also given. Bold type highlights where the SFD, in the unknown-speaker configuration, significantly ($p < 0.05$) outperforms the baseline.

	-9 dB	-6 dB	-3 dB	0 dB	3 dB	6 dB	Average
SS	**38**	**37**	**34**	**37**	**54**	**73**	46
SG	**43**	**42**	**37**	**47**	**70**	**79**	53
DG	**39**	**40**	**38**	**42**	**73**	**80**	52
Overall	40	40	36	42	66	77	50

Table 8.13. Results for the SFD in the known-speaker configuration. All speaker configurations are shown: same speaker (SS), same gender (SG) and mixed-gender (DG). The overall score is also given. Results are highlighted, where the known-speaker configuration performs significantly better ($p < 0.05$) than the unknown-speaker configuration.

	-9 dB	-6 dB	-3 dB	0 dB	3 dB	6 dB	Average
SS	39	37	34	37	55	74	46
SG	**49**	**56**	**65**	**72**	**77**	80	66
DG	**54**	**63**	**70**	**76**	**79**	81	71
Overall	47	52	56	62	70	78	61

Table 8.14. Results for a missing data decoder using *a priori* masks and speaker-independent models. All speaker configurations are shown: same speaker (SS), same gender (SG) and mixed-gender (DG). The overall score is also given. Accuracies which are significantly better ($p < 0.05$) than the known-speaker configuration are highlighted.

	-9 dB	-6 dB	-3 dB	0 dB	3 dB	6 dB	Average
SS	**70**	**81**	**86**	**88**	**91**	**91**	84
SG	**78**	**87**	**91**	**93**	**93**	**93**	89
DG	**83**	**89**	**92**	**92**	**91**	**92**	90
Overall	76	85	89	91	92	92	88

-3 *dB*. This might be attributable to a sharp reduction in informational masking that outweighs the effects of the increase in energetic masking that accompanies a decrease in TMR (Brungart, 2001); this is further explored in Section 8.3.3..

The recognition performance of the SFD is virtually identical for both configurations, suggesting that prior knowledge of the target speakers' identity is not an advantage in this

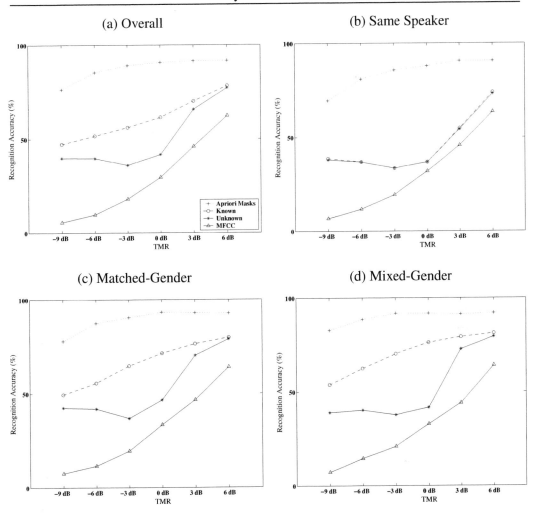

Figure 8.7. Results for the speech fragment decoder compared against the baseline system. The SFD results are shown separately for the known- and unknown-speaker configurations.

condition. It must be noted that this does not imply that the SFD is doing well in the unknown-speaker condition, on the contrary, it is doing poorly. What is happening is that the SFD, in the known-speaker configuration, is performing as poorly as it does in the unknown-speaker condition.

For the matched-gender condition, the SFD outperforms the baseline system at all TMRs and for both configurations. In the unknown-speaker configuration, recognition accuracy decreases as TMR does, until TMR reaches $-3\ dB$, where accuracy begins to rise again.

In this condition the pattern of results for the different configurations are markedly different. At $6\ dB$ the accuracies are the same, however, the similarity ends there. While the recognition performance in the known-speaker condition is better than the unknown-speaker configuration, it decreases monotonically as TMR moves from positive to negative.

The pattern of mixed gender results is similar to that obtained in the matched-gender condition, in that the known-speaker configuration outperforms the unknown-speaker configuration, which in turn outperforms the baseline. The known-speaker results show an average improvement of 19%, across TMR, over the unknown-speaker configuration. For the unknown-speaker condition, there is a sharp decrease in accuracy at 0 *dB* which is likely due to the combination of informational and energetic masking. It does however, show an average improvement of 20% over the baseline system.

The performance of the missing data system using *a priori* masks falls off smoothly with decreasing TMR and is similar in pattern and actual accuracy across condition.

8.3.3.   Interim Discussion II

The results of the alpha-digit task provide several points worthy of discussion. Before examining any of these issues, it is important to recall that the experiments are performed on an unseen dataset (i.e., the parameters employed in the primitive segmentation stage are trained on a separate dataset and are not re-tuned for this task). This is indicative of the robustness of the segmentation process employed to generate fragments for the SFD.

The results presented have been shown to be subject to both *informational masking* and *energetic masking*, These terms have not been discussed in detail. As both are central to the discussion of the results of the SFD, some time is spent in extending the definitions already presented.

When asked to segment and identify speech that is monaurally mixed with a competing speech source, listeners find it more challenging to do so as the signal level of the masker is increased. As the target moves from being the overall dominant sound in the mixture, there are fewer regions where the target energy exceeds that of the masker, rendering the target less intelligible as TMR decreases. This process is often referred to as *energetic masking* (Kidd et al., 1994). In the event that energetic masking is working in isolation, the expected impact on the recognition would be a steady, monotonic, decrease in accuracy for recognition of the target sequence as TMR decreases (Brungart, 2001). It has been shown, however that at TMR values around 0 *dB*, there is a greater than expected decrease in target intelligibility that cannot be accounted for by energetic masking alone (Brungart, 2001; Brungart et al., 2001).

If the acoustic evidence of the target source is not completely concealed by a more energetic masker, the task remains of disambiguating the glimpses of acoustic energy that emerge from the mixture (i.e., to decide which source produced it). The uncertainty as to the origin of acoustic energy is referred to as *informational masking* (Pollack, 1975; Leek et al., 1991). Informational masking is also related to TMR, but in a different way; it is a function of the listeners ability to distinguish one source from the other when they are both audible. Thus, informational masking effects are greatest when TMR is close to 0 *dB*. The combination of these two effects has been shown to account for the majority of errors that listeners make in intelligibility tests (Brungart, 2001).

As the SFD has been put forward as a recognition system inspired by models of perception, it is expected that the recognition scores should model these effects. The discussion to follow seeks, among other things, to identify where these two processes combine to influence the pattern of results (see Barker et al., 2006; Shao and Barker, 2007, for discussions of the interplay between informational and energetic masking in the SFD). Section 8.4. considers the extent to which the performance, on the alpha-digit task, of the SFD mirrors that of listeners.

Same Speaker Condition

In the same-speaker condition the cues that could be used to distinguish the messages from each talker in the mixture are mostly absent. The talkers have the same range of fundamental frequency, making segmentation particularly difficult. The combination of energetic and informational masking can be seen in the performance below 3 dB. The sharp dip in performance at 0 dB is unlikely to be due solely to energetic masking; this is confirmed by the small increase at lower TMRs. The interaction of masking effects is partially responsible for the lack of improvement over the baseline at positive TMRs; the rest of the responsibility lies with the segmentation algorithm. The lack of distinguishing features between the two voices will likely have a detrimental effect on the segmentation algorithm, possibly leading to the production of poor quality fragments. The effects of energetic masking at high TMR is possibly exacerbated by having both masker and target utterances spoken by the same person.

Matched-Gender Condition

The matched-gender condition is similar to the same-speaker condition; both speakers are likely to have a very similar range of fundamental frequency, making segmentation more challenging. The differences in the individual speakers' acoustic output seem to be sufficient to provide a better recognition performance than in the same-speaker condition (7% for the unknown-speaker configuration and 21% for the known-speaker configuration, averaged across TMR). This can be related to less energetic masking, as spectral peaks for different speakers will not overlap as much as those for the same-speaker, leading to a greater ease of segmentation. The impact of informational masking is also seen in this condition, which has a similar pattern of results to the same-speaker condition: a sharp fall at 0 dB and an increase after -3 dB.

The larger increase in the recognition performance for the known-speaker configuration is evidence of the benefit derived by the decoder from the difference in speaker characteristics. The SFD, for this decoder configuration and mixture condition, is not subject to the effects of informational masking. This is confirmed by the lack of the characteristic dip in performance at 0 dB. The fragments belonging to the target will fit well to the models of the target, thus reducing the potential for confusing the messages of the different speakers.

Comparing the matched-gender performance in this task with the performance on the digit task (Section 8.2.4.) the benefit of employing speaker-dependent models can clearly be seen. With speaker-dependent models, it is less likely that the recognition accuracy will decrease significantly due to the erroneous recognition of the masker.

Mixed-Gender Condition

The segmentation of mixed-gender utterances is aided by the differences in speaker characteristics, especially the difference in male and female fundamental frequency ranges. This should be reflected in the recognition scores of the decoder. However, for the unknown-speaker configuration averaged across TMR, the performance was worse, by 1%, than the matched-gender condition. This is mainly due to a sharper falloff in recognition accuracy between 3 *dB* and 0 *dB*. Given that energetic masking is likely to be higher in the matched-gender case, it is reasonable to attribute this effect to informational masking. The pitch differences that mark the utterances as different cannot be exploited by the decoder itself, as the auditory representation employed is not sensitive to pitch. The acoustic models are thus, immune to the variability caused by changes in pitch. This makes for a robust decoder, but it also makes segmentation more difficult. Thus, the decoder is at times susceptible to confusions in source assignment. Pitch is used in the fragment-forming stage of the system, however, it is not used explicitly to group fragments through time. This level of sequential grouping is achieved by the decoder as it decides which fragments can be unambiguously grouped by scoring each fragment with the HMMs of the various speakers. It is possible that better pitch-based grouping could improve the results.

The results in the known-speaker configuration for the mixed-gender condition are, on average, 4% better than the matched-gender results.

8.4. Comparison with Human Performance

The SFD has been tested with two separate speech recognition tasks and has been shown to be able to outperform a standard ASR system. This is the major goal of the proposed system: to achieve a robust performance in noisy conditions. However, there is a secondary objective, which is to see how well the pattern of ASR results from the SFD matches to the pattern of results achieved by human speech recognition (HSR) on the same task. Section 8.4.1. will compare ASR and HSR results for the digit task, while Section 8.4.2. will repeat the analysis for the alpha-digit task.

8.4.1. Digit String Experiments

To determine human performance, the same set of mixtures that were presented to the ASR system in Section 8.2. were presented to 11 listeners. Each listener, aged between 18 and 30 years old, had received a hearing test in the year prior to the experiments and was found to have normal hearing, i.e. better than 20 dB hearing level in the range $50 - 8000\ Hz$. Listening sessions took place in an IAC single-walled acoustically isolated booth. Stimuli were re-sampled to 25 *kHz* and presented via a Tucker-Davis Technologies System 3 RP2.1, at comfortable listening levels. Stimulus presentation was controlled by a computer situated outside the booth. Signals were presented diotically over Sennheiser HD250 headphones. Listeners were required to perform the same task as the decoder. They were presented with the first two digits on a computer display and then played the stimulus once. The listeners were instructed to write down the other digits that came from the speaker uttering the first two. Both mixed- and matched-gender mixtures were presented to the listeners, however, (unknown to the listener) the target was always the male source. The TMR used for the mixtures was 0 *dB*. The average accuracy of the listeners' responses is presented in Table 8.15 and compared with the results from the decoder.

Table 8.15. Digit recognition accuracy for matched-gender and mixed-gender signals using the key sequence methodology described in Section 8.2.4.. Results compare human performance (HSR), ASR with *a priori* fragments (ASR Apr.), ASR with estimated fragments (ASR Est.) and a baseline MFCC system (MFCC).

	HSR	ASR Apr.	ASR Est.	MFCC
Matched-Gender	78	44	43	38
Mixed-Gender	97	75	66	57

Consider the comparison between the ASR and HSR results. In the mixed-gender condition, the performance of the decoder, even when using *a priori* fragments, is far below the almost perfect performance achieved by the listeners. When gender differences are removed there is a 19% drop in listener performance. This is in agreement with previous findings that masking is more effective when the masker and target are of the same gender (Brungart, 2001). This has been explained as an effect of informational masking, which is maximum when the statistical difference between the acoustics of the target and masker is at a minimum – in this condition listeners find it hardest to attend to the target without being distracted by the masker. As the mixtures used in this experiment are mixed at 0 *dB*, informational masking will play a significant role. At 0 *dB* listeners cannot track the target by attending to a particular level.

For the ASR system, removal of gender difference provokes an even larger drop in performance, with results barely above those of the baseline system. Analysis of the decoder's output reveals many instances where fragments of the masker are chosen in preference to those of the target. The problem here is that, as the decoder is using gender-dependent but speaker-independent models, it cannot reliably distinguish between a fragment of the target and the masker, since fragments of either speaker in the mixture may have a similarly good fit to models of the target source. The only cues come from sequential constraint imposed by the HMM word models (e.g. a fragment matching the first half of the word 'seven' should be followed by one matching the second half). However, listeners performing the matched-gender task are able to use speaker differences to track the target speaker. From the decoder's perspective, with a lack of speaker specific modelling, the task is more similar to that faced by humans when confronted with two simultaneous utterances from the same speaker. Human results in this condition are much poorer (Brungart, 2001).

8.4.2. Grid Corpus Experiments

Listener performance on the alpha-digit task is compared to the performance of the SFD in the unknown-speaker configuration. The listener results reported here were obtained in experiments conducted by Cooke et al. (2008).

The results from the known-speaker configuration were not considered for comparison because of a lack of informational masking effects, which suggest that they would not be similar to listener data. Also, the task faced by listeners is closer to that of the unknown-speaker configuration. The listeners are not provided with any knowledge of who the target speaker is, thus they do not have the advantage provided to the known-speaker ASR system. The results are plotted in Figure 8.8.

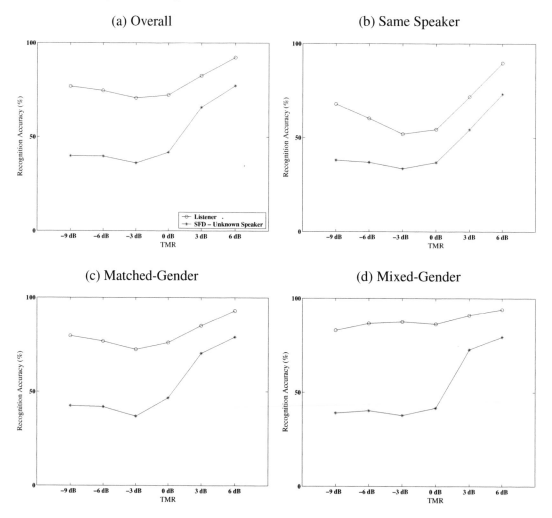

Figure 8.8. Results for the speech fragment decoder in the unknown-speaker configuration compared against listener performance on the same task.

As the TMR decreases from 6 *dB* down to −3 *dB* in the same-speaker condition, listeners' performance falls very sharply. As the target and masker utterances are from the same speaker, and hence have the same fundamental frequency range and identical vocal tract length, the level difference is possibly the main cue available to listeners for distinguishing the competing utterances. At 0 *dB* the level cue is removed and performance deteriorates. As the TMR continues to decrease, the recognition performance increases, despite the increased energetic masking that accompanies a decrease in TMR. This pattern is consistent with the effects of informational masking reported by Brungart (2001). The pattern of recognition in the SFD, despite being on average 36% lower, is very similar to listeners' performance. This is because it has the same difficulties that the listeners face. Namely, the spectral overlap between the speakers is highest in this condition, as the spectral peaks tend to occur in the same frequency regions for both target and masker, more often than in the other conditions.

For the same-gender condition both target and masker have a similar fundamental frequency range and a similar (but not identical) vocal tract length. This suggests that listeners should have less difficulty in identifying the target than they did in the same-speaker condition. The results show this to be the case, as the performance is better than in the same-speaker condition. The reduction in recognition accuracy around $0\ dB$ is present, but is less distinct. The SFD pattern is somewhat similar, however, the dip at $-3\ dB$ is quite pronounced. This is attributable to the decoder's inability to use the cues exploited by users to identify and track the target speaker.

In the mixed-gender condition there is a relatively constant decrease in accuracy for the listener performance. As the gender difference provides consistent cues for source segmentation, informational masking does not play a significant role in the degradation of intelligibility; the performance is largely determined by the degree of energetic masking. There is a slight reduction in performance at $0\ dB$, but negligible compared to the decrease seen in the other conditions. Compare this to the performance of the SFD in the mixed-gender condition. After a sharp decrease in recognition performance at $0\ dB$ the accuracy essentially plateaus, with a small decrease at $-9\ dB$ (this is likely an effect of energetic masking). As mentioned in Section 8.3.3. the difference in the patterns is due to the inability of the SFD to exploit pitch differences between the target and masker.

In the unknown-speaker configuration, the SFD seems to reproduce the pattern of listeners' behaviour for the same-speaker and same-gender conditions; however, it fails to do so in the mixed-gender condition. While it is encouraging that the SFD is able to reproduce, to some degree, patterns of human speech perception, there are some differences between HSR and the way the SFD performs recognition that make it unwise to draw strong conclusions. The ASR system has one distinct advantage over listeners: First, the ASR system uses a closed set of speaker-dependent models, furnishing it with complete descriptions of each speaker's characteristics, whereas listeners have no access to this information. However, listeners may be able to adapt rapidly to the target speaker which may mean that speaker-dependent models will still be a better model of listener performance than, say, for example, a fully speaker-independent model. This can be seen when a comparison is made between the performance of the SFD in the matched-gender condition for the different datasets. In Section 8.2.4., speaker-independent models are employed for the decoding in the digit task. The results are poor because all fragments matched well to the non-specific models and the SFD often chose fragments from the masking sequence. With the alpha-digit task, the speaker-dependent models more readily allow for the choice of the correct fragments, resulting in much improved performance.

The unknown speaker configuration of the SFD shows a surprisingly similar performance to listeners in two of the three conditions tested. While there are caveats, this similarity suggests that the SFD system is modelling human speech perception to some extent.

8.5. Summary

The chapter has shown a full evaluation of the perceptually motivated speech recognition system, in the form of speech recognition experiments using the SFD and employing the fragments derived from the segmentation system developed in previous chapters. The experiments were performed using the speech fragment decoder on two separate datasets: one with connected digit sequences and the other of sentence-length utterances. In the first set of experiments, decoding was performed with fragments derived from the voiced regions of mixed-gender utterances. The results of those experiments showed that the fragments, even without the inclusion of fragments from the unvoiced regions, can yield recognition results that are on average better than a baseline speech recognition system. The inclusion of unvoiced fragments led to an increase in recognition performance across TMR. The gender-dependent HMMs allowed for discrimination of the target speakers' fragments, which gave good recognition accuracy for the target utterance. A more challenging condition (matched-gender utterances) was then explored. The performance was found to be poor at negative TMRs. Further analysis revealed that the SFD was recognising the masker utterance more often than it was the target. With the use of speaker-independent models, and only level differences available for the decoder to distinguish between the fragments of target and masker, there is little chance that the decoder will always select the fragments corresponding to the target.

A comparison with human performance on the same test at 0 *dB* TMR, revealed that the pattern of performance is similar for listeners and the SFD – a significant drop in performance occurred in the matched-gender condition. The percentage decrease was smaller for listeners. This was found to be as a result of the listeners being able to use differences in speaker characteristics, which the decoder, employing speaker-independent HMMs, could not. The alpha-digit experiments attempted to verify this by employing speaker-dependent models.

The alpha-digit experiments employed mixtures in three different conditions: same-speaker, matched-gender and mixed-gender. The SFD was also deployed in two separate configurations: known-speaker and unknown-speaker. In the known-speaker configuration, only the target speakers' models were used; in the unknown-speaker configuration, HMMs from all speakers were used to decode the utterances and the best scoring model was chosen. The SFD, in both configurations outperformed the baseline system in all conditions. However, the known-speaker configuration performed better than the unknown-speaker configuration in all but the same-speaker condition. In this condition, there was no benefit to knowing the target speaker as both sets of fragments belonged to the same speaker. The results of listening tests were compared to the accuracy of the SFD in the unknown-speaker configuration as listeners did not have access to the target speakers' characteristics. Overall, the SFD was shown to mirror the pattern, though not the accuracy, of performance of the listeners. The listeners' performance in the mixed-gender condition was not modelled by the SFD. This seems, in part, to be due to the inability of the SFD to exploit differences due to gender, such as vocal tract length, as listeners generally do. The system also fails to utilise the continuity of pitch across fragments, even though pitch is employed in the primitive segmentation. Further, the SFD could not account for the reduced effect of informational masking in the mixed-gender condition. These points suggest that the SFD should not currently be put forward as a general model of human speech perception.

The speech recognition results shown above, as well as their pattern across TMR, provide encouragement for pursuing techniques for robust speech recognition that are motivated by the wide body of work in auditory scene analysis. More specifically, they highlight the utility of employing computational models of primitive grouping to segment an acoustic mixture; isolating regions of a target source for recognition. The following chapter highlights the significant contributions of this work and suggest directions for future work.

Chapter 9

Conclusion

9.1. Summary

A robust automatic speech recognition system has been presented which successfully merges auditory scene analysis (ASA) and automatic speech recognition (ASR). The coupling of the source segmentation and recognition processes by integrating source segmentation into the decoding process represents a shift in the way ASR is approached. This work draws equally from the perceptual insights of ASA and the well understood statistical framework of ASR to produce a framework that performs speech recognition in a manner that is arguably similar to humans in ways that conventional ASR is not. The system was presented as different modules, each of which acted upon the output of the previous one. The first module presented was the multiple-pitch determination algorithm (Chapter 4), which presented pitch candidates, for both sources in a two-source mixture, to the multiple-pitch tracker (Chapter 5). The output of the tracker was used in the segmentation of the voiced regions of speech in Chapter 6, after which, the unvoiced regions of speech were segmented (Chapter 7). The final module was an automatic speech recognition engine that took as input the segmented speech produced by the previous modules (Chapter 8).

9.2. Original Contributions

9.2.1. Pitch Determination

In Chapter 4 a novel approach to multiple-pitch determination was presented. Pitch candidates were determined by first computing an autocorrelogram and then summing the low frequency regions to form a summary autocorrelogram. There are two novel aspects of the algorithm: The first is the retention of multiple pitch points from the summary autocorrelogram. Similar algorithms typically retain n pitch points where there are n sources in the mixture; this often leads to an error in detection, where the pitch of one source is missed. By retaining multiple candidates, fewer detection errors occur.

The other novel aspect of the algorithm is the retention of pitch candidates which represent pitch doubling and halving errors. It is often the case that evidence of the pitch of a sound source is weak, or not present. There will, however, be harmonics of the pitch which can be used to identify the source. The multi-pitch determination algorithm was developed as part of a speech segmentation system, where it is important to extract the harmonic component of all sources. Thus, when the pitch is unavailable, but a pitch double or half can be detected, the pitch determination algorithm retains the double/half as evidence of the sound source.

9.2.2.   Pitch Tracking

A novel multiple-pitch tracker was presented in Chapter 5. The algorithm was developed based on the assumption that the candidates proposed by the pitch determination algorithm were generated by two speech sources and a separate noise source. As such, each source was modelled by an HMM, the parameters of which were estimated from training data. The novelty of the algorithm stems from two areas: 1) the way in which pitch doubling/halving is systematically modelled; and 2) the inclusion of a noise model to account for pitch points not generated by the speech HMM. The modelling of pitch doubling/halving allows the algorithm to continue a smooth segment, where the fundamental frequency is missing. Other pitch tracking algorithms would seek to correct for these effects either during or after completing the tracking. In a comparison with the multi-pitch tracker of Wu et al. (2003) the proposed algorithm generally made fewer detection and estimation errors – see Section 5.4.. However, it must again be made clear that the tracking of pitch is not an end in itself; it serves as a mechanism whereby contiguous segments of pitch can be assigned to a single source. The final goal is to segment voiced speech, thus applying a correction to pitch doubles/halves would likely lead to errors in segmentation.

Given that there are multiple candidates for the pitch tracker to consider, there will doubtless be spurious pitch points that act as 'distractors'. The algorithm deals with these by employing a noise model, coupled with a distribution of the number of distractor points that are likely to occur in a time frame.

A further point to note about the pitch tracking algorithm is that it does not enforce continuity across pitch breaks, as this is where the majority of errors in source assignment can occur. Source assignment errors would be detrimental to the final segmentation and would have implications for the recognition stage. Thus, the pitch track consists of a number of segments of contiguous regions of voiced speech, separated by breaks in voicing.

This highlights another novel contribution of the work: the fact that pitch tracking is treated as part of the speech recognition problem. The voiced fragments labelled as foreground during the recognition process (see Section 3.6.2.) are associated with particular pitch track segments. These fragments can be recovered after the decoding. Connecting the fragments is effectively connecting the track segments, thereby tracking the pitch across the entire utterance. Similarly, grouping the background segments allows the other source to be tracked. This approach treats the pitch tracks, as well as the final segmentation, as emergent from the recognition process rather than an input. This is the first known recognition system to adopt this approach.

9.2.3.   Voiced Speech Segmentation

Chapter 6 deals with the segmentation of voiced speech. The segmentation employs the autocorrelogram, summary autocorrelogram and the pitch tracks. The pitch track segments are used to recruit spectro-temporal regions of the mixed signal that correspond to voiced speech by checking at each frame, whether the pitch points found in a segment match to peaks in the channels of the autocorrelogram or envelope autocorrelogram. The channels in which matches occur are labelled, such that the regions corresponding to each contiguous segment have a unique label. Regions with similar labels are called fragments. The novel aspects of this stage are: 1) the development of a confidence map based on the relative contributions of each source in a frequency channel; and 2) the evaluation measure that was proposed as a measure of determining the extent to which a fragment overlaps both sources.

The aim of the segmentation algorithm is to produce coherent fragments, fragments that can be unambiguously assigned to a single source. If, however, there are errors in the process, assignment errors will be made. Where both sources are active in a channel, the confidence map serves to introduce a measure of reliability, which indicates how likely it is that a spectro-temporal point was generated by a particular source.

The coherence of each fragment is calculated and used as a measure of the quality of each fragment produced by the segmentation algorithm. This was employed as it gave a good indication of how well the speech recogniser would perform when it utilised fragments derived from the segmentation algorithm.

9.2.4.   Unvoiced Speech Segmentation

The novel algorithm employed for the segmentation of unvoiced speech was presented in Chapter 7. The algorithm applied a well-known image processing tool – the watershed transform – to the task of segmenting unvoiced speech. By exploiting the coherent spectro-temporal glimpses that are present in overlapping speech, the algorithm segments the unvoiced-regions of speech based on the energy contours of the mixture. Recognition experiments show that the inclusion of unvoiced speech improves recognition performance.

9.2.5.   Speech Recognition Studies

The speech fragment decoder (SFD) was proposed as a novel approach to ASR (Barker et al., 2005). Prior to the current study, however, there had been no concrete demonstration of its power. The original idea was tested with speech corrupted with simple noises and segmented using *a priori* knowledge of the pre-mixed sources.

The experiments performed in Chapter 8, which employed fragments derived from a systematic segmentation algorithm, were the first concrete demonstration of its utility for speech recognition with challenging and, somewhat, realistic tasks. Since this early work, several studies have been done that confirm this – see (Barker et al., 2006; Coy and Barker, 2007; Christensen et al., 2007; Ma et al., 2007; Barker et al., 2010). The study has also inspired work being carried out in *audio-visual speech recognition* (Shao and Barker, 2006, 2007).

9.3.   Directions for Future Work

This work has presented a complex SFD system that is built from many relatively simple components. The modular nature of the system presents many opportunities for increasing the performance of the system. This section will identify some of the current limitations of the system components and present suggestions for future work that could serve to enhance them. Firstly, the pitch determination algorithm has some weaknesses that need to be addressed. The retention of multiple peaks has been shown to be one method of developing a pitch determination algorithm with few errors. However, the retention of an arbitrary number of peaks from the summary is not an optimal solution. In the first instance, it is not clear how many peaks need to be retained to ensure that all the correct pitch candidates are retained. Furthermore, it is possible that the cross-frequency integration, achieved by summing the channels, is itself removing valuable evidence for the sources in the mixture. In the event however, that the evidence is present in the summary, a more systematic approach to determining its value could be employed.

The shortcomings of the multiple-pitch tracker have been mentioned in Section 5.5., but they are worth repeating here. The assumption that the pitch is generated by a first order Markov process ignores the relationship between the neighbouring pitch points. It is possible that including a model of temporal continuity to simulate the pitch trajectory could produce more accurate pitch tracks. Though the tracks themselves are not the final goal, their accuracy has direct implications for the quality of the voiced fragments. This could further provide increased constraint for the segmentation model of the decoder, leading to improved segmentation and possibly lower error rates.

The model of pitch dynamics employed assumes a Gaussian fit, however this is only an approximation. A better fit to the data could improve the model. A third approximation is the treatment of the distractor point as independent-and-identically-distributed noise. It is possible that modelling the relationship between the distractor and true pitch points could make for a better pitch tracker.

The voiced-fragment generation process depends on the pitch determination and tracking stages which come before it, thus any errors made at that stage can affect the segmentation. The actual segmentation process is subject to its own errors. There are a number of tuning parameters that have been set empirically. While this is common practice in systems that perform primitive segmentation, it may be that the values set by experiment are not optimal; this would affect the fragment generation and ultimately, the decoding process.

The multi-stage segmentation described in this work has its advantages, but it also has disadvantages. For instance, the errors made in the segmentation of voiced speech carry over to the module in which the segmentation of unvoiced speech is carried out. If these errors are such that regions of voiced speech are labelled as unvoiced, the algorithm used for unvoiced speech segmentation would be required to segment voiced speech as well. Fortunately, the algorithm is not one that will fail if the input is voiced.

The unvoiced-speech segmentation algorithm is relatively simple, and yet it yields fragments that lead to improvements in recognition results. While there is no guarantee that a more complex algorithm will produce fragments that will lower recognition errors, it might be useful to develop an algorithm that exploits some of the classification cues for segmentation.

Within the current recognition framework, both schema-driven and primitive grouping processes are effectively coupled because the ASR system evaluates multiple segmentation hypotheses that are constrained by primitive grouping. As suggested by Coy and Barker (2007), however, a more tightly coupled version of the decoder can be imagined. For example, if the pitch track information were preserved in the fragments, the decoder could then modify the likelihood of a decoding by factoring in probabilities for a sequence of fragments to be consistent with a pitch track. That is, if there is a large pitch jump between two fragments separated by a short time interval then they are less likely to both belong to the same source. Taking this idea to its logical conclusion, separate harmonic fragments could be defined at every frame, and the pitch tracking step in the current system could be completely incorporated into the top-down search. In such a system, the pitch track of a source would emerge as a by-product of segmentation, rather than as a primitive feature employed in the process of source segmentation. The current system takes inspiration from human perception, but does not attempt to model it. It is however, encouraging that the system, in some small way, seems to mimic human speech recognition.

Within such a system, primitive grouping would be imposing a weaker constraint. It is arguable whether the removal of an accurate, primitive grouping constraint is necessarily a positive thing. For example, it would be more difficult for humans to recognise speech if primitive processes were not involved in grouping individual formants.

The recognition system proposed has been evaluated and shown to have good performance in challenging tasks. That performance is not nearly as good as that of humans – see Section 8.4.. Work is needed to better understand the origins of this difference. This would include a study to determine the extent to which the performance difference is due to weaknesses in primitive processing, schema-driven processing or the manner in which the two are coupled.

A natural extension of the current study would be to perform large-vocabulary decoding with the speech fragment decoder. It has been suggested that the missing data approach to speech recognition is unsuitable for large vocabularies (Srinivasan et al., 2006). However, this assertion is made based on recognition results that employed *a priori* masks and a basic missing data decoder. The speech fragment decoder does not suffer from some of the constraints of basic missing data decoders and with the use of uncertainty decoding, such as soft masks, it could lead to better results on large vocabulary tasks. While there are several challenges that will have to be overcome in developing such a system, it is well worth attempting to do so.

The fragment generation processes could be revisited. The two-stage segmentation process employed here could possibly be replaced by a single stage, in which both voiced and unvoiced speech is segmented simultaneously. Such an algorithm need not be a radical departure from the current system, but could, in the first instance, simply exploit several primitive cues in an iterative and complimentary manner to achieve full segmentation. An algorithm of this type would likely be performing segmentation in a manner similar to the way that humans do it.

Finally, the current work does not take into account the effects of reverberation. Reverberation would make pitch determination more challenging by disrupting pitch cues. Temporal smearing could make the effects of energetic masking more severe by filling in the gaps that would allow the detection of a less energetic source. Other effects, such as the mismatch between reverberant speech and acoustic models trained on clean speech, would make segmentation, as well as recognition, a very challenging task. Future work could investigate this and propose a method of handling reverberation for two-source mixtures.

9.4. Implications of the Approach for Automatic Speech Recognition

Given the encouraging performance of the system discussed, one must consider the potential benefits of further research into coupling ASR and studies of human speech recognition (HSR). Since as early as the 1980s there has been a general shift in the way that ASR is approached. This shift has been away from an attempt to model HSR and toward system-based approaches, where the goal is improved recognition accuracy and where little consideration is given to whether or not the system is a replica of human speech processing (see Huckvale, 1998, for a discussion). While it may be argued that there is no need for an ASR system to faithfully reproduce the method of speech processing employed by humans, it may be beneficial for such systems to incorporate insights gained from research into HSR. It may be the case that studies of HSR could offer the means of addressing some of the problems faced by automatic recognition systems, which humans handle with seeming ease, and in the process erase the disparity in recognition performance between ASR and HSR (see Huckvale, 1998; Carpenter, 1999; Dusan and Rabiner, 2005; Scharenborg, 2007).[30]

For the purpose of discussion, the areas in which ASR systems can be improved by HSR can be crudely grouped into: feature extraction; acoustic modelling; and language modelling. Human speech contains a multiplicity of acoustic cues, which provide a strategic redundancy (Assmann and Summerfield, 2004) that is useful, especially in the presence of interference, for accurate recognition. The most common features used in ASR systems (Mel-frequency Cepstral Coefficients and Perceptual Linear Predictive features, for instance) aim to remove this redundancy in order to match the independence assumptions made by the acoustic models employed in recognition. Experimental evidence from recognition studies in the Missing Data framework has shown, to some limited extent, that retaining some redundancy in the acoustic feature representation can provide a boost in ASR performance.[31] However, taking full advantage of the extra information present in the speech signal would require that there be a change in the way that acoustic models are trained and likely, in the way that recognition is performed.

The Hidden Markov Model (HMM), which is used almost universally as an acoustic model for ASR systems, is known to be a poor model of speech. Bob Carpenter refers to the acoustic models employed in traditional ASR systems as both "dumb and lazy" (Carpenter, 1999, pg. 1). Among the specific criticisms levelled against these models is that the assumptions made about frame independence do not hold; duration, temporal fine structure and fine phonetic detail are all poorly modelled (Barker and Cooke, 2007). Because of these shortcomings, HMM models have relatively poor performance where there is competition between acoustically similar sounds. Template-based models have been proposed as a possible alternative to the HMM framework (Wachter et al., 2003; Maier and Moore, 2005; Strik, 2006). These approaches take inspiration from Goldinger's *episodic* theory of HSR, in which stored templates of speech are compared to incoming speech signals using some distance metric (Goldinger, 1998). The template with the smallest distance to the incoming

---

[30]A full discussion of the manner in which ASR can be improved through the incorporation of knowledge gained from HSR is beyond the scope of the current work. The references given in the text serve as a good starting point for a study of the various issues.

[31]See Chapter 2 and references therein for a discussion.

signal is chosen as the correct one. Initial results using this approach have been promising and encourage further exploration.

Currently the statistical language models employed in ASR systems are complex multi-level structures trained on hundreds of millions of words from various sources. And yet the *n-gram*-based language models are still crude approximations of 'language modelling' as seen in HSR. In ASR the semantic and syntactic constraints are applied at the sentence level, whereas HSR applies these constraints at the concept level, where word recognition is influenced by concept recognition and vice versa (Dusan and Rabiner, 2005). This coupling of top-down and bottom-up processing appears to be a recurring feature in human auditory processing, which allows for complex interactions between high- and low-level processes leading to more robust behaviour. While the benefits of this approach has been demonstrated in this current work for acoustic features, there has yet to be a system that exploits this behaviour at the level of language processing. A further difference between ASR and HSR is evident in the manner in which context is utilised. N-gram language models are forced to treat the issue of context as a highly localised phenomenon, even though psycho-linguistic studies have shown that linguistic relationships are not limited to 'nearest-neighbour' associations (see Carpenter, 1999, and references within).

This discussion does not provide a full coverage of the potential for HSR to influence ASR; it does however, highlight some of the major areas of difference, where perceptual and psycho-linguistic studies can improve the performance of ASR systems. While some suggestions have been made as to how these observations may be implemented in ASR systems, there remains an issue of how closely it is possible, or even practical, to follow the lead of HSR. This is important, as it is unlikely that a technique will be given serious consideration if it does not show that it can lead to significant improvement over the state of the art, regardless of how sound the method may be. In other words, recognition accuracy must not be made to suffer in an effort to implement a theoretically pleasing approach. Rather than serving as a deterrent, this should encourage researchers in both fields to collaborate in the effort to find those solutions; for as the current work – and other emerging evidence – has shown, ASR can be significantly improved by applying the principles of HSR.

References

S. Ahmad and V. Tresp. Some solutions to the missing feature problem in vision. In S. J. Hanson, J. D. Cowan, and C. L. Giles, editors, *Advances in Neural Information Processing Systems*, volume 5, pages 393–400, San Mateo, California, 1993. Morgan Kaufmann Publishers.

C. Alain and A. Izenberg. Effects of attentional load on auditory scene analysis. *Journal of Cognitive Neuroscience*, **15**:1063–1073, 2003.

C. Alain, S. Arnott, and T. W. Picton. Bottom-up and top-down influences on auditory scene analysis: Evidence from event-related brain potentials. *Journal of Experimental Psychology: Human Perception and Performance*, **27**:1072–1089, 2001.

C. Alain, K. Reine, Y. He, C. Wang, and N. Lobaugh. Hearing two things at once: Neurophysiological indices of speech segregation and identification. *Journal of Cognitive Neuroscience*, **17**:811–818, 2005.

A. M. A. Ali, J. Van der Spiegel, and P. Mueller. Acoustic-phonetic features for the automatic classification of fricatives. *Journal of the Acoustical Society of America*, **109(5)**: 2217–2235, 2001a.

A. M. A. Ali, J. Van der Spiegel, and P. Mueller. Acoustic-phonetic features for the automatic classification of stop consonants. *IEEE Transactions on Speech and Audio Processing*, **9(8)**:833–841, 2001b.

S. Anstis and S . Saida. Adaptation to auditory streaming of frequency-modulated tones. *Journal of Experimental Psychology*, **11**:257–271, 1985.

P. F. Assmann. Tracking and glimpsing speech in noise: Role of fundamental frequency. *Journal of the Acoustical Society of America*, **100**:2680, 1996.

P. F. Assmann. Fundamental frequency and the intelligibility of competing voices. In *14th Int. Congress of Phonetic Sciences*, pages 179–182, 1999.

P. F. Assmann and D. D. Paschall. Pitches of concurrent vowels. *Journal of the Acoustical Society of America*, **103**:1150 – 1160, 1998.

P. F. Assmann and A. Q. Summerfield. The perception of speech under adverse conditions. In S. Greenberg, W. A. Ainsworth, A. N. Popper, and R. Fay, editors, *Speech Processing in the Auditory System*, pages 231–308. Springer-Verlag, New York, 2004.

P. F. Assmann and Q. Summerfield. Modelling the perception of concurrent vowels: Vowels with different fundamental frequencies. *Journal of the Acoustical Society of America*, **88**: 680–697, 1990.

P. F. Assmann and Q. Summerfield. The contribution of waveform interactions to the perception of concurrent vowels. *Journal of the Acoustical Society of America*, **95**:471–484, 1994.

F. R. Bach and M. I. Jordan. Discriminative training of hidden markov models for multiple pitch tracking. In *ICASSP '05*, pages 489–492, 2005.

J. Barker. Robust automatic speech recognition. In D. Wang and G. J. Brown, editors, *Computational Auditory Scene Anaysis: Principles, Algorithms, and Applications*, pages 297–350. IEEE Press/Wiley-Interscience, 2006.

J. Barker and M. Cooke. Modelling the recognition of spectrally reduced speech. In *Proceedings Eurospeech '97*, pages 2127–2130, 1997.

J. Barker and M. Cooke. Modelling speaker intelligibility in noise. *Speech Communication*, **49**:402–417, 2007.

J. Barker and A. Coy. Towards solving the cocktail party problem through primitive grouping and model combination. In *Proc. Forum Acusticum, Budapest*, 2005.

J. Barker, L. Josifovski, M. P. Cooke, and P. D. Green. Soft decisions in missing data techniques for robust automatic speech recognition. In *Proceddings ICSLP '00*, pages 373–376, 2000.

J. Barker, M. Cooke, and D. Ellis. Combining bottom-up and top-down constraints for robust ASR: The multisource decoder. In *CRAC Workshop*, 2001a.

J. Barker, M. Cooke, and P. Green. Robust ASR based on clean speech: An evaluation of missing data techniques for connected digit recognition in noise. In *Proceedings Eurospeech '01*, pages 213–216, 2001b.

J. Barker, M. Cooke, and P. Green. Linking auditory scene analysis and robust ASR by missing data techniques. In *Proceedings WISP '01*, pages 295–307, 2001c.

J. Barker, M. Cooke, and D. Ellis. Decoding speech in the presence of other sources. *Speech Communication*, **45**:5–25, 2005.

J. Barker, A. Coy, N. Ma, and M. Cooke. Recent advances in speech fragment decoding techniques. In *Interspeech '06*, pages 85–88, 2006.

J. Barker, N. Ma, A. Coy, and M. Cooke. Speech fragment decoding techniques for simultaneous speaker identification and speech recognition. *Computer Speech and Language*, **24(1)**:94 – 111, 2010.

L. E. Baum, T. Petrie, G. Soules, and N. Weiss. A maximization technique occurring in the statistical analysis of probabilistic functions of markov chains. *Annals of Mathematical Statistics*, **41**:164–171, 1970.

M. W. Beauvois and R. Meddis. Computer simulation of auditory stream segregation in alternating-tone sequences. *Journal of the Acoustical Society of America*, **99**:2270–2280, 1996.

M. Benzeghiba, R. De Mori, O. Deroo, S. Dupont, T. Erbes, D. Jouvet, L. Fissore, P. Laface, A. Mertins, C. Ris, R. Rose, V. Tyagi, and C. Wellekens. Automatic speech recognition and speech variability: A review. *Speech Communication*, **49**:763–786, 2007.

M. Berouti, R. Schwartz, and J. Makhoul. Enhancement of speech corrupted by acoustic noise. In *ICASSP '79*, pages 208–211, 1979.

J. Bird and C. J. Darwin. *Psychophysical and Physiological Advances in Hearing*, chapter Effects of a difference in fundamental frequency in separating two sentences, pages 263–269. Whurr, London, 1998.

R. Bolia, W. Nelson, M. Ericson, and B. Simpson. A speech corpus for multitalker communications research. *Journal of the Acoustical Society of America*, **107**:1065–1066, 2000.

S. Boll. Suppression of acoustic noise in speech using spectral subtraction. *IEEE Transactions on Speech and Audio Processing*, **27**:113–120, 1979.

A. S. Bregman. *Auditory Scene Analysis*. MIT Press, 1990.

A. S. Bregman. Auditory streaming is cumulative. *Quarterly Journal of Experimental Psychology*, **4**:380–387, 1978.

A. S. Bregman. Use of psychological data in building asa models. In *IEEE Workshop on Applications of Signal Processing to Audio and Acoustics*, pages 1–3, 1995.

J. P. L. Brokx and S. G. Nooteboom. Intonation and the perceptual separation of simultaneous voices. *Journal of Phonetics*, **10**:23–36, 1982.

A. Bronkhorst. The cocktail party phenomenon: A review of research on speech intelligibility in multiple-talker condition. *Acoustica*, **86**:117–128, 2000.

G. J. Brown. *Computational auditory scene analysis: A representational approach*. PhD thesis, University of Sheffield, 1992.

G. J. Brown and M. Cooke. Computational auditory scene analysis. *Speech Communication*, **8**:297 – 336, 1994a.

G. J. Brown and M. P. Cooke. Computational auditory scene analysis. *Computer Speech and Language*, **8**:297–336, 1994b.

G. J. Brown and D. Wang. Modelling the perceptual segregation of double vowels with a network of neural oscillators. *Neural Networks*, **9**:1547 – 1558, 1997.

D. S. Brungart. Informational and energetic masking effects in the perception of two simultaneous talkers. *Journal of the Acoustical Society of America*, **109**:1101–1109, 2001.

D. S. Brungart, B. D. Simpson, M. A. Ericson, and K. R. Scott. Informational and energetic masking effects in the perception of multiple simultaneous talkers. *Journal of the Acoustical Society of America*, **100**:2527–2538, 2001.

D. S. Brungart, N. Iyer, and B. D. Simpson. Monaural speech segregation using synthetic speech signals. *Journal of the Acoustical Society of America*, **119**:2327 – 2333, 2006.

E. Buss, J. W. Hall, and J. H. Grose. Effect of amplitude modulation coherence for masked speech signals filtered into narrow bands. *Journal of the Acoustical Society of America*, **113**:462–467, 2003.

E. Buss, J. W. Hall, and J. H. Grose. Spectral integration of synchronous and asynchronous cues to consonant identification. *Journal of the Acoustical Society of America*, **113**: 2278–2285, 2004.

R. Carhart, T. W. Tillman, and E. S. Greetis. Perceptual masking in multiple noise background. *Journal of the Acoustical Society of America*, **45**:694 – 703, 1969.

P. Cariani. Neural timing nets for auditory computation. In S. Greenberg and M. Slaney, editors, *Computational models of auditory function*, pages 233–247. IOS Press, Amsterdam, 2001.

P. A. Cariani and B. Delgutte. Neural correlates of the pitch of complex tones. I. Pitch and pitch salience. *Journal of Neurophysiology*, **76**:1698–1716, 1996.

R. P. Carlyon. How the brain separate sounds. *Trends in Cognitive Sciences*, **8**:465–471, 2004.

R. P. Carlyon and T. M. Shackleton. Comparing the fundamental frequencies of resolved and unresolved harmonics: Evidence for two pitch mechanisms? *Journal of the Acoustical Society of America*, **95**:3541–3554, 1994.

R. P. Carlyon, R. Cusack, J. M. Foxton, and I. H. Robertson. Effects of attention and unilateral neglect on auditory stream segregation. *Journal of Experimental Psychology: Human Perception and Performance*, **27**:115–127, 2001.

B. Carpenter. Human versus machine: psycholinguistics meets asr. In *IEEE Workshop on Automatic Speech Recognition and Understanding*, pages 225–228, 1999.

W. A. Castleman and R. L. Diehl. Acoustic correlates of fricatives and affricates. *Journal of the Acoustical Society of America*, **99(4)**:2546(A), 1996.

M. Chalikia and A. Bregman. The perceptual segregation of simultaneous auditory signals: Pulse train segregation and vowel segregation. *Perceptual Psychophysics*, **46**:487–496, 1989.

D. Chazan, Y. Stettiner, and D. Malah. Optimal multi-pitch estimation using the EM algorithm for co-channel speech separation. In *Proceedings ICASSP '93*, pages 728 – 731, 1993.

E. C. Cherry. Some experiments on the recognition of speech, with one and two ears. *Journal of the Acoustical Society of America*, **25**, 1953.

C. Chesta, O. Siohan, and C. H. Lee. Maximum a posteriori linear regression for hidden markov model adaptation. In *Eurospeech '99*, pages 211–214, 1999.

H. Christensen, N. Ma, S. Wrigley, and J. Barker. Integrating pitch and localisation cues at a speech fragment level. In *Interspeech '07*, pages 2769–2772, 2007.

A. Cohen, J. F. Scheuten, and J. 't Hart. Contribution of the time parameter to the perception of speech. In *Fourth International Congress of Phonetic Sciences*, pages 555–560, Mouton, The Hague, 1962.

M. Cooke. *Modeling Auditory Processing and Organization*. Cambridge University Press, Cambridge, UK, 1993.

M. Cooke. A glimpsing model of speech perception in noise. *Journal of the Acoustical Society of America*, **119**:1562–1573, 2006.

M. Cooke, A. Morris, and P. Green. Missing data techniques for robust speech recognition. In *Proceedings ICASSP '97*, pages 893–896, 1997.

M. Cooke, P. Green, L. Josifovski, and A. Vizinho. Robust automatic speech recognition with missing and unreliable acoustic data. *Speech Communication*, **34**:267–285, 2001a.

M. Cooke, P. Green, L. Josifovski, and A. Vizinho. Robust automatic speech recognition with missing and uncertain acoustic data. *Speech Communication*, **34**:267 – 285, 2001b.

M. Cooke, M. Garcia Lecumberri, and J. Barker. The foreign language cocktail party problem: energetic and informational masking effects in non-native speech perception. *Journal of the Acoustical Society of America*, **123**:414–427, 2008.

M. P. Cooke. Glimpsing speech. *Journal of Phonetics*, **31**:579–584, 2003.

M. P. Cooke, M. D. Crawford G. J. Brown, and P. Green. Computational auditory scene analysis: Listening to several things at once. *Endeavour*, **17**:186–190, 1993.

M. P. Cooke, J. Barker, S. P. Cunningham, and X. Shao. An audio-visual corpus for speech perception and automatic speech recognition. *Journal of the Acoustical Society of America*, **120**:2421–2424, 2006.

A. Coy and J. Barker. A multipitch tracker for monaural speech segregation. In *Interspeech '06*, pages 1292 – 1295, 2006.

A. Coy and J. Barker. An automatic speech recognition system based on the scene analysis account of auditory perception. *Speech Communication*, **49**:384–401, 2007.

A. Coy and J. Barker. Soft harmonic masks for recognising speech in the presence of a competing speaker. In *Interspeech '05*, volume 1, pages 2641–2644, 2005.

J. F. Culling and C. J. Darwin. Perceptual and computational separation of simultaneous vowels: Cues arising from low frequency beating. *Journal of the Acoustical Society of America*, **95**:1559–1569, 1994.

J. F. Culling and C. J. Darwin. Perceptual separation of simultaneous vowels: Within and across formant grouping. *Journal of the Acoustical Society of America*, **93**:3454 – 3467, 1993.

J. E. Cutting and B. S. Rosner. Categories and boundaries in speech and music. *Perceptual Psychophysics*, **16**:564–570, 1974.

C. J. Darwin. *Pitch: Neural Coding and Perception*, volume 24 of *Springer Handbook of Auditory Research*, chapter Pitch and Auditory Grouping, pages 278–305. Springer, New York, 2005.

C. J. Darwin. Perceptual grouping of speech components differing in fundamental frequency and onset time. *Quarterly Journal of Experimental Psychology*, **33(A)**:185–207, 1981.

C. J. Darwin. Auditory grouping. *Trends in Cognitive Sciences*, **1**:327–333, 1997.

C. J. Darwin and C. E. Bethell-Fox. Pitch continuity and speech source attribution. *Journal of Experimental Psychology: Human Perception and Performance*, **3**:665–672, 1977.

C. J. Darwin and R. W. Hukin. Effectiveness of spatial cues, prosody, and talker characteristics in selective attention. *Journal of the Acoustical Society of America*, **107**:970–977, 2000.

C. J. Darwin, D. S. Brungart, and B. D. Simpson. Effects of fundamental frequency and vocal-tract length changes on attention to one of two simultaneous talkers. *Journal of the Acoustical Society of America*, **114**:2913–2922, 2003.

B. A. Dautrich, L. R. Rabiner, and T.B. Martin. On the effect of varying filter bank parameters on isolated word recognition. *IEEE Transactions on Acoustics, Speech and Signal Processing*, **31**:793–806, 1983.

M. H. Davis and I. S. Johnsrudeb. Hearing speech sounds: Top-down influences on the interface between audition and speech perception. *Hearing Research*, **229**:132–147, 2007.

A. de Cheveigné. Multiple f0 estimation. In D. Wang and G. J. Brown, editors, *Computational Auditory Scene Analysis Principles, Algorithms, and Applications*, pages 45–79. John Wiley & Sons, New Jersey, 2006.

A. de Cheveigné. Concurrent vowel segregation III: A neural model of harmonic interference cancellation. *Journal of the Acoustical Society of America*, **101**:2857–2865, 1997.

A. de Cheveigné. Separation of concurrent harmonic sounds: fundamental frequency estimation and a cancellation model of auditory processing. *Journal of the Acoustical Society of America*, **93**:3271–3290, 1993.

A. de Cheveigné. Speech f0 extraction based on Licklider's pitch perception model. In *ICPhS*, volume 4, pages 218–221, 1991.

A. de Cheveigné. Pitch perception models. In *Pitch*, pages 169–233. Springer Verlag, New York, 2005.

A. de Cheveigné and H. Kawahara. Yin, a fundamental frequency estimator for speech and music. *Journal of the Acoustical Society of America*, **111**:1917–1930, 2002.

A. de Cheveigné and H. Kawahara. Multiple period estimation and pitch perception model. *Speech Communication*, **27**:175 – 185, 1999.

A. de Cheveigné, H. Kawahara, M. Tsuzaki, and K. Aikawa. Concurrent vowel segregation I: Effects of relative level and f_0 difference. *Journal of the Acoustical Society of America*, **101**:2839–2847, 1997.

P. B. Denes. On the statistics of spoken English. *Journal of the Acoustical Society of America*, **35**:892–904, 1963.

M. F. Dorman, M. Studdert-Kennedy, and L. J. Raphael. Stop consonant recognition: Release bursts and formant transitions as functionally equivalent, context-dependent cues. *Perception and Psychophysics*, **22**:109–122, 1977.

W. J. Dowling. The perception of interleaved melodies. *Cognitive Psychology*, **5**:322–337, 1973.

R. Drullman and A. W. Bronkhorst. Multichannel speech intelligibility and talker recognition using monaural, binaural, and three-dimensional auditory presentation. *Journal of the Acoustical Society of America*, **107**:2224–2325, 1990.

H. Duifhuis, L. F. Willems, and R. J. Sluyter. Measurement of pitch in speech: An implementation of Goldstein's theory of pitch perception. *Journal of the Acoustical Society of America*, **71**:1568–1580, 1982.

A. J. Duquesnoy. Effect of a single interfering noise or speech source on speech intelligibility. *Journal of the Acoustical Society of America*, **74**:739–743, 1983.

S. Dusan and L. R. Rabiner. Can automatic speech recognition learn more from human speech perception. In *Trends n Speech Technology: Third Conference on Speech Technology and Human-Computer Dialogue*, pages 21–36, 2005.

J. P. Egan. *Signal detection theory and ROC analysis*. Series in Cognition and Perception. Academic Press, New York, 1975.

D. P. W. Ellis. *Prediction-driven computational auditory scene analysis*. PhD thesis, Massachusetts Institute of Technology, 1996.

D. P. W. Ellis. Using knowledge to organize sound: The prediction-driven approach to computational auditory scene analysis and its application to speech/nonspeech mixtures. *Speech Communication*, **27**:281–298, 1999a.

D. P. W. Ellis. Model-based scene analysis. In D. Wang and G. J. Brown, editors, *Computational Auditory Scene Anaysis: Principles, Algorithms, and Applications*, pages 115–146. IEEE Press/Wiley-Interscience, 2006.

D. P. W. Ellis. Evaluating speech separation systems. In *Speech separation by humans and machines*, pages 295–304. Kluwer Academic Publishers, 2005.

D. P. W. Ellis. Using knowledge to organize sound: The prediction-driven approach to computational auditory scene analysis and its application to speech/nonspeech mixtures. *Speech Communication*, **27(3-4)**:281–298, 1999b.

L. D. Erman, F. Hayes-Roth, V. R. Lesser, and R. Reddy. The Hearsay-II speech-understanding system: Integrating knowledge to resolve uncertainty. *Computing Surveys*, **12**:213–253, 1980.

M. Every and P. J. B. Jackson. Enhancement of harmonic content of speech based on a dynamic programming pitch tracking algorithm. In *Interspeech '06*, pages 81–84, 2006.

T. Fawcett. An introduction to ROC analysis. *Pattern Recognition Letters*, **27**:861–874, 2006.

J. M. Fellowes, R. E. Remez, and P. E. Rubin. Perceiving the sex and identity of a talker without natural vocal timbre. *Perceptual Psychophysics*, **59**:839–849, 1997.

J. M. Festen and R. Plomp. Effects of fluctuating noise and interfering speech on the speech-reception threshold in impaired and normal hearing. *Journal of the Acoustical Society of America*, **88**:1725–1736, 1990.

F. Flego. *Fundamental frequency estimation techniques for multi-microphone speech input*. PhD thesis, DIT - University of Trento, 2006.

R. H. Fraizer, S. Samsam, L. Braida, and A. Oppenheim. Enhancement of speech by adaptive filtering. In *Proceedings ICASSP '76*, pages 251–253, 1976.

N. R. French, C. W. Carter, and W. Koenig. The words and sounds of telephone conversations. *Bell System Technical Journal*, **9**:290–324, 1930.

B. J. Frey, L. Deng, A. Acero, and T. Kristjansson. ALGONQUIN: Iterating Laplace's method to remove multiple types of acoustic distortion for robust speech recognition. In *EUROSPEECH '01*, pages 901–904, 2001.

R. L. Freyman, U. Balakrishnan, and K. S. Helfer. Effect of number of masking talkers and auditory priming on informational masking in speech recognition. *Journal of the Acoustical Society of America*, **115**:2246–2256, 2004.

S. Furui. Toward robust speech recognition under adverse conditions. In *ESCA Workshop on Speech Processing in Adverse Conditions*, pages 31–42, 1992.

S. Furui. Cepstral analysis technique for automatic speaker verification. *IEEE Transactions on Acoustics, Speech and Signal Processing*, **29**:254–272, 1981.

M. J. F. Gales. *Model-based techniques for noise robust speech recognition*. PhD thesis, Cambridge University, 1995.

M. J. F. Gales and S. J. Young. Robust continuous speech recognition using parallel model combination. *IEEE Transactions on Speech and Audio Processing*, **4**:352–359, 1996.

J. Garofolo, L. Lamel, W. Fisher, J. Fiscus, D. Pallet, and N. Dahlgren. DARPA TIMIT acoustic-phonetic continuous speech corpus. Technical Report NISTIR 4930, National Institute of Standards and Technology, Gaithersburg, MD, 1993.

J. Gauvain and C. Lee. Maximum a posteriori estimation for multivariate Gaussian mixture observation of Markov chains. *IEEE Transactions on Speech and Audio Processing*, **2**: 291–298., 1994.

Z. Ghahramani and M. I. Jordan. Factorial hidden Markov models. In *Advances in Neural Information Processing Systems, (NIPS)*, volume 8, pages 472–478, 1995.

M. Gibson and T. Hain. Temporal masking for unsupervised minimum Bayes risk speaker adaptation. In *Interspeech / Eurospeech '07*, pages 238–241, 2007.

L. Gillick and S. Cox. Some statistical issues in the comparison of speech recognition algorithms. In *ICASSP '89*, pages 532–535, 1989.

D. Godsmark and G. J. Brown. A blackboard architecture for computational auditory scene analysis. *Speech Communication*, **27**:351–366, 1999.

S. D. Goldinger. 'echoes of echoes? an episodic theory of lexical access. *Psychological Review*, **105(2)**:251–279, 1998.

J. L. Goldstein. An optimum processor theory for the central formation of the pitch of complex tones. *Journal of the Acoustical Society of America*, **54**:1496–1516, 1973.

Y. Gong. Speech recognition in noisy environments: A Survey. *Speech Communication*, **16**:261–291, 1995.

R. Gonzalez, R. Woods, and S. Eddins. *Digital image processing using MATLAB*. Prentice Hall, 2004.

S. Gordon-Salant. Recognition of natural and time/intensity altered cvs by young and elderly subjects with normal hearing. *Journal of the Acoustical Society of America*, **80**: 1599–1607, 1986.

P. Green, P. Cooke, and M. Crawford. Auditory scene analysis and Hidden Markov Model recognition of speech in noise. In *Proceedings ICASSP '95*, pages 401–404, 1995.

P. Green, J. Barker, M. Cooke, and L. Josifovski. Handling missing and unreliable information in speech recognition. In *Proceedings AISTATS*, pages 49–56, 2001.

Y. H. Gu and W. M. G. van Bokhoven. Co-channel speech separation using frequency bin non-linear adaptive filter. In *Proc. ICASSP '91*, pages 949–952, 1991.

J. Häkkinen and H. Haverinen. On the use of missing feature theory with cepstral features. In *CRAC Workshop*, Aalborg, Denmark, 2001.

B. A. Hanson and D. Y. Wong. The harmonic magnitude suppression (HMS) technique for intelligibility enhancement in the presence of interfering speech. In *Proceedings ICASSP '84*, pages 65–68, 1984.

W. M. Hartmann and D. Johnson. Stream segregation and peripheral channeling. *Music Perception*, **9**:155–183, 1991.

S. Haykin and Z. Chen. The cocktail party problem. *Neural Computation*, **17**:1875–1902, 2005.

V. Hazan and A. Simpson. The effect of cue-enhancement on the intelligibility of nonsense word and sentence materials presented in noise. *Speech Communication*, **24**:211–226, 1998.

M. S. Hedrick and R. N. Ohde. Effect of the relative amplitude of frication on the perception of place of articulation. *Journal of the Acoustical Society of America*, **94**:2005–2006, 1993.

M. S. Hedrick and R. N. Ohde. Effect of the relative amplitude, presentation level, and vowel duration on perception of voiceless stops by normal and hearing impaired listeners. *Journal of the Acoustical Society of America*, **100**:3398–3407, 1996.

H. Hermansky. Should recognizers have ears? *Speech Communication*, **25**:3–27, 1998.

H. Hermansky. Perceptual linear predictive (PLP) analysis for speech. *Journal of the Acoustical Society of America*, **87**:1738–1752, 1990.

H. Hermansky and N. Morgan. Rasta processing of speech. *IEEE Transactions on Speech and Audio Processing*, **2**:578–589, 1994.

D. J. Hermes. Pitch analysis. In M. Cooke, S. Beet, and M. Crawford, editors, *Visual representations of speech signals*, pages 3–25. John Wiley & Sons, Inc., 1993.

D. J. Hermes. Measurement of pitch by subharmonic summation. *Journal of the Acoustical Society of America*, **83(1)**:257–264, 1988.

W. Hess. *Pitch determination of speech signals : algorithms and devices*. Springer Series in Information Sciences, 1983.

H. G. Hirsch and D. Pearce. The Aurora experimental framework for the performance evaluation of speech recognition systems under noisy conditions. In *Proc. ICSLP '00*, pages 29–32, 2000.

J. Holmes and W. Holmes. *Speech Synthesis and Recognition*. London, UK: Taylor and Francis, 2 edition, 2001.

A. J. M. Houtsma and J. Smurzynski. Pitch identification and discrimination for complex tones with many harmonics. *Journal of the Acoustical Society of America*, **87**:304–310, 1990.

P. A. Howard-Jones and S. Rosen. Uncomodulated glimpsing in 'checkerboard' noise. *Journal of the Acoustical Society of America*, **93**:2915–2922, 1993.

G. Hu and D. Wang. Auditory segmentation based on event detection. In *ISCA Tutorial and Workshop on statistical and perceptual audio processing*, 2004a.

G. Hu and D. Wang. Separation of stop consonants. In *ICASSP '03*, pages 749–752, 2003.

G. Hu and D. L. Wang. Monaural speech segregation based on pitch tracking and amplitude modulation. *IEEE Transactions on Neural Networks*, **5**:1135–1150, 2004b.

M. Huckvale. Opportunities for re-convergence of engineering and cognitive science accounts of spoken word recognition. In *Institute of Acoustics Conference Speech and Hearing*, pages 9–20, 1998.

M. J. Hunt. Spectral signal processing for ASR. In *Proceedings ASRU99*, 1999.

T. Irino, R. D. Patterson, and H. Kawahara. Speech segregation using an auditory vocoder with event-synchronous enhancements. *IEEE Transactions on Audio, Speech and Language Processing*, **10**:2212–2221, 2006.

T. Ito, K. Takeda, and F. Itakura. Analysis and recognition of whispered speech. *Speech Communication*, **45**:139 – 152, 2005.

D. T. Ives, D. R. R. Smith, and R. D. Patterson. Discrimination of speaker size from syllable phrases. *Journal of the Acoustical Society of America*, **118**:3816–3822, 2005.

B. H. Juang. Speech recognition in adverse environments. *Computer Speech and Language*, **5**:275–294, 1991.

Z. Jun, S. Kwong, W. Gang, and Q. Hong. Using Mel-frequency cepstral coefficients in missing data technique. *Eurasip Journal on Applied Signal Processing*, **3**:340–346, 2004.

M. Karjalainen and T. Tolonen. Multi-pitch and periodicity analysis model for sound separation and auditory scene analysis. In *Proceedings ICASSP '99*, pages 929–932, 1999.

K. Kasturi and P. Loizou. The intelligibility of speech with "holes" in the spectrum. *Journal of the Acoustical Society of America*, **112**:1102 – 1111, 2002.

H. Kawahara, I. Masuda-Katsuse, and A. de Cheveigné. Restructuring speech representations using a pitch-adaptive time-frequency smoothing and an instantaneous-frequency based f0 extraction: possible role of a repetitive structure in sounds. *Speech Communication*, **27**:187–207, 1999.

H. Kawahara, A. de Cheveigné, H. Banno, T. Takahashi, and T. Irino. Nearly defect-free f0 trajectory extraction for expressive speech modifications based on STRAIGHT. In *Interspeech '05*, pages 537 – 560, 2005.

A. Khurshid and S. L. Denham. A temporal analysis based pitch estimation system for noisy speech with a comparative study of performance of recent systems. *IEEE Transactions on Neural Networks*, **15**:1112–1124, 2004.

G. J. Kidd, C. Mason, P. Deliwala, W. Woods, and H. Colburn. Reducing informational masking by sound segregation. *Journal of the Acoustical Society of America*, **95**:3475–3480, 1994.

A. Klapuri. A perceptually motivated multiple-f0 estimation method. In *IEEE Workshop on Applications of Signal Processing to Audio and Acoustics*, pages 291–294, 2005.

A. P. Klapuri. Multiple fundamental frequency estimation based on harmonicity and spectral smoothness. *IEEE Transactions on Speech and Audio Processing*, **11**:804–816, 2003.

D. H. Klatt. Software for cascade/parallel formant synthesizer. *Journal of the Acoustical Society of America*, **67**:971–995, 1980.

T. Kristjansson, H. Attias, and J. Hershey. Single microphone source separation using high resolution signal reconstruction. In *ICASSP '04*, pages 817–820, 2004.

T. Kristjansson, J. Hershey, P. Olsen, S. Rennie, and R. Gopinath. Super-human multi-talker speech recognition: The IBM 2006 Speech Separation Challenge System. In *Interspeech '06*, pages 97–100, 2006.

R. Kuhn, J. C. Junqua, P. Nguyen, and N. Niedzielski. Rapid speaker adaptation in eigenvoice space. *IEEE Transactions on Speech and Audio Processing*, **8**:695–707, 2000.

H. Kuwabara and T. Takagi. Acoustic parameters of voice individuality and voice-quality control by analysis-synthesis method. *Speech Communication*, **10**:491–495, 1991.

J. Laidler, M. Cooke, and N. D. Lawrence. Mode-driven detection of clean speech patches in noise. In *Interspeech '07*, pages 922–925, 2007.

C. K. Lee and D. G. Childers. Cochannel speech separation. *Journal of the Acoustical Society of America*, **83**:274–280, 1988.

M. R. Leek, M. E. Brown, and M. F. Dorman. Informational masking and auditory attention. *Perception and Psychophysics*, **50**:205–214, 1991.

C. Leggetter and P. Woodland. Maximum likelihood linear regression for speaker adaptation of continuous density hidden Markov models. *Computer Speech and Language*, **9**:171–185, 1995.

V. R. Lesser, R. D. Fennell, L. D. Erman, and D. R. Reddy. Organization of the Hearsay-II speech understanding system. *IEEE Transactions on Acoustics, Speech, and Signal Processing*, **23**:11–23, 1975.

J. C. R. Licklider. A duplex theory of pitch perception. *Experientia*, **7**:128–134, 1951.

R. Lippmann. Speech recognition by machines and humans. *Speech Communication*, **22**:1–15, 1997.

R. Lippmann and B. Carlson. Using missing feature theory to actively select features for robust speech recognition with interruptions, filtering and noise. In *Proceedings Eurospeech '97*, pages 37–40, 1997.

C. Liu and D. Kewley-Port. Vowel formant discrimination for high-fidelity speech. *Journal of the Acoustical Society of America*, **116**:1224–1233, 2004a.

C. Liu and D. Kewley-Port. STRAIGHT: A new speech synthesizer for vowel formant discrimination. *Research Letters Online*, pages 31–36, 2004b.

D. Liu and C. Lin. Fundamental frequency estimation based on the joint time-frequency analysis of harmonic spectral structure. *IEEE Transactions on Speech and Audio Processing*, **9(6)**:609–621, 2001.

P. Lockwood and J. Boudy. Experiments with a nonlinear spectral subtractor (NSS), Hidden Markov Models and the projection, for robust speech recognition in cars. *Speech Communication*, **11**:215–228, 1992.

P. Lockwood, C. Baillargeat, J.M. Gillot, J. Boudy, and G. Faucon. Noise reduction for speech enhancement in cars: Non-linear spectral subtraction - Kalman filtering. In *Proceedings Eurospeech '91*, pages 83–86, 1991.

R. F. Lyon. Computational models of neural auditory processing. In *ICASSP '84*, pages 36.1.1–36.1.4, 1984.

N. Ma, P. Green, J. Barker, and A. Coy. Exploiting correlogram structure for robust speech recognition with multiple speech sources. *Speech Communication*, **49**:874–891, 2007.

M. W. Macon and M. A. Clements. Sinusoidal modeling and modification of unvoiced speech. *IEEE Transactions on Speech and Audio Processing*, **5**:557–560, 1997.

V. Maier and R. K. Moore. An investigation into a simulation of episodic memory for automatic speech recognition. In *Interspeech '05*, pages 1245–1248, 2005.

B. Mak, J. T. Kwok, and S. Ho. Kernel eigenvoice speaker adaptation. *IEEE Transactions on Speech and Audio Processing*, **13**:984–992, 2005.

S. Makin. *The Role of Static and Dynamic F0 Cues in Concurrent Vowel Segregation*. PhD thesis, University of Sheffield, 2006.

D. Marr. *Vision: a computational investigation into the human representation and processing of visual information*. W. H. Freeman, San Francisco, 1982.

P. Martin. Comparison of pitch detection by cepstrum and spectral comb analysis. In *ICASSP '82*, pages 180–183, 1982.

R. Martin. Noise power spectral density estimation based on optimal smoothing and minimum statistics. *IEEE Transactions on Speech and Audio Processing*, **9**:504–512, 2001.

MathWorks. *MATLAB version 6.5 Image Processing Toolbox 5.3*.

S. L. Mcabe and M. J. Denham. A model of auditory streaming. *Journal of the Acoustical Society of America*, **101**:1611 – 1621, 1997.

S. E. McAdams and A. S. Bregman. Hearing musical streams. *Computer Music Journal*, **3**:26–43, 1979.

J. D. McKeown. Perception of concurrent vowels: The effect of varying their relative level. *Speech Communication*, **11**:1–13, 1992.

J. D. McKeown and R. D. Patterson. The time course of auditory segregation: Concurrent vowels that vary in duration. *Journal of the Acoustical Society of America*, **98**:1866–1877, 1995.

R. Meddis and M. Hewitt. Modelling the identification of concurrent vowels with different fundamental frequencies. *Journal of the Acoustical Society of America*, **91**:233–245, 1992.

R. Meddis and M. J. Hewitt. Virtual pitch and phase sensitivity of a computer model of the auditory periphery. I: Pitch identification. *Journal of the Acoustical Society of America*, **89**:2866–2882, 1991a.

R. Meddis and M. J. Hewitt. Virtual pitch and phase sensitivity of a computer model of the auditory periphery. II: Phase sensitivity. *Journal of the Acoustical Society of America*, **89**:2883–2894, 1991b.

R. Meddis and L. O'Mard. A unitary model of pitch perception. *Journal of the Acoustical Society of America*, **102**:1811–1820, 1997.

D. Mehta and T. Quatieri. Pitch-scale modification using the modulated aspiration noise source. In *ICSLP '06*, pages 2490–2493, 2006.

D.K. Mellinger. *Event formation and separation in musical sound*. PhD thesis, Stanford University, 1991.

B. Meyer, T. Wesker, T. Brand, A. Mertins, and B. Kollmeier. A human-machine comparison in speech recognition based on a logatome corpus. In *Proceedings of the Workshop on Speech Recognition and Intrinsic Variation*, 2006.

F. Meyer and S. Beucher. Morphological segmentation. *Journal Visual Communication and Image Representation*, **1**(1):21–46, 1990.

G. A. Miller. *Language and Communication*. McGraw-Hill, 1951.

G. A. Miller. The masking of speech. *Psychological Bulletin*, **44**:105 – 129, 1947.

G. A. Miller and J. C. R. Licklider. The intelligibility of interrupted speech. *Journal of the Acoustical Society of America*, **22**:167–173, 1950.

S. Mitani, T. Kitama, and Y. Sato. Voiceless affricate/fricative distinction by frication duration and amplitude rise slope. *Journal of the Acoustical Society of America*, **120**(3): 1600–1607, 2006.

B. C. J. Moore. *Cochlear Hearing Loss.* Whurr Publishers, London, 1998.

B. C. J. Moore. *An Introduction to the Psychology of Hearing.* Academic Press, 4 edition, 1997.

R. K. Moore and A. Cutler. Constraints on theories of human vs. machine recognition of speech. In *Workshop on Speech Recognition as Pattern Classification*, pages 145–150, 2001.

D. M. Moreno, P. J. B. Jackson, J. Hernando, and M. J. Russell. Improved ASR in noise using harmonic decomposition. In *Proceedings of the International Congress of Phonetic Science*, pages 751–754, 2003.

D. P. Morgan, E. B. George, L. T. Lee, and S. M. Kay. Cochannel speaker speaker separation by harmonic enhancement and suppression. *IEEE Transactions on Speech and Audio Processing*, **5**:407 – 421, 1997.

S. Morii, T. Morii, M. Hoshimi, S. Hiraoka, T. Watanabe, and K. Niyada. Noise robustness in speaker independent speech recognition. In *ICSLP '90*, pages 1145–1148, 1990.

A. C. Morris, M. Cooke, and P. Green. Some solutions to the missing feature problem in data classification, with application to noise robust ASR. In *Proceedings ICASSP '98*, pages 737–740, 1998.

A. C. Morris, J. Barker, and H. Bourlard. From missing data to maybe useful data: Soft data modelling for noise robust ASR. In *Proceedings WISP '01*, pages 737–740, 2001.

T. Nakatini and H. G. Okuno. Harmonic sound stream segregation using localization and its application to speech stream segregation. *Speech Communication*, **27**:209 – 222, 1999.

J. A. Naylor and S. F. Boll. Techniques for suppression of an interfering talker in co-channel speech. In *Proceedings ICASSP '87*, pages 205–208, 1987.

J. A. Naylor and J. Porter. An effective speech separation system which requires no a priori information. In *Proceedings ICASSP '91*, pages 937–940, 1991.

U. Neisser. *Cognitive Psychology.* Appleton Century Crofts, New York, 1967.

T. Nishimoto, S. Sagayama, and H. Kameoka. Multi-pitch trajectory estimation of concurrent speech based on harmonic GMM and nonlinear Kalman filtering. In *Interspeech '04*, pages 2433–2436, 2004.

A. M. Noll. Cepstrum pitch determination. *Journal of the Acoustical Society of America*, **41**:293–309, 1967.

A. M. Noll. Pitch determination of human speech by the harmonic product spectrum, the harmonic sum spectrum and a maximum likelihood estimate. In *Symposium on Computer Processing in Communication*, volume 19, pages 779–797. University of Brooklyn Press, 1970.

R. N. Ohde and K. N. Stevens. The effect of burst amplitude on the perception of consonant place of articulation. *Journal of the Acoustical Society of America*, **74**:706–714, 1983.

L. Ottaviani and D. Rocchesso. Separation of speech signal from complex auditory scenes. In *Proceedings of the Conference on Digital Audio Effects*, 2001.

D. S. Pallet, W. M. Fisher, and J.G. Fiscus. Tools for the analysis of benchmark speech recognition tests. In *ICASSP '90*, pages 97–100, 1990.

A. Papoulis. *Probability, random variables, and stochastic processes*. McGraw-Hill, New York, 1991.

G. Parikh and P. Loizou. The influence of noise on vowel and consonantal cues. *Journal of the Acoustical Society of America*, **118**:3874 – 3887, 2005.

T. W. Parsons. Separation of speech from interfering sounds by means of harmonic selection. *Journal of the Acoustical Society of America*, **60**:911–916, 1976.

R. D. Patterson, M. H. Allerhand, and C. Giguère. Time-domain modeling of peripheral auditory processing: A modular architecture and a software platform. *Journal of the Acoustical Society of America*, pages 1890–1894, 1995.

G. H. Peterson and H. L. Barney. Control methods used in a study of the vowels. *Journal of the Acoustical Society in America*, **24**:175–184., 1952.

P. Placeway, S. Chen, M. Eskenazi, U. Jain, V. Parikh, B. Raj, M. Ravishankar, R. Rosenfeld, K. Seymore, M. Siegler, R. Stern, and E. Thayer. The 1996 Hub-4 Sphinx-3 system. In *DARPA Speech Recognition Workshop*, pages 85–89, 1997.

I. Pollack. Auditory informational masking. *Journal of the Acoustical Society of America*, **82**:S5, 1975.

P. Price, W. M. Fisher, J. Bernstein, and D. S. Pallet. The DARPA 1000 word resource management database for continuous speech recognition. In *ICASSP '88*, pages 651–654, 1988.

T. F. Quatieri and R. G. Danisewicz. An approach to co-channel talker interference suppression using a sinusoidal model for speech. *IEEE Transactions on Acoustics Speech and Signal Processing*, **38**:56–69, 1990.

L. R. Rabiner. On the use of autocorrelation analysis for pitch detection. *ITASSP*, **25**:24–33, 1977.

L. R. Rabiner and M. R. Sambur. An algorithm for determining the endpoints of isolated utterances. *The Bell System Technical Journal*, **54(2)**:297–315, 1975.

L. R. Rabiner, M. J. Cheng, A. E. Rosenberg, and C. A. McGonegal. A comparative performance study of several pitch detection algorithms. *ITASSP*, **254**:399–417, 1976.

N. Rabiner and L.Y. Juang. *Fundamentals of Speech Recognition*. Englewood Cliffs, NJ: Prentice Hall, 1993.

B. Raj. *Reconstruction of incomplete spectrograms for robust speech recognition*. PhD thesis, Carnegie Mellon University, 2000.

B. Raj and R. M. Stern. Missing-feature approaches in speech recognition. *IEEE Signal Processing Magazine*, **22**:101–116, 2005.

B. Raj, M. Seltzer, and R. M. Stern. Reconstruction of damaged spectrographic features for robust speech recognition. In *Proceedings ICSLP '00*, pages 357–360, 2000.

B. Raj, M. Seltzer, and R.M. Stern. Robust speech recognition: The case for restoring missing features. In *CRAC Workshop*, 2001.

B. Raj, M. L. Seltzer, and R. M. Stern. Reconstruction of missing features for robust speech recognition. *Speech Communication*, **43**:275–296, 2004.

P. Renevey and A. Drygajlo. Detection of reliable features for speech recognition in noisy conditions using a statistical criterion. In *Proceddings Consistent and Reliable Acoustic Cues for Sound Analysis Workshop '01*, pages 71–74, 2001.

N. Roman, D. L. Wang, and G. J. Brown. Speech segregation based on sound localisation. In *IJCNN*, pages 2861–2866, 2001.

N. Roman, D. Wang, and G. Brown. Speech segregation based on sound localisation. *Journal of the Acoustical Society of America*, **114**:2236–2252, 2003.

D. F. Rosenthal and H. G. Okuno, editors. *Computational Auditory Scene Analysis*. Lawrence EarlBaum, Mahwah, NJ, 1998.

M. J. Ross, H. L. Shaffer, A. Cohen, R. Freudberg, and H. J. Manley. Average magnitude difference function pitch extractor. *ITASSP*, **22**:353–362, 1974.

J. Rouat, Y. C. Liu, and D. Morissette. A pitch determination and voiced/unvoiced decision algorithm for noisy speech. *Speech Communication*, **21**:191–207, 1997.

S. T. Roweis. One microphone source separation. In *Advances in Neural Information Processing Systems, (NIPS)*, pages 793–799, 2000.

S. T. Roweis. Factorial models and refiltering for speech separation and denoising. In *Eurospeech '03*, pages 1009–1012, 2003.

T. Saitou, M. Unoki, and M. Akagi. Development of an f0 control model based on f0 dynamic characteristics for singing-voice synthesis. *Speech Communication*, **46**:405–417, 2005.

O. Scharenborg. Reaching over the gap: A review of efforts to link human and automatic speech recognition research. *Speech Communication*, **49**:336–347, 2007.

M. T. M. Scheffers. *Sifting Vowels: Auditory Pitch Analysis and Sound Segregation*. PhD thesis, Rijksuniversiteit te Groningen, The Netherlands, 1983.

R. Schlüter and H. Ney. Using phase spectrum information for improved speech recognition performance. In *Proceedings ICASSP '99*, pages 133–136, 1999.

M. R. Schroeder. Period histogram and product spectrum: new methods for fundamental frequency measurement. *Journal of the Acoustical Society of America*, **43**:829–834, 1968.

M. L. Seltzer, B. Raj, and R. M. Stern. Classifier-based mask estimation for missing feature methods of robust speech recognition. In *ICSLP*, pages 538–541, 2000.

M. L. Seltzer, B. Raj, and R. M. Stern. A Bayesian classifier for spectrographic mask estimation for missing feature speech recognition. *Speech Communication*, **43**:379–393, 2004.

X. Shao and J. Barker. Audio-visual speech recognition in the presence of a competing speaker. In *Interspeech '06*, pages 1292–1295, 2006.

X. Shao and J. Barker. Audio-visual speech fragment decoding. In *AVSP '07*, 2007.

E. Shlomot, V. Cuperman, and A. Gersho. Hybrid coding: Combined harmonic and waveform coding of speech at 4 kb/s. *IEEE Transactions on Speech and Audio Processing*, **9**: 632–646, 2001.

P. G. Singh. Perceptual segregation of complex-tone sequences: A trade-off between pitch and timbre? *Journal of the Acoustical Society of America*, **82**:886–895, 1987.

O. Siohan. On the robustness of linear discriminant analysis as a preprocessing step for noisy speech recognition. In *Proceedings ICASSP '95*, pages 125–128, 1995.

O. Siohan, Y. Gong, and J. P. Haton. A Bayesian approach to phone duration adaptation for lombard speech recognition. In *Proceedings European Speech Communication Technology*, pages 1639–1642, 1993.

K. Sjolander. The Snack sound toolkit version 2.2b1. http://www.speech.kth.se/snack/, 2002.

M. Slaney. A critique of pure audition. In D. Rosenthal and H. Okuno, editors, *Computational auditory scene analysis*, pages 27–41. Lawrence Erlbaum Associates, Inc., Mahwah, NJ, USA, 1998.

M. Slaney and R. Lyon. A perceptual pitch detector. In *ICASSP '90*, pages 357–360, 1990.

P. Smaragdis. *Redundancy Reduction for Computational Audition, a Unifying Approach*. PhD thesis, Massachusetts Institute of Technology, 2001.

D. R. R. Smith and R. D. Patterson. The interaction of glottal-pulse rate and vocal-tract length in judgements of speaker size, sex and age. *Journal of the Acoustical Society of America*, **118**:3177–3186, 2005.

S. Srinivasan. *Integrating computational auditory scene analysis and automatic speech recognition*. PhD thesis, Ohio State University, 2006.

S. Srinivasan, N. Roman, and D. L. Wang. Binary and ratio time-frequency masks for robust speech recognition. *Speech Communication*, **48(11)**:1486–1501, 2006.

J. J. Sroka and L. D. Braida. Human and machine consonant recognition. *Speech Communication*, **45**:401–423, 2005.

K. N. Stevens. *Acoustic Phonetics*. MIT Press, Cambridge, 1998.

K. N. Stevens. Acoustic correlates of phonetic categories. *Journal of the Acoustical Society of America*, **68(3)**:836–842, 1980.

S. S. Stevens, J. Volkmann, and E. B. Newman. A scale for the measurement of the psychological magnitude pitch. *Journal of the Acoustical Society of America*, **8**:185–190, 1937.

H. Strik. How to handle pronunciation variation in asr: by storing episodes in memory? In *Workshop on Speech Recognition and Intrinsic Variation*, pages 33–38, 2006.

H. Strik, C. Cucchiarini, K. Catia, and M. Judith. Comparing the performance of two CSRs: how to determine the significance level of the differences. In *EUROSPEECH '01*, pages 2091–2094, 2001.

R. J. Stubbs and Q. Summerfield. Algorithms for separating the speech of interfering talkers: Evaluations with voiced sentences, and normal-hearing and hearing-impaired listeners. *Journal of the Acoustical Society of America*, **87**:359–372, 1990a.

R. J. Stubbs and Q. Summerfield. Algorithms for separating the speech of interfering talkers: Evaluations with voiced sentences, and normal hearing and hearing-impaired listeners. *Journal of the Acoustical Society of America*, **87**:359–372, 1990b.

Q. Summerfield and J. F. Culling. *Fundamentals of speech synthesis and speech recognition*, chapter Auditory computations that separate speech from competing sounds: a comparison of monaural and binaural processes, pages 313–338. Wiley, Chichester, 1994.

E. Sussman, I. Winkler, M. Huotilainenc, and R. Näätänene W. Ritterd. Top-down effects can modify the initially stimulus-driven auditory organization. *Cognitive Brain Research*, **13**:393–405, 2002.

E. S. Sussman. Integration and segregation in auditory scene analysis. *Journal of the Acoustical Society of America*, **117**:1285–1298, 2005.

J. A. Swets, R. M. Dawes, and J. Monahan. Better decisions through science. *Scientific American*, **283**:82–87, 2000.

D. Talkin. A robust algorithm for pitch tracking (RAPT). In W. B. Kleijn and K. K. Paliwal, editors, *Speech Coding and Synthesis*, pages 495–518. Elsevier Science, 1995.

L. ten Bosch. ASR-HSR from an ASR point of view. In R. Smits, J. Kingston, T. M. Nearey, and R. Zondervan, editors, *Workshop on Speech Recognition as Pattern Classification*, pages 49–54, 2001.

T. Tolonen and M. Karjalainen. A computationally efficient multipitch analysis model. *IEEE Transactions on Speech Audio Processing*, **8**:708–716, 2000.

R. van Dinther and R. D. Patterson. Perception of acoustic scale and size in musical instrument sounds. *Journal of the Acoustical Society of America*, **120**:2158–2176, 2006.

H. Van hamme. Robust speech recognition using missing feature theory in the cepstral or lda domain. In *Proceedings Eurospeech '03*, pages 3089–3092, 2003.

D. A. van Leeuwen, L. G. van den Berg, and H. J. M. Steeneken. Human benchmarks for speaker independent large vocabulary recognition performance. In *Proceedings Eurospeech*, pages 1461–1464, 1995.

L. P. A. S. van Noorden. *Temporal coherence in the perception of tone sequences*. PhD thesis, Eindhoven University of Technology, 1975.

A. P. Varga and R. K. Moore. Hidden Markov Model decomposition of speech and noise. In *Proceedings ICASSP '90*, pages 845–848, 1990.

L. Vincent and P. Soille. Watersheds in digital spaces: an efficient algorithm based on immersion simulations. *IEEE Transactions on Pattern Analysis and Machine Intelligence*, **13**:583–598, 1991.

J. Vliegen and A. J. Oxenham. Sequential stream segregation in the absence of spectral cues. *Journal of the Acoustical Society of America*, **105**:339–346, 1999.

J. Vliegen, B. C. J. Moore, and A. J. Oxenham. The role of spectral and periodicity cues in auditory stream segregation, measured using a temporal discrimination task. *Journal of the Acoustical Society of America*, **106**:938–945, 1999.

K. von Kriegstein, J. D. Warren, D. T. Ives, R. D. Patterson, and T. D. Griffiths. Processing the acoustic effect of size in speech sounds. *NeuroImage*, **32**:368–375, 2006.

M. De Wachter, K. Demuynck, D. Van Compernolle, and P. Wambacq. Data driven example based continuous speech recognition. In *EUROSPEECH*, pages 1133–1136, 2003.

D. Wang. Feature-based speech segregation. In D. Wang and G. J. Brown, editors, *Computational Auditory Scene Analysis Principles, Algorithms, and Applications*, pages 81–114. John Wiley & Sons, New Jersey, 2006.

D. Wang and G. Hu. Unvoiced speech segregation. In *ICASSP '06*, pages 953–956, 2006.

D. L. Wang. Primitive auditory segregation based on oscillatory correlation. *Cognitive Science*, **10**:684 – 697, 1996.

D. L. Wang and G. J. Brown. Separation of speech from interfering sounds based on oscillatory correlation. *IEEE Transactions on Neural Networks*, **10**:684 – 697, 1999.

M. Weintraub. *A theory and computational model of auditory monaural sound separation*. PhD thesis, Stanford University, 1985.

A. Witkin and J.M. Tenenbaum. On the role of structure in vision. In J. Beck, B. Hope, and A. Rosenfeld, editors, *Human and Machine Vision*, pages 481–543. Academic Press, New York, 1983.

S. N. Wrigley and G. J. Brown. A computational model of auditory selective attention. *IEEE Transactions on Neural Networks*, **15**:1151–1163, 2004.

M. Wu, D. L. Wang, and G. J. Brown. A multipitch tracking algorithm for noisy speech. *IEEE Transactions on Speech and Audio Signal Processing*, vol. **11**:229–241, 2003.

E. Zwicker. Subdivision of the audible frequency range into critical bands. *Journal of the Acoustical Society of America*, **33**:248, 1961.

U. T. Zwicker. Auditory recognition of diotic and dichotic vowel pairs. *Speech Communication*, **3**:265–277, 1984.

Index